Grass Roots to New Suits

GRASS ROOTS TO NEW SUITS

THE F.A. CUP DREAM

Paul Eastman
&
Kevin Slocombe

Aureus

First Published 2001

ISBN 1 899750 11 8

Printed in Great Britain.

A catalogue record for this book is available from the British Library.

Aureus Publishing Limited, 24 Mafeking Road, Cardiff, CF23 5DQ, UK.
Tel: (029) 2045 5200 Fax: (029) 2045 5200
Int. tel: +44 29 2045 5200 Int. fax: +44 29 2045 5200
E-mail: sales@aureus.co.uk
         meuryn.hughes@aureus.co.uk
Web site: www.aureus.co.uk

CONTENTS

Ladies and Gentlemen - The Prologue

(stop tittering, missus)

The Relief of Mafeking

Have you ever tried to get a publishing deal? If you have, you will know that the first time is far from easy, virtually impossible in fact. But this book constitutes our 'first time', and what follows is a brief synopsis from conception to achievement.

Chicago Rock Café, Bristol. September 1995

Two men prop up the bar at the bar at the end of the longest, hottest Summer that they can recall since the heady days of 1976, when they were swaggering around Bristol in cheesecloth shirts and denim waistcoats, while the sound of *Jeans On* by David Dundas crackled from transistor radios everywhere.

Having taken a few pensive moments, one of them declares:

"I've got an idea for a book – about the FA Cup."

The other puts down his half-empty bottle of Michelob and looks up:

"That's a massive job. You'll need to contact the FA – Y'know, press passes and all the rest of it, and that's just the tip of the iceberg."

"Yep – already done!" retorts the perfectly prepared perpetrator.

"You're serious about this aren't you!"

The pitch is sold with ideas exchanged accordingly, and:

By September '98, absolutely nothing has been done about it.

But with motivation suitably reinstated, galvanisation at last occurs and the attentions of potential publishers are sought. Then, as some of you will appreciate, the full difficulties of launching our inaugural work are experienced as the rejection slips begin to flood in and numerous companies unwittingly place themselves within the same category as the man who rejected the Beatles.

But to cut a long story short, a visit to Mafeking Road in Cardiff (appropriately?) - headquarters of the clearly discerning Aureus publishing house - results in celebration, when the deal that is this book is sealed in May 1999. Now, with much hard work behind us, we would like to thank the man behind the company, Meuryn Hughes, for his patience, professionalism and faith during the creation of the project. Indeed immediately upon our first entry into his office, we could smell success in the air as copies of 'Loaded' and numerous soccer books *in situ*, revealed him to be a true kindred spirit. Mind you, we only found the copies of Loaded amongst other dodgy literature, whilst one of us looked around his house as the other engaged him in conversation in the lounge.

Thanks are also due, to all friends and family who tolerated the blood sweat and tears that went into this publication (and they did) not to mention the invaluable contribution made by numerous players, managers, officials, fans and scribes of newspaper, fanzine and website alike. These credits cover every town and club we visited on our journey and are too numerous to mention in full, but Mangotsfield club historian Dave Blackmore, Rotherham fanzine 'Moulin Rouge' editor, Steve Exley and Burnley exile crew, the London Clarets, deserve special reference. Keep an eye out for the brilliant London Clarets website on your surfing travels, it's definitely worth a read.

In addition, a debt of gratitude is owed to Bristol's biggest Chelsea fan, our bud Ian Scott, who raided the family photo album in the name of sports literature and a desperate bid to get a mention somewhere, although we never did use his photos.

And last but by no stretch of the imagination least, it should also be known that this undertaking could not have gone ahead without the large chunks of assistance rendered by Steve Clark and Liz Coley at the FA Competitions Department, Tim Collins at JTI (AXA's PR people) and the phenomenal support and assistance of Tony Williams, our editor at Team Talk magazine, and Britain's number one non-league guru.

So, whether you have purchased it or robbed it, Enjoy!

Introduction

What's the Story?

After the trophy has been hoisted high and celebrations transferred to appropriate pubs and clubs around the country, the dust around Wembley, Cardiff (or wherever!) will barely have a chance to settle, before the giant FA Cup machine grinds into life once again. Indeed, many will still be playing allegedly hilarious cucumber games on the beach, fending off time-share touts or forking out thirty quid to get into Manumission at the time, as it is the hazy days of late August that herald the humble qualifying stages of this grand old tournament. A time when the rain sodden, snowbound, fixture backlog-inducing, encounters to come, seem scheduled for a different planet.

The less than clement weather of course, is the most frequent back-drop during the involvement of the league clubs, with their own relative aspirations and fear of ignominious despatch in the cramped back yard of lesser mortals, perhaps courtesy of a bunch of likely lads that started their campaign in the sunshine.

But similar feelings exist for the hundreds of Non-League clubs in the Qualifying stages, for these massed ranks have their own hierarchy, giving rise to all manner of David and Goliath encounters before a Nationwide or Premiership club has even entered the draw. Every season there are 'massive' games in these rounds, which capture the imagination of whole towns and villages and there are bouts of 'cup fever' that never make it anywhere near Football Focus.

With memories of Manchester United's historic treble still sharp in the mind, on Saturday 21 August 1999, a quite unique FA Cup competition kicked–in, as the first 394 of the season's official 580 entries (579 without Manchester United) took the field for the Preliminary Qualifying Round of the 119th tournament. As always, for some, it would be a passport to fame and fortune, while for others, it would be over before much of the bigger world knew it had begun. And amazingly, for the holders, it was never to start.

The concept was simple, to take a club - any club entered in the Preliminary Qualifying Round of the FA Cup, and to follow it through the competition until it was defeated. Then to transfer allegiance to the victors until they were defeated and so on, until the Final itself and the subsequent parade of spoils on the open-topped bus.

And it is these bare facts that base the template for our story which tells you of a journey. A journey that began at a place called Mangotsfield.

The traditional worldwide intensity of feeling for the old pot goes much of the way to explaining our choice for this snapshot of sporting history. But so too does the Cup's allegedly loosening grip on the public imagination and the demolition of Wembley Stadium at season's end giving rise to the possibility that the next Final will be held in Cardiff! Swansong or new beginning? Either way, the FA Cup remains the premier domestic knockout tournament, the culmination of which takes place in a showpiece national stadium. The beginnings however, are not far removed from your local park.

And this leads us to the inception of our odyssey - Cossham Street, Mangotsfield, Bristol - home of Mangotsfield United Football Club, of the Western League, Premier Division, there being only one other division, the First. But why start our journey through this labyrinth of football here? Simple, the Western League and it's regional counterparts embody more-or-less the lowest standard of club that can hope to have their FA Cup entry accepted. And as we were to start at the very beginning, surely the initial club had to be as junior a member of the hierarchy as was workable. But that's not all – the West Country is hardly a hot-bed of FA Cup (or any soccer) success and what harm in raising its profile a little? That not withstanding, the authors live just around the corner from Cossham Street!

I

Any chance of a game?

S o just who is eligible to enter the FA Cup? Not just any old team that's for sure. And it will come as no surprise to learn that the FA have a comprehensive set of prerequisites. These are issued in the form of a booklet to any club that shows an interest, but aspiring entrants should be warned, the criteria are both strict and exhaustive and at the end of the day, pub and parks teams may as well forget it.

There are firstly a whole host of minimum requirements regarding the club's home ground, which include provision of the following:

- Adequate entrances and exits for spectators, with an admission fee charged of at least the FA minimum rate - currently £3.

- The facility to record the precise attendance.

- Goal nets.

- Ladies and gents toilets for spectators.

- A covered area for spectators and hard standing (concrete/paving slabs) of at least one metre in width, on at least the entire length of one touchline and one goal line.

- A playing area enclosed entirely by a fixed barrier, the only exception being those areas excluded from spectator viewing. Wire must not be used in rope form to connect any fence posts that constitute this barrier, due to the potential danger to spectators, players and match officials.

- Some kind of separate hospitality area for visiting club officials.

- Separate toilet facilities for players and match officials, that are not available for use by the public and that are located in the appropriate dressing rooms.

- Separate dressing and washing accommodation for each team and the match officials, each with hot water available.

- First aid facilities and a stretcher, with a qualified person on hand to administer the treatment.

- Insurance for registered players and club officials, with public liability.

- A protected walkway for players and match officials between the dressing room and the pitch. (If a caged or covered area cannot be provided, a post and rail structure is essential, as roping off is not acceptable).

- Separate home and visitors' trainers' boxes (dugouts) – clearly marked for home and away staff.

- Clearly marked home and away technical areas.

- A non-artificial pitch of dimensions between 110-120 by 70-80 yards.

- A matchday programme or team-sheets at the very least.

- And crucially - to really sort the men from the boys – floodlights to certain specifications, including a minimum lux value of 120, with no single reading less than 25% of the highest reading.

- And interestingly, clubs that share their ground with cricket teams thus preventing the exclusive use of the playing surface for football, will be allowed to apply only if they submit acceptable details in writing, to confirm the situation regarding home football matches in August and September.

If your team can manage all of the above, they must also have an administration that is 'capable of understanding and complying with the requirements needed to compete in the FA Cup,' (which certainly eliminates any of the teams for which the authors have played). And it is emphasised/expected that club secretaries ensure their complete familiarity with the general duties relating to entering national competitions.

Still in with a shout? Next up, the club must compete in one of the leagues detailed by the FA as being of sufficient standard. And where deemed necessary, references will be sought from the county FA to which the side in question is affiliated.

But teams outside the Premiership and Football League can forget the whole thing unless they are currently competing in either of the major Non-League knockout competitions, those being the FA (Umbro) Trophy and FA (Carlsberg) Vase, which are considered a clear barometer of standard. (Both finals are played at showpiece stadia).

The Trophy represents the competition of the higher standard, and sides are allowed to enter only if they compete in the Football (Nationwide) Conference, the Isthmian (Ryman) League Premier or First Division, the Northern Premier (Unibond) League or the Southern (Dr Martens) League.

Clubs competing in the FA Trophy are not eligible to enter the Vase and vice-versa. The Vase is for teams in certain leagues immediately below the requisite Trophy standard, although clubs must nevertheless meet rigorous entry criteria.

Taking no chances, even if a team meets all these standards and has been a regular entrant in the FA Cup itself, the FA reserves the right to issue warnings or reject entries in the event of an alarming drop in playing standards or league position.

Successful applicants will automatically be sent an application form for the following year's tournament. Those not in that category will need to contact the FA and ask for one. And if your club meets the requirements, simply fill in the form, enclose the requisite £75 entry fee (payable by every team entering. Cheque or postal order only – no cash accepted) make sure it gets to Lancaster Gate by the closing date – usually 1 April – and, at the FA's ultimate discretion, you're away. All entries are closely scrutinised every year, but don't worry; you'll get your £75 back if they reject you.

In short, to make a successful application to enter the FA Cup, a team must almost certainly be playing at a semi-professional standard, with its own 'stadium' of sorts. A loose definition of the absolute lowest standard acceptable would therefore be for a club to have attained senior status within its county. 'County League' teams *per se* however, do not usually fit the bill and you would normally have to look one step up into the leagues they feed, in order to find the minimum level from which teams will be accepted.

Income/Prizes

Having successfully entered the great competition, the lucky applicants will receive a booklet setting out the pre-determined draw for the qualifying stages, which will be covered in more depth later. But now they have made it into the big time, aside from the taking part in such a prestigious tournament, the rewards are plentiful:

This table sets out the prizes available for winning matches before the Third Round Proper.

Preliminary Round winners	£400
1st Qualifying Round winners	£500
2nd Qualifying Round winners	£600
3rd Qualifying Round winners	£800
4th Qualifying Round winners	£1,200
1st Round Proper winners	£2,000
2nd Round Proper winners	£3,000

No financial awards are made for winning matches beyond the Second Round Proper, as gate receipts and TV rights will supply substantial incomes in their own right.

Teams that reach certain stages of the competition also become eligible to apply for a grant, which comes out of a pot which the FA put aside from their TV contract earnings. But these must be used for reasons such as ground maintenance/improvements and not for example, to pay a player's wages. Appropriate justification and proof such as receipts etc must also be provided.

The amounts available are as follows:

Clubs losing in the 2nd Qualifying Round: £5,000
Clubs losing in the 3rd Qualifying Round: £5,000
Clubs losing in the 4th Qualifying Round: £7,500
Clubs losing in the competition proper: £12,500

There are also awards for the following:

Award:	Prize:	1999-2000 Winners:
Non-League FA Cup Team of the season:	£500	Hereford United (1-0 home wins v York City and Hartlepool and 0-0 home draw v Leicester City before 2-1 away defeat)
Top Non-League FA Cup scorer:	£500	Stuart Taylor (Eccleshill - 8 goals)
Giant killer of the Tournament (Open to all)	£5,000	Gillingham (3-1 home wins v Bradford City and Sheff Wed)
Fastest Goal (Open to all)	No prize	Paul Hunt (Forest Green Rovers - 22 Seconds)
AXA Silver Boot (Top scorer from 1st Rnd proper onwards)	Silver Boot	Gustavo Poyet (Chelsea – 6 goals)
Last team left in with no exemption	£8,000	Shared equally between: Oxford City, Whyteleafe, Worthing, Chelmsford and Eastwood Town

And AXA – in association with 'Team Talk,' Britain's biggest, national Non-League soccer magazine - arrange a regional 'Performance of the Round' award for the Qualifying stages, which consists of a special plaque.

It must be emphasised at this point, that the FA have designed many of these awards, in order to give significant financial assistance to Non-League sides. Indeed this is further demonstrated by the fact that they will donate towards certain expenses incurred by teams during FA Cup activity, e.g. travel and accommodation for away games.

The ultimate prize of course is the Cup itself, but if you win it you have to look after it, as you are held responsible for any loss, theft or damage between presentation and it's compulsory return on the first day of March in the following year.

The FA also make payments for TV appearances (only in the tournament Proper) as follows:

Round:	Live/Highlights:	Payment:
First/Second	Live	£75,000
First/Second	Highlights	£18,750
Third to Semis	Live	£150,000
Third to Semis	Highlights	£18,750

A sum does get paid into the gate receipts for the Final, although this is not simply split two ways. 25% of the profit goes to the FA, 32.5% to the clubs contesting the Final and 10% to the 'Pool.' The Pool is made up of contributions from the Football League and Premiership clubs, and constitutes 10% of the profits from all their matches in that season's tournament. This is then divided up at the end of the competition, between all those clubs, regardless of the size of their contribution.

The above payments also apply to replays, which are no longer a feature of the Semi-Finals and Final as they are now decided on the day, by penalties if necessary. This is due to a decision taken by the Challenge Cup Committee, which they made in order to avoid fixture congestion at that stage of the season, especially in view of the increased number of matches in the European club competitions. (Obviously this does not apply to the World Club Championship).

The Qualifying Tournament

Contrary to popular belief, Non-League sides do not appear in the First Round Proper each year by magic. A five round Qualifying tournament must be negotiated first, with exemptions awarded depending on the team's status. We are all familiar with the exemption format for the competition proper, which dictates that the Football League clubs from Divisions 2 and 3 enter in the First Round Proper, while the Division 1 and Premiership sides come in at the Third Round stage.

And the arrangements for the Qualifying Rounds are very similar, in spite of a recent revamp, with the 22 Conference sides entering in the Fourth Qualifying Round and the 67 clubs that comprise the Premier Divisions of the three leagues immediately below the Conference, exempt until the Second Qualifying Round.

Every other team goes directly into the Preliminary Round, which is drawn on a strictly regional basis. The regional theme carries on until the Fourth Qualifying Round, by which time however, it has broadened simply to a 'north and south' scenario. Past performance in the competition by Non-League sides contributed towards their exemptions until recently, but this is now no longer the case.

The very early stages of the competition will often feature sides that derive from works teams which have gone on to slightly better things, the various Police and Navy sides being excellent examples, not to mention the likes of Dunston Federation Brewery and Jarrow Roofing. Other delightful names that encapsulate the romance of theses early rounds include Viking Greenford and Billingham Synthonia, although closer inspection of this year's Preliminary Qualifying Round will reveal an ex-League club from not so long ago – Bradford Park Avenue.

Attendances at this stage of the competition can vary greatly, ranging from less than 50 to over 750 and teams pulling out or being 'removed from the competition' for various administration reasons at the eleventh hour is not unheard of - in some ways a bit like Third Round Proper 1999-2000!

When this happens the removed club's opponents simply receive a 'walkover' as happened in the 1999-2000 tournament for Hertford Town when Barkingside were expelled. Clubs progressing via the walkover system however, do not receive the 'winners' prize money.

The Non-League Hierarchy:

The elite Non-League clubs compete in the Football (Nationwide) Conference, the champions of which will enter the Football (Nationwide) League Division 3 providing their ground comes up to scratch. Teams can be relegated from the Conference into one of three existing leagues of equal standard, depending on their geographical location. And promotion can take place the other way, again depending upon whether the ground requirements are met. These requirements are a major pre-requisite in making progress through all levels of the Non-League set-up, with each stadium receiving a specific grading or 'Category.'

The three leagues into which relegation from the Conference can take place are:

Northern Premier (Unibond)   (Teams basically from anywhere in the north of England)

Isthmian (Ryman)   (Teams mainly from London and the Home Counties)

Southern (Dr Martens)   (Teams mainly from the south and south west)

These location ID's remain flexible and it is not unheard of for 'borderline' teams to move sideways from one league to another in order to ensure numbers remain constant.

The leagues are usually referred to by their sponsor names. All of them have a Premier Division. The Unibond has a First Division, which is a parallel standard to the Ryman Division One and Dr Martens Eastern and Western Divisions.

The Ryman has Divisions Two and Three of which there are no equivalent in the Unibond and Dr Martens Leagues and the parallel standard will therefore constitute the top two divisions of any leagues that feed directly in to the Unibond and Dr Martens.

This structure is referred to as the pyramid, with one league at the top, and an increasing number of parallel leagues the lower you fall, until you get to the bottom which represents the level of your common or garden parks team. The Pyramid is particularly keenly felt immediately outside the professional leagues. The closer teams get to the Football League, the more obsessive the detailed understanding of the pyramid and its rules. Indeed, it is the fans of non-league clubs striving towards the league and the Conference who have the biggest number of anoraks for whom The Pyramid fills their dreams. If you want to meet a non-league anorak, simply stand in any decent non-league ground and say something erroneous about the Pyramid. Without warning the local statistician will descend on you, pull out his biro and his special Pyramid chart and explain the error of your ways. If you still fail to understand, you will be asked to leave.

Greater still, is the competition between leagues set at the same level. Try standing on the terrace at a Ryman League 1st Division ground and saying the standard is not as good as the Dr Martens League Eastern Division. Expect a punch in the mouth.

Suffice to say for our story that Mangotsfield United inhabits a berth one promotion away from the Dr. Martens Western Division, and if you count the Conference as Non-League Division 1, then Mangotsfield's level constitutes Division 4.

And this weaves us invitingly back into our story, where the Preliminary Round draw has provided the Bristol club with a home tie against Hungerford Town from the parallel division of the Isthmian (Ryman) League.

2

The Palace kit that looked like a cigarette packet

PRELIMINARY QUALIFYING ROUND

MANGOTSFIELD UNITED

V

HUNGERFORD TOWN

21 AUGUST 1999

@ COSSHAM STREET, MANGOTSFIELD, BRISTOL

ATTENDANCE: 183

Mangotsfield United reside in the far north-eastern reaches of Bristol, just off the A432 to Chipping Sodbury to be precise. The area itself was once classified as a village in it's own right, but with the erosion of green spaces over the years, the village eventually became the suburb that it is today. The Cossham Street ground remained in relatively rural surroundings until very recently, but a renewed obsession with the building of housing estates in the Bristol area, has ensured that the ground is now flanked on two sides by neat, gleaming residences.

The ambience of the third side, upon which are the impressive new facilities of a local rugby club, is also down to a housing developer, who bought the fields on which the club played originally for a sum sufficient to relocate them very nicely, thank you. And it would be understandable if those connected with Mangotsfield

United FC looked upon their new neighbours with envious eyes, for those particular egg chasers compete much lower in rugby's equivalent ladder.

A mile or so down the road, the local factory team who have battled their way up to County League standard (the equivalent of two divisions below Mangotsfield) will soon be moving on for the same reason. Their pitch and indeed the whole factory are to be razed to the ground accordingly.

Meanwhile, the developers hope to complete a hat trick, as similar plans are afoot for Cossham Street's fourth side. But for now, fields prevail in that particular quarter, with Mangotsfield school providing the only bricks and mortar in sight. Aside from this, the picturesque hills and dales that form part of Bristol and Bath's green buffer zone dominate the scene.

Mangotsfield, like many other semi–professional sides at this level, must compete both for players and support with a host of other local clubs. Back across the city, the grounds of relative giants Bristol Rovers and Bristol City are no more than 15 and 30 minute drives away respectively, not to mention the dozen or so other Non - League teams scattered around the area. And this type of circuit also brings with it the rivalry to attract the best local players. Whilst it is accepted that the cream of the crop may go on to professional clubs, loyalty can count for very little at this level, given that many are not under contract and can therefore move around virtually at will. With teams like Bath City, Yate Town and a generous helping of Western League rivals within easy driving distance, many of the decent players have been known to 'do the rounds' accordingly. Their travels can take them to places as far afield as Swindon or the scene of the West Country's biggest success story of late, Nailsworth, near Stroud, where a number of Bristolians have featured in the line up of Forest Green Rovers, now of the Conference.

Clearly clubs must remain attractive to players in order to keep their heads above water, which is something that Mangotsfield do very well not least of all due to the fact that they are perceived by many as Bristol's 3rd biggest club. Strictly according to the Pyramid rules, a chart-mapping anorak will be able to prove beyond any doubt that Yate Town have actually held that honour for a few years. However, any self-respecting MUFC fan will then quickly divert to the geographical issue that Yate isn't technically in Bristol anyway. Indeed, this argument could also be applied to any such loftier rival as Clevedon or Weston Super Mare. Whatever the facts however, Mangotsfield have held the reputation in much the same way as the consumer has always decided Sony

Playstation is greater than Sega or Nintendo. Perception is everything in this game, and Mangotsfield have always taken advantage of the perhaps misconception. Whatever the arguments however, they have an excellent reputation for attracting the best local talent, both on the playing and managing side and then looking after it. Although, as with so many clubs at this level, there is no board of directors, the club has a sound infrastructure in the shape of the committee, which contains local businessmen well - versed in financial matters, ensuring that the bank balance remains consistently in the black. At the sharp end, they have a newly–recruited manager in Andy Black, veteran of some 450 games for the club and head–hunted from Bitton, a Bristol side just finding their feet in the Western League First Division, after recent promotion from the County League. He was with them for only 29 days, before Mangotsfield made their move, safe in the knowledge that their local status and Black's affinity for the club would bring him on board. Nigel Gillard, another stalwart of the side is Black's number 2. Both are still registered as players, with only Gillard in reality actually making appearances.

And in real-life, both earn their living in the building trade.

With the scene set, the time is right for our journey to commence, so its first stop Cossham Street, where the new season is one week old:

6.30 pm, Thursday 19 August 1999

'MUFC' says the sign outside the diminutive stadium. But that is where the similarity between Mangotsfield and their more illustrious namesakes ends. Not only because the other lot have found this year's competition less attractive, but also because there are no 40 grand a week salaries here. Nor are there any 40 grand a year salaries for that matter. But there are salaries. Since the semi–pro structure was set up in 1973, thus doing away with the practice of paying players with surreptitious 'boot money,' Western League players and their like, have been receiving remuneration of an above board nature. Indeed, the subject of boot money is nowadays more likely to be on the mind of the David Beckhams of this world, as his advisors negotiate new terms with Adidas. Payment at Western League level will usually take the form of appearance fees and goal/win/clean sheet bonuses, or straightforward wage payments with no bonuses. Either way, those deemed valuable

22

enough to warrant contracts will be on better rates, in the same way as first team squad members will command higher amounts than the reserves, if indeed the reserves are paid at all. The wage frameworks and amounts earned at this level can vary enormously, even between clubs in the same division, although certain sides are able to attract better players more often, due to the amounts they can afford to pay. The precise sums earned are very closely guarded, but it is known that fees in excess of £100 a game are available. And word up is that Mangotsfield are almost certainly able to compete with this figure, although by all accounts they choose to pay straight salaries, with bonuses a rarity.

Nobody in the game wants to be too specific about the actual levels of payment for various reasons. However, it is not difficult in practice to identify the better paying clubs for exactly the same reasons as in the Premiership: they seem to be either top of the league or the managers disappear at regular intervals. It is also relatively easy to spot a club that has a sudden influx of cash, usually in the form of new benefactors, in that there is a sudden arrival of bigger names from the local playing circuit. Mangotsfield themselves have parted company with a number of managers in recent years including ex-Liverpool player Nicky Tanner.

Payment and salary at this level is not a wage. Western League players and those who perform in equivalent standards around the country, will usually have day jobs. They can be found sitting next to you in the office, carrying hods on the building site, or maybe sorting your mortgage out. In fact, the bloke who fitted your double-glazing will almost certainly be playing in the FA Cup next week! Whilst wages for football at this standard are unlikely to keep the wolves from the door in their own right, but a normal salary can be supplemented rather nicely by three games a month if you play for the right club. However, most of these guys play for the love of it, often turning out for Sunday morning sides and paying their subs like everyone else, although this is strictly forbidden for those under contract, mainly due to the risk of injury. To provide some perspective for the uninitiated, if you take an average Western League player and stick him in a standard parks side, he will probably stand head and shoulders above the rest, a bit like a decent footballer in the England side.

Western League managers coaches and sometimes, staff, are also looked after financially, but there are a whole host of people that help to run this type of side as a labour of love, a prime example being Mangotsfield's club secretary Rodger Gray.

As we pull into the car park, we are greeted by the sight of Rodger outside the clubhouse, with his car boot open and stacked to the hilt with paperwork, box-files and assorted clerical bi-products. This is Rodger's role, and at this stage he belies his efficiency as a modern secretary of a growing football club, and looks like a car boot seller. Rodger's commitment means that swathes of time from his personal life are handed over to all things Mangotsfield, but this is a labour of love. He goes on to tell us that there is a degree of financial incentive for club success, with the league awarding £1500 to the Premier Division champions, £1000 to the runners up and £600, £375 and £250 to the third, fourth and fifth placed sides respectively. A Premier Division Manager of the Month meanwhile, will pick up a cool £20 worth of Western League sponsors 'Screwfix Direct' (DIY firm) vouchers, with the club in question pocketing £25 in cash.

"And it's worth entering the FA Cup if you can get a good run," he adds. The money can start to add up nicely the further you go." It was nice for us to see that the Cup still means something for some people.

Anybody fancying a bet on Mangotsfield to lift the trophy in May however, could almost certainly name their own price with William Hill and Joe Coral battering each other with their account books in the rush to reach the punter.

Meanwhile, the Mangotsfield players are rolling up and changing up, for this, their second training session of the week and final work-out before the commencement of another FA Cup campaign. And many are still wearing the clothes that reveal a drive straight from a day - job. The small frame of manager Andy Black is now, also to hand:

"These guys are workers first and footballers second," he admits. "That's why we can only realistically expect them to train two nights a week."

Diminutive though he may be, Black was a highly respected player on the local circuit and will still turn out for Mangotsfield if the need arises. A greying head of hair betrays the fact that he is only in his early forties, although this is rescued by a still - youthful face. Thirty five year old Gillard by comparison, is a tall, thick –set powerhouse of a man, with a reputation for '100% commitment' on the pitch. Just the kind of concrete head we all hated playing against.

The players waste no time and begin limbering up on the training ground, which consists of a patch of grass sandwiched between the smaller touchline stand and the housing estate.

"There's no point in not using this time wisely," explains Black. "To coin a phrase, you're only fooling yourself otherwise. And they all know that in order to compete on a Saturday they have to use our limited development time to its fullest extent."

They bang a ball about to each other, glazier to builder to teacher to student. All ready to go again after a day's labour, while Black and Gillard convene to plan the evening's torture.

"They've got good attitudes and they're really well-focused on this FA Cup game for a start. Hungerford are halfway decent, but we should be able to beat them". Hungerford's manager is Don Rogers. Readers might remember him from his playing days? You should certainly remember his very own special Wembley goal, one that some would claim is right up there with the best of the Wembley goals. And after a good pre-season, confidence is high.

The players are now well and truly being put through their paces. The training shows similarities to that of any local pub or parks team. But this is more intense and the accuracy and efficiency with which they perform the required functions is noticeably superior. And in accordance with today's lifestyle, where designer gear is king, the days of motley old kit for training are long gone and everyone is resplendent in Nike, Adidas or smart t–shirts bearing the logos of businesses owned by the club officials. The barracking, piss taking and sub-conscious bonding however, remain an integral part of the proceedings, the same as you will see from Hackney to Hampden, but no one loses sight of the seriousness. Indeed the proceedings are scrutinised throughout by at least ten club officials including the chairman.

Our presence has generated interest among the locals and a scattering meet us in the clubhouse, all wanting to know what we are about and then to tell us their anecdotes. Enter lifelong fan, club historian and multi–role fulfilling, Dave 'Statto' Blackmore, (surprisingly without anorak) who revels in the prospect of recounting the club's history for the umpteenth time in his life, as a result of which we learn, amongst other things that the club can be traced back to 1886.

The ground is being re-developed with a 300 seater stand. Trees and houses still overlook the ground from all angles. Some cynics always claim that the status of a ground can be judged by the amount of washing that can be seen hanging on lines, when looking from the centre circle. In this case, plenty.

The bar is getting busier by the minute and is by all accounts a thriving hub most every night. Apart from locals and supporters there for a drink, it is leased out as the home venue for skittles teams (a major local sport in Bristol) and the function room caters for numerous occasions, all of which brings in valuable revenue. We dutifully join Rodger in purchasing tickets for tonight's home team's raffle, as if we had a choice.

At this point the players begin to filter in for some post training refreshment with the banter ongoing. "I hope you lot get more past Churchy (Hungerford's ex-Mangotsfield keeper Allen Churchward) on Saturday than you did past me tonight", laughs Mangotsfield's reserve team 'keeper (he points to the authors) otherwise this lot'll be following Hungerford. A suitably vitriolic barrage ensues from those within earshot.

When asked about their realistic ambitions within the FA Cup, players, officials and supporters basically share one dream, to top their current personal best of the Third Qualifying Round and go two stages further by reaching the First Round Proper:

"We'll be taking it seriously" says Andy Black. "A good run in the Cup can mean a lot of money for us. And we can do it. I'll definitely put our strongest side out. We are a decent side, and we're perfectly capable of holding our own against higher graded opposition, especially at home. So who's to say, we could end up playing a top Conference side".

The fans however want one better. They would dearly love to see their heroes entertain a league club, not least of all Bristol Rovers or Bristol City. Statto Dave tells us though, that this would cause divided loyalties, for the ranks of the Cossham Street faithful are regularly swelled by fans that have not followed one of the professional sides away from home. It is in fact fair to say that Mangotsfield lies deep within the traditional blue quarter of the city and has always been geographically so, whether Rovers have been based at Eastville, Bath or the Memorial Stadium. And Dave assures us that Mangotsfield gates are usually bigger when Rovers are on their travels.

Meanwhile Andy continues:

"But our real hope of getting to Wembley is in the Vase. That's the big one. We reached the semis in 96 and I'd love us to go one better. Imagine that. Mangotsfield at Wembley. And we'd have loads of support. Half the Rovers and City lot would be there I bet!" This analysis demonstrates the reality of the situation at this stage of the Cup. Mangotsfield's real aim at a Cup is the Vase, as the bigger non-league clubs come in their real aim will be the Trophy. In the modern game nobody who has entered the Cup prior to the 3rd round has ever won it. However, the dream of a fantastic run and a match against a league club is always in the back of the mind every time the Cup comes around. And if that fails there is still some magic in kicking off in the same competition that Alan Shearer and Michael Owen will also kick off in, albeit 4 months later.

The conversation between officials, players, supporters and authors carries on until time is called at the bar and beyond. With confidence for a win on Saturday growing by the pint, we end up predicting a Mangotsfield victory, based on a combination of their great start to the season and a 3-0 victory over Hungerford, en route to the much–vaunted FA Vase Semi-Final appearance. This is in spite of Don Rogers' previous Wembley success (League Cup with Swindon in 1969, if you haven't worked it out) and the fact that the visitors from down the M4 actually reached the First Round Proper, in season 1979/80.

And we take it as a sign when Rodger wins the skittles raffle, on ticket number 4-4-2!

Saturday, 21 August 1999

Tabloid sub-editors everywhere must have been straining to resist another 'Hotta Than The Costa' headline, for it truly is a proverbial 'scorcher'. But the fact that our greatest domestic tournament is about to commence seems of little interest to the media, proving worthy of no more than an inch of column space in some papers and none at all in others.

Indeed there is little evidence of Cup fever as the authors take their pre-match meal in the nearest pub to Cossham Street. As we sit outside at around midday and bask in the fine weather, a group of lads on the table next to us show allegiance only to Liverpool and Arsenal via their respective replica kits. And a solitary man in the new Bristol Rovers shirt sips a pint inside, presumably readying himself to attend their first home fixture of the season. And even he will be ignorant of the start of a competition he will be hoping his heroes can perform well in later this year.

But there is not a solitary instance of the maroon and blue in which Mangotsfield play.

Cossham Street 1.00 p.m. And the existence of FA Cup action is at last evident, if only through the bold lettering on the fixture noticeboard. There are a number of individuals busying themselves with their respective pre-match tasks and the social club is beginning to fill with supporters. And at last the maroon and sky blue of Mangotsfield replica kits can be seen.

As kick–off time nears, Rodger and the club officials change out of their MUFC polo shirts and don the *de rigeur* shirts and blazers with club ties.

Just before 3pm - bathed in sunshine - the Cossham street ground is looking good. The brightness makes every colour sharper and more defined. The impressive main stand and pitch - perimeter provided by Ralph's Wall (named after a previous chairman who paid for its construction) are speckled with shirt – sleeved punters ready for the off. It's going to be a sweltering encounter for fans and players alike.

One man however, is noticeable for being the only person left in the ground (and you can virtually count them) with more than one layer on. He is sporting a blazer where even the club officials have had to admit defeat and go into shirt – sleeve order. The only difference being, this particular blazer bears the FA insignia and the wearer is none–other, than FA heavyweight Adrian Titcombe, up from Taunton for the day having been in attendance at Somerset Cricket Club, where he is a member. There are a few nudges and looks from the more well – informed punters in the vicinity. But the vast majority in attendance today will be oblivious to the fact, that the next time they see this man will probably be on their TV sets on 20 May, as he leads the FA Cup finalists out at Wembley.

Meanwhile, Andy gives a few last shouts of motivation and Mangotsfield are

The 'Field Faithful leaning on Ralph's Wall

ready to go out. A Blast from Colin's air horn signals the eagerly anticipated emergence of the teams, from the far corner of the ground, to the right of the main stand, where the dressing rooms adjoin the back of the clubhouse. The adversaries run on to the pitch side by side–to a ripple of applause–and more air horn, as the locals set about trying to create Fortress Cossham. The Mangotsfield kit is reminiscent of Aston Villa, but the colours are officially classed as maroon and sky blue. The burr of one or two isolated, West–Country voices can be heard, "Come on the Field," being the cry. There is no corresponding vocal encouragement or indeed any obvious following for the white shirts (with red, white and blue trimmings on the sleeves) and dark blue shorts and socks of Hungerford.

Statto Dave is standing beside us:

"You can spot our casual supporters a mile off" he explains. "Not that they're unwelcome of course, but you can tell them apart because odds are they'll shout 'come on United'. During our FA Vase Semi - Final run there were loads of 'em giving it United, United. But the hardcore shout here's always been 'Come On the Field.' That's our nickname you see."

Glorious weather or not, there are precious few to witness the start of our FA Cup adventure. "I reckon on about 200 here today," declares one enthusiastic Bristolian. "Not bad seeing as though Hungerford've brought sod all with 'em. And plenty of our lot are still on holiday!"

Kick-off of the great competition takes place all over the country at 3pm sharp. At Cossham Street, the home side miss an immediate chance as target man Martin Boyle heads a cross just over.

Before long, the highly-rated Boyle is in the thick of the action again, with an overhead kick from the edge of the six yard box. His effort is charged down by the combined efforts of Hungerford defenders Daniel Gray and Andy Weller but the ball squirts up nicely for his striking partner Darren Edwards, giving him a free header at four yards range. Edwards nods the ball towards the target, but Hungerford keeper Allen Churchward throws himself across the goalmouth to deny Mangotsfield the lead.

The Field are dominating the early exchanges and, of no relevance to anything in particular, we begin to notice, that often when the ball is kicked, it sends a strange 'pinging' echo around the compact ground. A few chances go begging. It's classic backs–to–the–wall stuff for Hungerford as Mangotsfield throw the kitchen sink at them. And shots begin to rain in, including one that almost knocks a couple of watching kids out of the tree behind the school end.

The onslaught is momentarily abated with a trio of back-to-back Hungerford forays into Bristol territory instigated by Don Rogers' other great hope, frontman Chris Brown. Brown's speed down the right first provides him with a shooting opportunity from the edge of the box. This necessitates a save from Tony Court (The Bosnian) who does well to smother a nasty ricochet. Then it's a ball played inside to midfielder Gary Horgan whose 30-yard daisy cutter catches the unsighted Mangotsfield keeper by surprise, but Court's split-second recovery results in another save. And it's third time unlucky as Hallett gets the measure of Brown and slides in to brilliantly intercept another powerful run down the right.

Then the pendulum swings again and Mangotsfield begin to take control. Midfielder Neil Rosslee plays a brilliant crossfield ball to Martin Boyle. Boyler is unmarked and within shooting range. He brings the ball under control with consummate ease – pulls the trigger – and – pokes it timidly over the top with the goal at his mercy. Cue more West Country groans.

Chances come and are squandered, but our West Country heroes are beginning to boss the midfield. Up front, Edwards and Boyler are constantly involved as balls are pumped and stroked around Hungerford territory. Mangotsfield's approach play is of a high standard.

There are gasps from the crowd as Noel O'Sullivan smashes the ball against a post from point blank range.

The sounds of foot smacking ball and ball smacking post in quick succession send a host of echoes around the stadium.

A minute or so later, Loyden crosses for O'Sullivan who heads wide from six yards. The lack of marking and closing down is all too much for Churchward and half the 'crowd' hear him ask:

"What the fuck's going on out there?"

The inevitable proximity of the players to Ralph's Wall in this type of compact arena, combined with the relatively low background noise, means that spectators can hear most of the verbal action on the pitch. And by the same token, easily audible messages can be despatched the other way if desired. The gaggle of Mangotsfield management committee members congregated to the frustrated keeper's right, utilise this acoustic phenomenon accordingly.

"Watch the language keeper, there's women and young 'uns 'ere". We look but cannot identify James Stewart in his Sheriff uniform.

But the keeper's words of 'encouragement' seem to give heart to battle - weary Hungerford. And a Brown cross finds Jason Brizell unmarked in front of the Mangotsfield goal, though his header is placed well wide of the mark. A minute later, Mangotsfield's defence goes AWOL again - a real sitter falls to Brizell about a yard out- but the striker somehow contrives to slice the ball out of the ground, and whilst it should have been in the net, it's most likely resting-place is in someone's front garden. Many an astute observer believes that the most profound difference in standard as you march up football's ladder is in the finishing and this game is certainly proving that point. In the third round proper even Andy Cole won't need this many chances to notch.

Another minute passes and it's the stroke of half–time. The proverbial great psychological time to score. And Mangotsfield's defence seem to choose this moment to act like they are still on holiday, as Hungerford Striker David Gee stands unchallenged, in the exact place from which Brizell has just missed. Knowing that lightning can't strike twice, Gee strides in to a first time shot – and blasts another one into the garden!

It can only be hoped this neighbour is not the type to keep the ball, sonny.

Half time arrives scoreless. The turnstile doors are opened and a couple of locals gleefully make their gratis entrance. "Bloody half-timers" murmurs Dave.

Where it all began - Mangotsfield v Hungerford

In the dressing room the Hungerford players are on an unexpected high. They know they could easily be ahead. And this gives rise to a torrent of perhaps over-optimistic opinions: "Their heads are down, they're knackered", "we can fuckin' do this". Andy Black has not yet followed his players into the Mangotsfield dressing room and hears the enemy's adrenaline-fuelled expressions of optimism.

"That's my half-time talk sorted out", says Black quietly, pointing to the visitors' dressing room. "When I tell my lot how Hungerford have been mouthing off, that's all the motivation they'll need". The Mangotsfield door is gently shut.

"Right listen" - Black is more assertive than we have yet seen him – "did you hear them next door, they're saying you're knackered… got nothing left - and that they're gonna do you second half. You've pissed all over 'em and now they think they're gonna get something". Captain Lee Barlass plays his part "Yeah come on lads I heard 'em on the way in, let's prove 'em wrong". A throng of concurrence shows the medicine is taking effect.

Significantly, there's no moaning, no bitching, only encouragement. The club has a good spirit and they motivate and work for each other.

As the time to re-enter the arena comes about, Black's parting shot is ready. "Right, forget those last few minutes, they didn't deserve that did they? Let's put it right". Now get out there and get straight back into it, run them hard straight from the whistle – remember what they said about you". The gladiators are re-energised and it is difficult to imagine them not fighting to the death for the cause.

More gentle applause signifies the second phase of combat and inside five minutes, Mangotsfield have won a corner. It's head tennis in the Hungerford box, until the ball falls to Darren Edwards who makes no mistake this time and nods home. A barely audible 'cheer' goes up and Mangotsfield are back in the groove. Hungerford heads drop visibly and the lethality of such a loss in spirit is demonstrated almost immediately, when some indifferent defensive play leaves Martin Boyle completely unmarked, six yards out. Could he too put the burden of earlier misses behind him?…Yes! He prods home and the entire Mangotsfield bench are punching the air like they've won the cup.

Despite Don Rogers' frenetic attempts from the other side of the white line, the slide in Hungerford morale continues unabated. Wing–back Danny Hallett is running them ragged down the left, Neil Rosslee is bossing the midfield and Boyle is really putting himself about up front. Before long Boyle intercepts a stray pass and engineers another chance for Hallett, but the youngster pulls his shot just wide.

A further minute passes and Boyle intercepts another demotivated Hungerford pass. From just inside his own half he plays a great through ball to Noel O'Sullivan, who sees the advancing Churchward and although 30 yards out, promptly lobs the ball over the keeper's head and... into the net! Three-nil and more ripples of applause. Cue another Hungerford revival: Greg Horgan shoots wide from a free kick just outside the box. Livewire striker Mickey Durkin suddenly steps it up a gear and is at long last causing the problems for which Don Rogers had hoped. And Chris Brown's powerful runs down the right have re-materialised. But the only result is a booking on the hour for frustrated defender Martyn Churchward, brother of the keeper. His subsequent suggestion that Mr Mills should "Fuck Off" changes nothing and fortunately for the player the punishment is not increased, perhaps against FA Directives. James Stewart says nothing, but fingers his holster.

Black is on his feet, he's noticed dangerous lapses in concentration and there's still half an hour to go. "Don't let them amble around here" he points to the Mangotsfield left-back zone – which Chris Brown has been plundering with renewed success. "Remember - professional to the end". Captain, Lee Barlass acknowledges Black's shout and cascades the advice accordingly.

With all Hungerford resistance suppressed accordingly, Mangotsfield play out the last fifteen well on top and Mr Mills' whistle hails a well-deserved Bristol victory. Cue pockets of polite applause all around Ralph's Wall.

Hungerford trudge off, they know they're well beaten and this time it's the Mangotsfield dressing room that sounds like an excerpt from the Jerry Springer show, with whoops and chanting in abundance. "Listen to them," says Black in his laid back tone, "they think they're unbeatable now" – as if to echo his theory the throes of "We're gonna win the cup" begin to bounce around the corridor – "They've got to come back down to earth". He is genuinely concerned about over-confidence.

But the beat goes on: "We're all pissed up an' we're going to Wemberlee, Wem-ber-lee, Wem-ber-lee!"

William Hill and Joe Coral arrive at the door in hope, but there are no takers.

Allowing them their moment, Black explains to us: "The furthest we've been is the Third Qualifying Round and my intention is to beat that this year. I think it's realistic to aim for the First Round Proper. And I'd love us to get a league club. And yeah you guessed it, preferably Rovers or City at home". Club secretary Rodger Gray interjects:

"And we wouldn't switch it either."

Black gives a wry smile. He knows they would.

The perennially sporting Don Rogers comes to the home dressing room to offer his congratulations: "Well done Blacky." They shake hands.

Memories are immediately evoked of Don haring down the wing in his heyday, initially for Swindon in countless HTV West sports broadcasts and then in that Palace kit that looked like a cigarette packet, with Brian Moore drooling over his every move. Although the rigours of battle have unfortunately left him with a bad limp, Don's face is still instantly recognisable from 'The Big Match' or so many bubble-gum picture cards. And the famous droopy moustache remains. We tell him so.

"Showing your bloody age a bit aren't you," he laughs.

Don is more than willing to discuss those heady days, but becomes serious when the conversation turns to his team's performance today:

"I'm really upset by that." He is genuinely perturbed.

"It's difficult to understand what went wrong. I was relying heavily on my centre-backs to keep it sewn up for us, but they didn't want to know it, especially after the first goal went in. And they're normally the first two on my teamsheet!"

He pauses to take a sip of a pint that's been thrust in his hand by his number two. "The less I say about it the better I think."

"Who've we got in the next round", asks one of today's subs Nick Wilson. Demonstrating a knowledge of theory equal to his practical abilities, with a few other players listening in, Club Captain Lee Barlass announces that the draw (pre–determined at this stage) pits Mangotsfield at home to the winners of the all - Western League Premier Division tie, Paulton Rovers v Odd Down.

Overhearing the conversation, a well - informed punter in the bar shouts that Odd Down have battled to an impressive 2-1 away win. "Odd Down," says Lee philosophically, they'll be a tough nut to crack – They always dig in, they're well renowned for it. And being from Bath, they'll want to put one over on Bristol, especially in the FA Cup - They're bound to be up for it big time. But - so will we!"

"Hey Lee,"shouts the barman with the clubhouse phone n his hand. "It's Alex Ferguson. He wants to know what you're doing next Saturday!"

"How about that lads, good story for you there eh?"

Lee just shakes his head and laughs.

Mangotsfield are enjoying the Limelight.

3

Oi Goaly, you'm a wanker

FIRST QUALIFYING ROUND

MANGOTSFIELD UNITED

V

ODD DOWN

SATURDAY 4 SEPTEMBER 1999

@ COSSHAM STREET, MANGOTSFIELD, BRISTOL

ATTENDANCE: 183 – Yes, the same as against Hungerford

On Thursday 2 September, Bristol is still consumed in a heatwave. But, by 7pm the day's full fervour is at last spent, meaning blessed relief for those rolling up to the week's second training session. And the high spirits engendered by the new management team are still very much in evidence. This is no doubt helped along, by the fact that Mangotsfield's 100% record for the season is still intact due to a 4-0 victory at Cossham Street on Saturday, against Bristol rivals Bishop Sutton.

A lot of fitness work is being done tonight, in accordance with earlier promises made by the management team and to compensate for the lack of stamina - building midweek matches. "When their fitness levels are up, I want them to be maintained," continues Blacky, so Gilly and I have designed a programme to keep them in top condition. We want them to work the opposition hard for ninety minutes, week in week out and that's exactly what we'll need to do on Saturday for a start. But it won't be easy 'cos Odd Down have a crucial extra game under their belts."

Next cup opponents Odd Down may not exactly be title contenders, they are very much the 'Wimbledon' of the Western League, with a reputation for battling until the end and working hard for each other. Whilst Wimbledon are currently going through a period of increased sophistication, the Bathonians are not, but possess a team spirit to rival the heady days of the Crazy Gang, which was underlined by their away victory at Paulton in the previous round. Paulton were clear favourites at the start and one-nil up at half-time, but reports made it clear that Odd Down's never-say-die spirit played a big part in seeing them through with two second half goals. Like Wimbledon, Odd Down on their day can well and truly upset the apple cart. And ominously, on the Tuesday of this week, they ground out another good result, a 4-3 league victory at home to more Bristolians in the form of Brislington, this time after being 3-1 down at the break. Gilly, was at that game checking out the opposition, and is in no doubt as to what will be required if the Field are to progress in the tournament. Although far from a shrinking violet on the pitch, Gilly is a most amenable chap and takes time out from training to confirm his findings:

"We're gonna have to roll our sleeves up, there's no doubt about that."

These sides are very familiar with each other and Gilly's scouting mission only confirmed what he already knew:

"If we score against them we can't let up, you can get two or three and they just won't roll over and die. But we're like that ourselves these days, so we'll be confident on Saturday, but like Blacky says, if we get over confident we'll be done for!"

Cutting back Tarantino–style to Tuesday 31 August, confidence is not something that appears to be oozing from the enemy camp:

"We certainly haven't got their kind of money and I don't think we can compete with them," bemoans full time carpenter and part time Odd Down boss, Vic Flippance:

"We have to make do with what we've got. We're only the number two team in Bath (behind Bath City) competing with top-class rugby as well, so it's difficult to bring in support and we get virtually no local press coverage. And that makes it difficult to compete in the wages department too. So the better players aren't always willing to come here. I don't think our interest in the Cup will extend beyond Saturday."

Only two real points are learnt from our evening out. The manager rates Glen Witts as their main man and the management team is called Vic and Bob.

Saturday 4 September, sees a national press still conspicuous by their lack of interest. The barest inch of column space is all that any paper can spare for these early Cup contests, with some giving no mention at all. But at a sun-drenched Cossham Street at around 1pm, the FA Cup is very much top of the agenda.

With preparatory work in full swing, staff flit from place to place, carrying out their ubiquitous labours of love. 'Shreddy' the groundsman fetches out the corner flags, in blissful ignorance of a nickname earned through the similarity between his Bobby Charlton circa 1973 hairstyle and a well-known breakfast cereal. Rodger is rushing around as usual and supporter and volunteer Meg has just removed the 'wet paint' sign in the gents, having added a second coat. The usual gaggle of committeemen stands pitchside talking pounds, shillings and pence and the bar is beginning to fill up.

Our presence plus Mangotsfield's sparkling form are without doubt the catalyst for widespread bar talk of Cup run. The pre-determined draw at this stage of the tournament, dictates that today's victors will be on their travels in the next round, where either fellow Western League Premier Division outfit Chippenham Town or South Western League St Blazey will await them. And this has put the Field faithful in good heart. They know that either way, the opposition will come from a parallel standard and as far as they are concerned, Mangotsfield's rich vein of form should take them past just about any opposition from this level. "We wouldn't even mind playing Taunton - that much," quips one wag from a nearby table. Noticeably though, this draws a number of frowns.

Most of the support is familiar with the early format of the Cup and the place is buzzing with the proximity to the really big game that victory over Chippenham or St Blazey would bring. Indeed it would take Mangotsfield to the Third Qualifying Round, and the brink of a possible Fourth Qualifying Round (last phase before the competition proper) tie, quite possibly against Conference opposition, which would constitute a massive occasion.

But in the car park, things come crashing down to Earth. "There's no guarantee we'll even get past Odd Down!" asserts Lee Barlass pragmatically.

Lee is fully aware of and very interested in, the permutations and combinations of the draw, but remains frustrated by the onslaught of optimistic speculation. He knows that football matches aren't won by divine right and of the immense effort, concentration and skill required, to overcome any side from this level of the game:

"Make no mistake about it, the Bristol versus Bath thing is a big factor today and they'll be wanting to put one over on us in a big way. The same as we do to them. There's a lot at stake and no way can we take anything for granted. But it's good that we've got Nathan (Rudge) back, to give us extra bite. He's what we need in a game like this.

At 2pm both sides are carrying out their respective warm up rituals on the pitch. Blacky has done his homework thanks to Gilly's Tuesday night observations, but is unaware of the esteem in which Glen Witts is held by the opposition. Instead, he's concentrated on his own players, the defence in particular:

"It's important we keep a clean sheet against these, because they'll be difficult to break down if they get one. They're strong through the middle, especially at the back, so we'll be looking to get it wide. And we'll see how they can handle three up front."

Flippance meanwhile, is in no mood to discuss his side's chances and it's quite obvious that contrary to the implications referred to on Tuesday night, he hasn't brought them here to make up the numbers. He and Bob Lardner can be seen entering into intense discussion with every one of their players, geeing them up, giving instructions. It's plain to see that on the quiet they believe they can do it.

One or two fans sporting Bristol City colours filter into the stadium to take in their second game of the day. They are in good spirits having just watched City dispose of Blackpool 5-2, in a Nationwide Division Two fixture with an experimental midday kick off. "Right, let's hope for a Bristol fuckin' double," says one, sporting a vest and City tattoo, rubbing his hands in anticipation as best he can with a pasty in one of them.

It's blisteringly hot again and certainly more conducive to watching than playing. Ten years ago, it would have been a classic case of 'letting the ball do the work'. But in these days of supreme fitness, speed and strength, at all levels of the game touched by any sort of professionalism, such weather will make little difference. And you can bet they'll come out fighting today. Colin's air horn and a ripple of applause from the shirt sleeved faithful, signal the arrival of the teams once again into the brightness. The players squint and hold hands up to faces in order to protect their eyes from the sun. Flippance's midweek prediction of ten followers cheering his side on seems about right. "Come on 'Down" is the shout, and it isn't Bath's own Lesley Crowther either.

Mangotsfield line up in their familiar maroon and sky blue and Odd Down in their away strip of black and white striped shirts, black shorts and black socks. Only one change for Mangotsfield from the Hungerford starting line–up, Nathan Rudge replaces Gilly, leaving them pretty much at full strength. Barlass and Fuller shake hands and the formalities are over. It's showtime!

So Martin Boyle kicks–off for the home side. The ball goes to his striking partner Darren Edwards and for the next couple of minutes or so, Mangotsfield stroke it around in style. But as per Blacky's promise it is not long before they're getting forward and chances are created and missed. Keeper Mark Batters saves comfortably on a couple of occasions.

Odd Down of course are not fazed by this energetic big-city start and signal their own intentions with the first in a series of tricky runs and penetrating crosses from right wing back Dean Book. Book is the brother of Cheltenham goalkeeper Steve, and nephew to 70's icon Tony, who lifted the Cup itself, as captain of the cult, Manchester City side that emerged some thirty years ago. In addition, Dean's father, Kim, played in goal for Northampton Town and indeed featured in memorable, 70s FA Cup action on *Match of the Day* against Manchester United. Unfortunately for Kim however, it was a resurgent George Best who provided the memories, as he celebrated return from suspension, by scoring six times in an 8-2 victory for United.

Back to FA Cup 2000 and Lee Barlass rises to head Book's cross, clear. To Odd Down's credit, they're trying to bring the ball down and play it, but in spite of this and Book's efforts, it is more or less all Mangotsfield and not long before ex-Bath City midfielder Gareth Loydon is on the end of a through ball from Lee Barlass. Loydon lets fly from 30 yards. The ball screams just over the bar. And the fencing behind the Odd Down goal prevents an unwelcome thud against the window for one of the nearby residents.

Meanwhile, one of the Odd Down followers congregated by the away dugout, decides that it's time to indulge in a little light conversation with Mangotsfield 'keeper Tony Court:

"Oi goaly, you'm a wanker!"

Unable to believe his ears, a startled Court looks over. With crowds this size it's not difficult to pick out individuals, and he soon identifies the perpetrator, who looks like an extra from 'Far From the Madding Crowd.' And there's more profanity to follow:

"You'm a fuckin' wanker goaly."

"Yeah?" laughs Court

"Fuckin' yeah," comes the response.

Court knows full well that the best way to deal with situations like this is through silence. But for reasons best known to himself, perhaps because

Mangotsfield's supremacy has provided enough spare moments to do so, Court cannot resist making a gesture from the front of his shorts, that would suggest it is indeed the spectator himself, who indulges in the aforementioned activity.

"Reck'n yer 'ard do yer goaly, come on then!" The perpetrator, knows full well that Court is not in the position to accept this challenge in the middle of an FA Cup-tie. And given the keeper's considerable stature, one gets the impression that our agricultural friend may not be so keen to make the offer in a more private place.

"Anytime" shouts Court, gradually losing patience in the heat. Unperturbed and safe within the backdrop of the game the abuser retorts: "Oi'm shittin' moiself goaly."

Court knows deep down that this is the oldest trick in the book, designed to break the concentration of a worthy opponent and as such is a back handed compliment. But he cannot resist waving his hand around his backside, to signify that his bowels too have been loosened. Before Court can run over and do an 'Eric Cantona,' the engagement is ended by the distraction of an Odd Down attack.

The supporters at Non-league football are allowed to develop their own identity at matches and this may well be a good proportion of the attraction of the "semi-pro" code, the lower leagues allowing a personal touch between supporters, club officials, and even players alike. And the identity of one individual is on display at close quarters, compared with the anonymity of the Holte End or the Bobby Moore Stand. It is likely that persons attracted to the professional "big" games enjoy the greater standard of football, and the vast electric atmosphere of the Premier league, but in there somewhere for many must be the comfort of the pack and the identity of the herd not the individual.

At Mangotsfield and it's like, the possibility of a stranger questioning you on your club normally supersedes the 'enjoyment' of hostile taunts at supporters 100 yards away. Indeed at any Nationwide League or Premiership stadium, that 100 yards can be 1 yard and 1 mile at the same time due to the strict security in place. And yet the intensity of a packed stadium brings the illusion of two mobs in the same drawing room, separated only by the carpet. But in parallel, the safety of the security measures and/or the division created by the pitch itself gives the distance of two armies across an uncrossable border. While at Cossham Street, 20 yards is 20 yards!

As the enthralling contest evolves, differing hugely from it's big league brothers in terms of pace, Mangotsfield bare their teeth as the challenges go in, proving in the process that they will not be rattled by the Odd Down steel. And the 'anger' on the touchline is gradually transferred to the pitch as tempers fray in the heat. But the Field continue to put some impressive moves together.

Young Hallett is doing his customary damage down the left, consistently beating Fear and crossing towards Boyler. A couple of chances are fashioned in this manner but spawned by the striker under pressure from centre back Fuller.

"Ride the storm lads!" is the desperate instruction from Batters between the sticks. And they do. These are the kind of blokes you would want to have with you in the trenches. If indeed, you want to be in the trenches.

Meanwhile Glen Witts is beginning to make ominously serious incisions into the body of the home side, as the visitors ease into contention through sheer grit and determination. And it becomes clear that Mangotsfield have got a game on their hands.

As the sweltering first half rages on and Witts launches himself into yet another powerful run, fiery 19 year old defender Nathan Rudge puts in one of his traditional 'fully committed' challenges, to unceremoniously prevent further progress. The inevitable happens and handbags are extracted accordingly and waved.

With half time and a welcome cooling drink just around the corner, the fracas dies down and Hallett soon shows that he can match the effectiveness of Witts as yet another pinpoint cross rains down upon Batters' box. This time, Neil Rosslee is on the end, and he heads powerfully home at the far post, to break the deadlock, showing the strikers how to finish into the bargain. Cue the echoing ripple of applause and muffled cheer.

"Right, now we can shut up shop and go in one–up," declares a relieved pitchside punter, leaning on Ralph's wall.

With half time virtually upon us and referee Mr Logford from Oxford looking hard at his watch, one or two of the Field faithful are beginning to grow impatient for the break:

"Come on ref, oi needs a pint to caalm me nerves."

The ball breaks yet again to Witts, this time some thirty yards out, but there are plenty of Mangotsfield players behind the ball and nobody is panicking. Seeing the limited options available, Witts decides to let one go and it flies into the roof of the net to fulfil Vic's prophecy. And what were those words about this lot refusing to lay down and die? Well, we warned them about Witts, even if no-one else did.

Ten sets of arms are raised aloft behind the away dugout. And half-time again sees the scores level.

"More of the same lads," is the simple dressing room message from Blacky. "You're so much better than them it's a joke. But you need to keep working hard. I know it's hot but you've gotta keep going!"

Batters pulls off some early spectacular saves after the re-start, drawing admiration around the ground.

A fine selection of full–blooded challenges and associated scuffles, often revealing Odd Down's Francis Hodges to be a keen participant, and Batters making decent saves is the story of the game. With a minute to go, despite the best efforts of Rudge and Barlass, who join the attack on a regular basis, those keen enough among the shirt-sleeved Bristolians are beginning to check their diaries, as a replay looks the safest bet. But Barlass plays in sub "Zubey" (ex-keeper named after the obvious Spaniard) down the right who skips past tired legs to get a cross in, that finds Boyle waiting in the middle. He brings it under and escapes the attention of Fuller yet again to unleash a great shot into the corner of the net to break Odd Down's hearts. For a second! Somewhere in the melee however, Batters was fouled and Mr Logford has decreed that the goal will not stand.

A murmur of discontent emulates from the sweating customers dotted around the ground. Mr Logford's next duty is to signal the end of round 1 of this bout, sparking off big celebrations as Odd Down players punch the air, faces reflecting 100% adrenaline. They live to fight another day, this time in their own back yard. In direct contrast, those in maroon and blue are disconsolate. They know it was of paramount importance to do the business today and now face an intimidating trip on Wednesday. Blacky sees each one of them into the dressing room. "Well done Lee....well played Boyler.....come on, heads up......well done lads." The door closes. Meanwhile there is distinctly more noise coming from the away facilities.

"And we'll fuckin' 'ave you down at our place!" shouts a rejoicing Bath punter, at the departing Mangotsfield players, as he senses an early piece of Cup giantkilling.

After half an hour, a philosophical Mr Black emerges. His brow is furrowed, but due more to concentration than despair. A journalist from the local rag and one Hospital Radio reporter invite his comments:

"I thought we over elaborated at times. I wanted our lads to get forward quicker, but it just didn't happen. At least not often enough anyway. Witts? Yeah his pace surprised us, but we'll have something up our sleeve for him on Wednesday."…Intimidating? Yeah, I suppose their place is a bit of a nightmare… But we should have won today y'know. No way was Boyler's goal a foul for a start. Sure, Odd Down battled well. Yeah, they dug in as expected, but we still should have won. Their keeper basically kept them in it." (Mark Batters was indeed declared man of the match, in the only local paper that bothered with sufficient column space).

"And yep, I'm confident of winning the replay… In good spirits? Of course I am, we're still in the FA Cup aren't we?"

Having heard of our venture, the Hospital Radio reporter requests an interview – Fame at last!

Meanwhile, some 30 miles to the East, Chippenham Town have eased past St Blazey (where Leeds and England goalkeeper Nigel Martyn was unearthed by a Bristol Rovers tealady) by two goals to one.

The coveted prize on Wednesday night is now a trip to Wiltshire.

Monday 6 September – Cossham Street.

Penalty practise is the main focus tonight as Andy Black goes where Glenn Hoddle dared not.

It transpires that Court has been saving more than his fair share of penalties and confidently predicts an Odd Down win, to the howls from his team-mates. "I don't know whether to be pleased or not," laughs Blacky. "On the one hand, we can't score penalties and on the other we've shown we can keep 'em out! I'll be optimistic and say it's down to us having a top keeper, rather than bad penalty takers.

4

A little Anglo Saxon out there tonight isn't it?

FIRST QUALIFYING ROUND - REPLAY

ODD DOWN

V

MANGOTSFIELD UNITED

WEDNESDAY 8 SEPTEMBER 1999

@ COMBE HAY LANE, ODD DOWN, BATH

ATTENDANCE 127

"**O**k lads remember, this ref's a stickler for jewellery and bad language." Blacky makes sure the pre-match preparations are 100% thorough, as the Mangotsfield entourage enter the changing rooms. He has the usual air of infectious confidence about him and it will need to rub off on his players tonight, as Combe Hay Lane, a lone, windswept, hilltop outpost, near the southernmost tip of Bath is at it's most intimidating. The glorious weather that graced the earlier rounds at the altogether more civilised and encompassed surroundings of Cossham Street, has done a complete u–turn and floodlights accentuate silvery rods of rain as they are blown into spirals by North East Somerset's version of El Nino. Dark woods and rugged countryside provide the background on three sides of the 'stadium' and only one covered area is provided in the form of a small stand. Half-overgrown by grass and bushes, with one corner of its roof flapping in the wind, the stand covers about one quarter of the length of the touchline. Behind the opposite touchline is an old railway goods carriage and the scene is closer to 'A Fistful Of Dollars' than the FA Cup. It is difficult to believe the sun ever shines in this neck of the woods.

The Combe Hay playing surface is a notorious 'leveller' at the best of times, so in combination with tonight's conditions and the guaranteed determination of the home side, it is all adding up to a stern test for the visitors. Adjacent to the remaining side of the pitch however, is the sizeable and very importantly, warm and dry, clubhouse, which is without doubt the finest feature of this ground, and the one we immediately head for and set up base camp in. This is set next to the changing rooms, which although rustic in appearance, are given character through their construction from the famous Bath Stone. After a while, Blacky emerges from the creamy yellow construction with a bag of footballs and steely stare. Bobby Robson as England manager once said the next game was not for players who were "woolly upstairs" and if he had been here tonight he would have definitely have said it again. Unfortunately, Mr Robson is unlikely to ever visit this gaff. At this point, Gilly and the players filter out. They know that this encounter is not for the faint-hearted, especially if, as seems likely, there is 'afters' on the menu. But each replicates the cold look of focussed determination and it is clear that the management team have done the first part of their job well tonight. No wool in sight.

This time Blacky has prepared for the pace of Witts. "we'll play a bit deeper against him. We'll start with 3-4-1-2, and Boyler just behind the main strikers." He trots off to the players to continue the encouragement. Flippance and Lardner do the same.

There are numerous vacancies for seating in the small stand, but the 30 or so indefatigable Bristol souls that have made the 15-mile trip, elect to huddle by the touchline perimeter wall and not under the sparse roofing. We know not why.

Some locals meanwhile have no interest in the outdoor proceedings, and remain in the warm and dry, preferring England's televised, Euro 2000 qualifier against Poland and a game of pool as their evening's entertainment. It is unlikely this happens at Anfield.

Back outside, zero hour has arrived and the teams are out. Mangotsfield in their away kit of yellow shirts, sky blue shorts and yellow socks. And strangely, the home side in their black and white away colours as sported on Saturday. Barely audible applause is again the greeting.

Things get under way with the wind and rain getting stronger. The ball is being blown all over the place and the only sure thing about this game is that it won't be pretty. But during the first two minutes, it is clear that both managers have been successful in motivating their players, as tackle after rain-sodden teeth-clenched tackle goes in. And given the amount of handbags in the first match, it looks already as though dessert could well be served cold tonight.

First to show on the football front are Odd Down, in the inevitable form of Glen Witts, who embarks on a penetrating run from midfield. He puts over a dangerous cross, but it's headed confidently away by Barlass. Before long, hard working forward Paul Keen shows sheer, dogged, determination on the halfway line, winning a ball to which he has no right. Keen plays a short pass to Witts who makes nonsense of the conditions with a class through ball to the overlapping Dean Book on the right. Book sends in a low cross, but Barlass's partner in crime Dave Elsey smashes it clear.

With ten minutes gone, Witts is running riot, as Barlass and Elsey are called upon time and time again to repel the results of his work. A further cross from the man himself flies in, this time from the left and Mangotsfield's hearts are in their mouths. The unthinkable is on the cards as right wing back Dean Book shapes up, unmarked, for a close range header, but the ball is fractionally too high for him and the Field are off the hook. Cue a number of encouraging expletives among the Mangotsfield players and corresponding comments among the Odd Down ranks. Today's referee (Mr Restall)'s bad language policy appears to be having little effect!

Mangotsfield are fighting well, but being outpointed. Boyler is battling away in the hole behind the strikers, but his supply line is well policed. And Fuller and Fear are maximising the big man's difficulty in getting on the end of anything that does filter through. Responding, Mangotsfield keep competing and carve out a missed chance for Nathan Rudge, who fails to test Batters from 18 yards.

Tonight, it is Court's turn to impress in The Field goal, and he saves well from Paul Keen.

In true style though, minutes later he is the villain. Book has made one of many good runs down the right, his cross flies in, swirling in the wind and rain. Court comes for it, but fumbles. (In mitigation after the match, Court claimed it took a deflection whilst he was in mid-flight and that he'd done well to even get a hand to it!) Odd Down central defender Dave Hare has made a galloping run to supplement the attack and the fumble has presented him with a gilt-edged chance. He needs only to lunge forward and poke it over the line. A second invitation is not required and Hare gleefully rams the ball home. Microseconds later, he's up from the mud with Odd Down players running towards him, some with arms outstretched some punching the air.

"Fuckin' get in there," is his celebratory cry. Some are so fired up they're just shouting "yes...yes" at the top of their voices, faces contorted with emotion. 100% pure adrenaline, again. It clearly means plenty to them to win this one. And this would have been an ideal cue for Court's terrace tormentor from Saturday, but he is nowhere to be seen or heard.

Meanwhile Court sits dejectedly on the saturated turf. He knows that fairly or unfairly, a goalkeeping error can be very costly in a cup game!!

Most football fans would sneer at this level of the game and barely anybody, aside from tonight's 127 witnesses, will ever become aware of this particular slice of FA Cup action. But whilst the conditions and levels of ability, mean that we will not see the most skilful football in the world, this to us, has already become a more intriguing and exciting encounter than many Sky Sports mid-table Premiership offerings or ritual Manchester United victories. Mind you, this view isn't shared by the dozen still in the bar watching England.

After a few minutes of determined clashes and no real chances, Zubey Wilson takes advantage of some careless Odd Down passing and charges down the right to get a cross in. But the delivery is poor and Duncan Fear of the renowned 'Fuller and Fear' defensive and comedy partnership thumps the ball away. Wilson is clearly disappointed. This is an ideal opportunity to stake his claim for a regular first team place. But Mangotsfield have clearly grown in stature since the Odd Down goal and it is end to end stuff now as the game becomes more evenly balanced. Next up for a chance though, is Odd Down's Paul Keen. He sees the shooting opportunity and lets fly. The shot blazes just wide, but more significantly a certain, better placed, Glen Witts was waving furiously for the ball in the middle. A decent cross from Keen could have all but sealed it.

On the half-hour, Boyler at last finds some space and lashes a fearsome shot from fifteen yards against the bar.

"It's 0-0 and we're playing crap", comes a confusing shout from the back of the stand. However this turns out to be a match report on England. The supplier of the news is a young man who's voice has been prevalent since kick-off. A comment about a player here, a score update from Katowicz there and a little quip everywhere. But above all, an obvious knowledge of the game and the local circuit in particular. It comes as no surprise that this man is one Tommy Saunders, manager of Chippenham Town, weighing up the opposition. Our first notice of a larger-than-life character who is to feature large in our FA Cup run.

To a man, Mangotsfield seem to have taken heart since Boyle hit the bar and have now started to grab the game by the scruff of the neck, and Half Time ends up as a welcome relief for the Bath side and they go in one-nil up.

The players head for the changing rooms and virtually every spectator makes a beeline for the warmth and dryness of the clubhouse, where steaming cups of tea, in proper mugs are selling very well. Proper mugs, how often would you find that?

"Right, we can do them. We proved it last Saturday by dominating the game and for the last quarter of an hour you've proved it here. Away from home, crap

Andy Black in pensive mood during the deadlock against Odd Down

weather and all. Just keep putting it in. Dig in that bit harder. Be more like them in that way! If you do that, we'll win it. We can outplay them any day - you just have to work hard enough as well." This is the Andy Black school of halt-time motivation.

Still no sign of a let-up in the weather as the brave supporters trudge back out for the second half. And as things get under way again, Mangotsfield carry on where they left off. Within a minute of the restart, Batters has saved a point blank header from Nathan Rudge, who has shown his supreme fitness time and time again by joining the attack in open play and getting back to defend when possession is lost. Boyle is getting more space in the box, but fires a good chance wide.

Then with the second half five minutes old, a cross comes in from a strangely quiet Danny Hallett and Darren Edwards is waiting in the middle to nod it home. At last the equaliser has come and the Mangotsfield players are going mental. Edwards is completely swamped with bodies in yellow and blue, right in front of the Field fans on the touchline. A very pleasurable contrast for them, between this and the sight of Odd Down's first half celebrations.

Boyler is now literally revelling in space as Down fail to get to grips with his withdrawn role. On the hour, Wilson is involved as some pantomime-style defending ends in a badly sliced clearance from Batters, which tees up a nice chance. Zubey volleys it over the bar, but this is all too much for Odd Down's Steve Fuller, whose jovial character is put to one side as he goes absolutely berserk and totally loses it with Batters and the rest of the defence. This gives rise to a heated debate with regard to blame and some of the comments float on the wind across to the perimeter fencing. "A little Anglo Saxon out there tonight, isn't it?" suggests one Mangotsfield supporter. And Odd Down's spirit seems to be breaking.

From the goal kick, the ball breaks to create a 50-50 challenge between Lardner and Loydon. The duel results in a few pushes and shoves, which in truth, is something the Odd Down number two appears to have been wanting for virtually the whole match. He must be a nightmare in the boozer. The only surprise is that this is the first real incident in another heated game.

Inside the last twenty minutes now and the revitalised Hallett wins a throw, which he takes to Wilson, who cuts inside from the left and unleashes a thirty-yarder. Batters tips it over the bar and Wilson is thwarted again. Nathan Rudge heads the corner on to Darren Edwards, who tries a spectacular overhead shot

Spot the ball - Mangotsfield v Odd Down

from ten yards, but blazes it over the bar. Just inside the last quarter of an hour, Rudge joins the attack again but his long-range shot is way wide of the mark.

With the physical stuff rumbling on, Mangotsfield win a free kick on the left, just outside the Odd Down box. Secret weapon Elsey runs up and blasts it into the wall. But Mr Restall signals for the kick to be taken again, due to an encroachment of the 10-yard rule. Elsey blasts it again, this time firmly into the net and now look at those Field players go. Such is the importance of victory tonight, that the celebrations are more furious than if the Cup itself had just been won. Even the perennially conservative statto Dave and co are punching the air.

Into the last ten minutes and man of the moment Dave Elsey puts in a crunching tackle on left wing back Francis Hodges to halt his progress just outside the Mangotsfield box. Hodges gets up immediately and without further ado delivers a right hook onto Elsey's jaw. Even from our position in the corner of the ground, diagonally opposite to the incident, the sickening sound of Hodges' fist making contact can be heard. A twenty two-man brawl breaks out. Afters has indeed been served. Cold and wet too. And inevitably Hodges walks.

Now it is wild tackles and adrenaline by the shedload. With five minutes to go, Tommy Saunders can be heard up in the stand confirming the latest England score as 0-0. His voice has been dominant for the entire match and he is proving his character, exchanging quips with us and all around him, in a dress rehearsal for our next meeting.

Out on the pitch, more defensive lapses result in Darren Edwards intercepting a terrible Odd Down pass down the right channel. He plays it square to sub Gillard who advances to the edge of the box in three strides and hits a screamer just wide of the far post. It is all Mangotsfield now and all over bar the shouting. Batters' save from Hallett's superb shot is academic and shortly afterwards Mr Restall signals the end of this pulsating tie. Mangotsfield have done it. The punching incident has clearly muted celebrations a little, but the joy on players' and supporters' faces alike is plain to see. Blacky's cup run is still on the rails and more importantly perhaps, Mangotsfield have come through a stiff character test, which will bode well for the league and cup campaigns ahead of them.

When everyone has had a chance to come out of the showers and down from the ceiling, Barlass confirms that he is (justifiably) pleased with his and Mangotsfield's performance: "Yeah I thought I did ok." (Understatement time again). "It's never easy coming here, always a bit of a leveller, but I suppose that's the idea isn't it, y'know, to make it as hard as possible for the visitors?" A few shouts from Mangotsfield followers go up, with regard to the pitch being "fucking awful, as usual." Their comments regarding Francis Hodges are largely unprintable, but the consensus of opinion is that his actions would be tantamount to GBH if carried out on the street. And we would be hard pushed to disagree.

The Odd Down players are nowhere to be seen and it seems safe to assume that they are on the receiving end of the wrath of Flippance. It is indeed a famous lock-in. Unfortunately, it is the only one of the night as the bar shuts promptly at 11.

It goes without saying that Hodges attracts little sympathy, least of all from the FA who subsequently handed him a thirty five-day ban.

Blacky finishes off the victory debrief: "Yeah it's a tough place to come, and on the whole, teams have to change their game to succeed here. But we had the low down from Gilly and we had them watched when they lost at Bridport, so we knew a bit about their weaknesses as well as their strengths. We came here with good players, but as I said to them at half time, you have to want it enough. And they proved in the second half that they did! But the signs were there towards the end of the first. I'll tell you what, Gilly and me are like the cat that's got the cream tonight, but we really should have finished it on Saturday! But tonight's shown me something else. Coming to places like this and winning after going behind–that's the stuff that championships are made of!" It is clear that tonight has meant more than just another stage further in the 99/00 FA Cup!

The Odd Down players begin to emerge and an unusually downbeat Steve Fuller takes up the post -mortem. "We lost it in eight crazy minutes. After half time we started to back off for some reason and our attitude was out of order, which is unusual for us. You don't get anywhere by arguing, least of all amongst yourselves."

And of the little incident near the end?

"Disgusting!" he states unequivocally. "In all my years of experience I've never seen a punch thrown. "It's ridiculous, you just can't condone it." No prizes for guessing that Hodges has gone AWOL.

The final word belongs to Vic Flippance. "We played well in the first half, but those eight minutes at the start of the second killed the whole thing off! We could've done without half time really."

But the final word belongs to Vic:

"Yeah I'm disappointed, of course I am. Once you go in front you should stay there. But at the end of the day we weren't gonna win the bloody FA Cup were we!"

5

Shut up – that's his girlfriend behind the bar

SECOND QUALIFYING ROUND

CHIPPENHAM TOWN

V

MANGOTSFIELD UNITED

SATURDAY 18 SEPTEMBER 1999

@ HARDENHUISH PARK, CHIPPENHAM

ATTENDANCE: 356

Cossham Street - Thursday, 16 September 1999

"**B**ollocks!"

The reply to Statto Dave's theory about the size of Odd Down's pitch is nothing if not incisive. But he is having none of it and the furious debate continues: "I'm telling you, it was two yards too narrow. The minimum width for the FA Cup is seventy yards and theirs is sixty eight!"

"Who gives a toss anyway? We won didn't we?"

"That's not the point is it?"

"Well, how the fuck do you know all this anyway?"

"It doesn't matter how - I just do. Alright? And it was rock hard and bumpy as well. Bloody disgusting."

But Dave is fighting a losing battle, as one by one the clubhouse crew have turned to different topics of conversation. Down now to the last two, the audience has quite simply refused to give his theories any credence and by no means do they share his obsession with statistics.

They are to a man, however, high on Mangotsfield's incredible start to the season, the latest victims being Bridport, to whom a 6-0 trouncing was dished out in Dorset, last Saturday. Indeed so awesome was the Field performance, that Bridport manager, Trevor Senior – yes, *the* Trevor Senior – was inspired to advise Blacky post-match, that he had never seen a showing of such quality at this level of the game, including anything served up by Taunton Town!

Meanwhile back in the clubhouse, Dave is able to recapture his audience by revealing how the pre-determined draw will pan out, if Mangotsfield can overcome Chippenham on Saturday. And if the truth be known, the faintest traces of Cup fever are now apparent at Cossham Street, with the likelihood of a full outbreak if any further progress is made. Dave of course, takes great delight in explaining precisely why:

"If we win on Saturday, which I'm confident we can, we'll be at home to Deal Town or Worthing in the next round. Now, Deal are top of the Bass Brewer's Kent League at the moment, but that's a parallel standard to us, so we'd be in with a good shout of getting through. As for Worthing, they're going well in the Ryman (Isthmian) League Division One, which is a step higher than us in the Pyramid, so that would be a big game in itself. And they'd bring a fair few fans, which would make for a great atmosphere y'know. It's not often the teams we play bring much support, except maybe Tiverton before they were promoted, Taunton and maybe Chippenham. Worthing would be a tough nut to crack mind. But the way we're going, I reckon we could turn anyone over at our place!

"Then it would be Dover Athletic at home in the Fourth Qualifying Round. Brilliant! They're a Conference club, what a day that would be! And that would break our record of the Third Qualifying Round." ...Dave has worked himself into a contagious frenzy:

"And the winners of the Dover match go into the draw for the First Round proper - with the League clubs!" We all take a moment to salivate at the thought.

"Better get the suits ready for Wembley then" quips Lee Barlass, as the players saunter in from training. One thing is for sure, Lee will keep his feet firmly on the ground during all this. But we and the clubhouse boys have had a few pints, and moved on to which league clubs it would be nice to meet in the First Round Proper. And beyond.

An interesting development has impacted on team selection for Cup Saturday, in that full back Gary Thomas has left the club. Gary has taken a step down the football ladder, by re-joining Cadbury Heath, a County League side. This league is a kind of buffer between parks and semi-pro football.

"He just said Western League football wasn't for him," groans Blacky. "Which is strange because he's played in every game, and done really well. I don't think he enjoyed the travelling though. It can be difficult to get used to, especially getting home late in midweek from places like Bridport and going to work the next day."

It is clear that these choices are made constantly by players. Mangotsfield are not Man Utd, as we have said. Long days, training commitments and Saturdays wiped out are a bind when work still plays first place in your life. Gary Thomas' decision may be strange in the cold confines of the football world, but in the real one it is easily understood.

Meanwhile, the money-men are focussing on their next move in the relentless drive towards the Southern League. The recently generated FA Cup income has been ploughed into underpinning the push for a more professional image, as a part of which, the tree behind the school end has now been cut-down. But far more exciting news could be on the horizon for that particular piece of land, as developers have today stepped-up their interest in acquiring it, with a view to expanding the operation right across the stadium. This of course, would necessitate the complete demolition of Cossham Street and a handsome pay-day for the Field, enabling a move to bigger and better things. For the moment though, Cossham Street remains in trust and is not theirs to sell. But having been turned on to the immense opportunity that dangles tantalisingly before them, the committee are desperately searching for loopholes.

The merry-go-round of the semi-pro circuit and the magic of the FA Cup, have blended to present one ex-Mangotsfield player with an ideal stage on Saturday. The man in question is Chippenham striker Tony Bennett, who left Mangotsfield last season, in quite ignominious circumstances, partly exacerbated - according to some of the clubhouse boys – by the way in which then manager, Nicky Tanner, handled the transfer.

For the uninitiated, Tanner, is a Bristolian, who started his career at Mangotsfield, but made his name with Bristol Rovers. The only thing is, that name was 'whoosher,' which signified the usual type of ball he played during a game, i.e. hit hard and hope, with accompanying shouts of 'whoosh' from the crowd. Given this implication of a shortfall in class, more than a few eyebrows were raised by Rovers fans when Liverpool came in for him. Indeed, the Bristol Evening Post headline that broke the news of the transfer had readers checking the date for April. However, although Tanner actually did reasonably well at Anfield, his playing career was cut short by injury and he ended up in management on the south-west Non-League scene, where he steered Almondsbury Town up the Hellenic (parallel to the Western) league table on a very low budget. This, plus the undoubted experience and pedigree that he picked up at Anfield, were seen by the Mangotsfield committee as being of the right stuff to fulfil the club's ambitions. But things did not work out that way and a series of big promises, including the signing of Bruce Grobelaar, did not come to fruition. A number of other problems and personality clashes saw to it that Tanner was gone within a year. And not a solitary Mangotsfield fan will speak of him now.

This notwithstanding, it must be noted that Tony Bennett is not particularly critical of Tanner and assures us that Whoosher was always good for a laugh and would keep you up to date on which birds the Liverpool players were shagging. In fact, there is one particular story about John Barnes... But we digress.

However, although Bristolian through and through, Bennett has certainly not left his heart in Mangotsfield and is known to harbour a strong desire, to be instrumental in dumping them out of the FA cup. This is all well and good of course, but Tony is also a personal acquaintance of the authors and if he does score the winner, we will never hear the end of it.

As the talk of Bennett escalates, alcohol increasing the volume of our voices to nauseating proportions (as is par for the course) we mention the many female admirers that we (unfortunately) know he has. But this guaranteed male-bonding technique generates only silence. Deciding that nobody heard first time round, we inject the same subject matter into the conversation again.

"Shut up," whispers Dave, that's his girlfriend behind the bar!" The non-league world is indeed a small one.

Cossham Street – Saturday 18 September 1999. 12.30 pm

The weather has improved from that wild night in Odd Down, but it is still raining and far more comfortable in the bar than the car park. But for those that have used this focal point of the club as today's meeting place, it is time to scamper out to the transport for the trip to Chippenham. The club has decided that players will make their own 28 mile way to the game.

Eventually, all car-sharing schemes have been sorted and players, officials and supporters alike are ready to go. The nine vehicle convoy, snakes its way out of the car park and within ten minutes all are heading east, on the M4. Some club colours are in evidence, especially in the supporter's car, but not many will look at us on our travels and deduce that we are on our way to a big FA Cup game.

Lee Barlass is keen to expand on his theory that "Chippenham are a sleeping giant at this level". "Saunders has been out buying Southern League players and I've heard there's still more money in the pot. I think he's got seven contract players now and that's difficult for us to compete with, and as I said, it's only a matter of time before they begin to gel. Then they'll be a force to be reckoned with. If Taunton go up, I can see that leaving Chippenham and us as main contenders for promotion in the not too distant future. But they've got some pretty heavy backing and I reckon they're aiming for the Conference, no holds barred, whereas realistically, we can only look to the Southern League, for the moment at least. We're both the same though, in that while we've got the potential to get out of this league, neither of us want to run before we can walk!"

Hardenhuish Park – Saturday 18 September 1999. 1pm

The Mangotsfield entourage arrives and parks up. The fans gather flasks, airhorns and various bits and pieces of maroon and blue paraphernalia, and make their way up the long leafy slope, amid the drizzle, to the stadium entrance, which is set back so far as to be virtually invisible from the main road. When Black and Gillard have gathered the team's equipment with Mr Hamilton, players, management and authors form the rearguard, with Black and Gillard cajoling and motivating all the while. The slope levels out and the stadium appears before us. Blacky and co disappear down the players' tunnel and into the changing rooms under the main stand.

With this, Tommy Saunders walks by and starts to make his way down the tunnel. We take the opportunity to ask whether he was impressed with Mangotsfield's hard-fought victory against Odd Down. "No," comes the snorted reply as he makes his way unstoppably into the depths of the dark entrance.

Located above the main stand is the bar and clubhouse, which becomes our first port of call, and inside, we find the Chippenham players relaxing with toast, tea and Sky Sports.

Club captain Lee Burns is initially a little more reserved than his Mangotsfield counterpart, but soon warms to the undoubted interpersonal skills of the authors and, when he has finished serving tea from the club urn to the rest of the players, takes time out for a chat. Like Barlass, Burns is a modest, yet quietly confident man and instantly likeable. And when all is said and done, he knows that Chippenham are classed by many as underdogs today. But in his view this is inaccurate:

"We're yet to get going, that's our problem," he philosophises. "I think we're

Another money making scheme for Chippenham Town

basically, every bit as good as Mangotsfield and I don't see why we can't beat them. In fact I think we will!" "Last season we only lost one game at home and we've done well in the Cup this year. Beating St Blazey was no mean feat for starters. Don't forget, the pressure's on Mangotsfield as they've been doing so well. And with home advantage, yeah we can do it. You wait and see!" He raises his voice. "Anyway they're from Bristol aren't they, it'll be easy!"

Cheers of agreement ring out from most of the players. And it comes as no surprise to learn that Burns is from Bath, and demonstrates eloquently the small town inferiority complex against the big city. When Barlass acknowledges that all the teams in this league want to beat the Bristol sides, it is an acknowledgement they are from the South West's big city, and it shows more in opponents attitudes than their own.

Enter Saunders stage right.

"Here's the man who'll have all the quotes for you," says Burns.

"Who, me? No, I've got nothing to say," comes the reply. It seems obvious to all that he is actually bursting to become centre stage, but trying to play it cool. Saunders then butters himself some toast and fills a cup from the urn, and immediately starts geeing up the players, getting them going with quips, jokes and piss-takes, including the accusation to one player that he possesses "the smallest knob in the league." We can't confirm or deny this, fortunately.

"We will beat Mangotsfield today." He says loudly to us. "I saw them at Odd Down and whatever they think, they were poor".

The large figure of Saunders may only be of some 28 summers (his playing career on the local circuit was cut short by injury at the age of 24) but he shows the guile and the girth of more mature years. His comments about today's match are clearly made in a volume sufficient for the players to hear, in the hope that they will become that little bit more fired up by his show of faith. He has already made it clear that he will milk any opportunity to squeeze every last drop of adrenaline from his men. And having earlier watched him guilefully prompting the bonding of his troops, as opposed to allowing vegetation in front of Sky Sports, the reports we have received regarding the motivational skills of this man begin to ring true.

Back outside, the crowd is swelling, although the stadium capacity of 4,000 will be far from attained. The space immediately surrounding the perimeter consists mainly of hard standing as opposed to terracing, but this is a slightly bigger set up than Mangotsfield, with a dedicated club shop *in situ* and bigger main stand. Although neither end is covered. From the main stand, there is a panoramic view of the local school on hills and dales. The school grounds rise above the level of the stadium and dominate the scenery both directly ahead and to the left, while Chippenham Cricket Club adjoins to the right. A local fan tells us that we are looking at the biggest state school campus in the country, at seventy-six acres, and that Nicholas Parsons once opened a fete there!

With the stand becoming more populated, the ambience begins to reflect the bigger than average occasion, that we are about to experience and interest in the FA Cup exploits of these two sides is clearly beginning to escalate. Indeed estimates as to the size of today's crowd go as high as 400, which is roughly double a normal home attendance for either team. The first real radio station involvement is also in evidence, with BBC Wiltshire Sound in full effect. They hear of our Cup venture and want an interview. First Bristol Hospital Radio, then this. Surely, tomorrow the world!

As kick off time draws closer, both sides are out for their pre-match warm ups. And, Blacky has decided upon his team. "Noel (O'Sullivan)'s just about fit, so I'm gonna risk him from the start. I need the experience up front. He'll partner Darren Edwards as normal. But I've not chosen a third front man. Lee (Barlass) can do a job up front actually and I considered that, but I've opted for Gilly to stiffen the midfield instead and he'll get forward whenever he can. And I've done a straight swap, Gary Davis for Thommo. Gary should be OK there. We'll play 3-5-2, with Gilly, Lee Barlass and Rudgey supporting the attack at every opportunity, as well as the wing-backs of course. Apart from me, there won't be that much experience on the bench today, unfortunately. Losing those players has been a big blow I can tell you, especially in Boyler's case. But there you go I suppose. We've just got to get on with it.

The tactics are straightforward today. We're looking to attack and do them. One blessing is that they're still missing Mark Cutler (a big name on the South West circuit) through suspension. He could have hurt us. And I reckon Dave Elsey's got the beating of Tony Bennett in the air. So yeah, I'm still confident. And I'm still fighting off that law of averages."

By the time the players go in for their final preparations, there is a healthy atmosphere around the ground, with just a touch of the 'big game' feel in the air. The expectancy among the Mangotsfield followers has reached fever pitch and the now familiar air horn is in full flow, while the murmur of conversation is interspersed with cries of "Come on the 'Field." Not to be outdone, one or two home fans are giving it "Come on Chip." There is still no organised chanting, but this is the first example of any type of fan rivalry on our journey. And one thing is for sure; it won't be the last!

One Mangotsfield player boots the closed Chippenham dressing room door on his way back in, and yells abuse directed at Saunders. There will be no love lost in some quarters today.

With talking done, the teams come out to do battle and those lazy, hazy Summer days at Cossham Street seem further away than ever as Burns, Barlass and today's referee Mr Gatzianidis from Hampshire, complete the formalities in the driving rain. With the protocol out of the way, combat commences, both sides in traditional colours, meaning blue shirts and shorts with white socks for Chippenham (hence their nickname – the Bluebirds).

Chippenham's tricky winger Steve Campbell is soon making his presence felt down the right, causing problems with the ball into the box. Everyone is definitely fired up for this one on and off the pitch. As the game goes on, the Chippenham defence in particular, look determined to prevail. Lee Burns is leading them by example and already looks the part, not least of all due to a great last-gasp challenge on Darren Edwards, who would have been clean through but for the captain's intervention.

The Wiltshiremen are just edging it on points in the early stages, but Mangotsfield force their way back into it, with Rudge picking the ball up on the half way line and bursting forward to shoot just wide. Mangotsfield look excellent going forward as always.

On 25 minutes Chippenham defender John Woods is pressured into a foul on right wing back Gary Davis, on the edge of the Chippenham box. Free kick specialist and saviour of the Battle of Bath, Dave Elsey strides up to take it once again. Can he do the business this time? The shot is parried but Elsey battles through to follow up... It's another shot...But ex-Mangotsfield keeper Ian Jones flies majestically through the air to his side, and makes a superb reflex-save.

On the half-hour, 30 year-old Chippenham defender, Civil Servant and dressing-room joker, Iain Murphy commits a bad foul on Noel O'Sullivan, which results in another MUFC free kick. Blacky goes mad. He knows the vulnerability of O'Sullivan today:

"Come on ref, you're supposed to stop that kind of thing aren't you!" He wasn't expecting a response and didn't get one.

The striker limps away and appears to run the pain off successfully. This time the kick is taken by Rudge, but an attempt at a sophisticated pass-based set-piece breaks down and Chippenham break to win a free kick of their own. Murphy floats the ball in, Bennett wins it in the air and it's a clear chance for winger Steve Campbell just inside the box...He blasts it way over the bar. "It fell to my weaker (left) foot" said Campbell in mitigation after the match.

Bennett gets the chance he covets on the half hour with a free header but puts it over from 6 yards. 10 minutes later he gets another. This time he converts a first time prod past Court after good work from the impressive Collier. Cue, the shirt over the head as the game mimics the Premiership TV exploits. The same combination worked again on the stroke of halt time, but this time Bennett missed the chance to double the margin.

In this interval, Mr Black is asking questions "Why was Lee (Barlass) isolated on the left, for that goal?" is his key question as a post mortem looks at the mistakes. He soon switches to the positive though and gets back to his motivational skills, aided by his trusty sidekick, Gillard.

Collier though is really beginning to pull the strings as they re-commence battle. Chippenham have started from where they left off. And before the half is ten minutes old, more pressure has won them a free kick on the right, just outside the Mangotsfield box. Tiley puts his dead ball specialist hat on and strides up to take the kick. He curls it around the wall, but it's going wide until an anonymous maroon sock comes from nowhere to deflect the ball slowly goalwards. Court scrambles across his line to no avail and it trickles in. Cue a brief cheer and more applause from the Chippenham fans. Some raise both arms to the skies in triumph:

Two nil. Mangotsfield are reeling on the ropes and Blacky's head, along with the visiting supporters, is in his hands:

"What a fuckin' soft goal," he mumbles to his palms, while his cup dreams collapse before him.

Mangotsfield show little invention and the game slides away from them. Into the last twenty and Chippenham's Tweddle shows why big brothers, Bath City tried to sign him in the close season. He turns Davis brilliantly to get a shot in, but Court's reflex save is equally impressive.

Blacky withdraws Gillard and O'Sullivan and sends youngsters Marcus Bloomfield and Bradley Andrews into the fray. And Barlass and Rudge add their weight to the attack at regular intervals. But still no breakthrough. Bloomfield is assigned to replace O'Sullivan up front, but it's Edwards who's next into striking action with a shot that's blocked in the box by a determined Lee Burns, who has been inciting regular purring from the blue portion of the crowd. Desperate Bristolian appeals for a penalty are turned down. Burns did not use his hand. Although he did manage to find his way into the book for a foul shortly afterwards.

Before long, Court is performing heroics to keep Mangotsfield in with any shout. First by flying across his line to palm a Collier free kick around the post, then from the resulting corner, he leaps acrobatically to tip a powerful Lea James shot over the bar. From that corner, the ball runs loose and Court throws himself upon it before anyone else has a chance to react. Superb stuff from the young keeper. Were it not for him, this tie would have been dead and buried long ago. Chippenham attack at will.

With ten minutes to go, Nathan Rudge shows his frustration by standing on Tony Bennett's ankle after a challenge. A move as unpopular with the crowd as with the now limping and usually unflappable Bennett, who gets up close and personal with Rudge to show his disapproval. Rudge and Bennett later stage a rematch, but before anybody can call Don King, Mangotsfield's dream is over. And when the whistle goes, we see a classic case of the agony and the ecstasy as the men in all-blue punch the air, while the disconsolate Mangotsfield players hang their heads and trudge off the pitch and the cheers and applause of the Chippenham fans rings out.

Black is brave in defeat. His dream is in tatters, but he is quick to offer congratulations to Tommy Saunders: "Well done Tom, well played mate." They shake hands. Then Black goes back to his own men: "Unlucky lads, come on, heads up."

A quick acknowledgement and saddened look towards the travelling Bristolians on the touchline, then completes the sad FA Cup exit for Mangotsfield.

As we munch on the generous buffet laid on in the Chippenham clubhouse, Tommy Saunders is more than happy to discuss the victory: "I don't wanna say I told you so, but..."

The Clubhouse TV fails to mention the Cup, but soon we learn from other sources that Deal and Worthing have drawn. So Chippenham won't know their next opponents just yet.

"It doesn't matter who we get," says Tommy. "When you consider what'll be at stake, it's gonna be a massive day." And he's not wrong. A home tie in the

Fourth Qualifying Round against well-supported Dover Athletic, is a guaranteed money-spinner.

'YESSS!' Lee Burns & Co. acknowledge the applause after dumping Mangotsfield out of the Cup

6

Don't worry about jet lag,
we'll let him sleep through the first half

THIRD QUALIFYING ROUND

CHIPPENHAM TOWN

V

WORTHING

SATURDAY 2 OCTOBER 1999

@ HARDENHUISH PARK, CHIPPENHAM

ATTENDANCE 496

Tuesday 28 September – Hardenhuish Park

Another day another clubhouse. And very picturesque it is too. Chippenham – on the River Avon - is the largest town in the district of North Wiltshire, and is sandwiched between the Marlborough Downs to the east, the Cotswolds to the north and west and Salisbury Plain to the south. And the view from the lofted position of the clubhouse window confirms the tranquil setting of their football club.

While the Chippenham players train, we climb the stairs at the back of the main stand again, this time to familiarise ourselves with the Hardenhuish support-base. They really are buzzing in the bar and who can blame them? Mangotsfield were beaten in style and Worthing have since despatched Deal Town at home in their Second Qualifying Round replay by three goals to nil, to set up a big occasion for Saturday. And it is widely acknowledged here, that whilst Deal - in spite of a new found heavy financial backing and consequent table topping position - would have proved infinitely more beatable, Worthing, currently in the upper reaches of the Isthmian (Ryman) League and their substantial support will undoubtedly provide the bigger day.

But possibly the most encouraging news of all is the fact that Chippenham held the almighty Taunton to a 0-0 draw on Saturday, in deepest Somerset at that. And slowly but surely, the confidence of many punters here is beginning to grow, as the crucial league form looks to be coming together, with the massive potential of this club perhaps coming to fruition.

First up for some male bonding is the natural replacement for Statto Dave. Chippenham's version is Wil Hulbert, Chairman of the Supporters' club, who have just celebrated the signing of their 100th member. He also has his finger on the pulse of the club's one hundred and twenty six-year history. Wil is however, not as happy as some today, due to a serious fixture clash in the form of a helicopter trip booked for the same day as the Worthing game. He is nevertheless determined find a compromise and will almost certainly be able to arrive by half time. Hopefully, not by helicopter in the Centre Circle.

He tells us Chippenham have good football roots. "Back in the Forties, we used to get spectators for the training sessions!" He enthuses and goes on to take us through the heady days of massive attendances, including a record four thousand one Christmas Day, against (now defunct) local rivals Chippenham United.

Chippenham have indeed progressed slowly but surely since then. The clubhouse in which we are drinking was built in 1979, followed in 1981 by the opening of the hard training surface by the FA's very own Ted Croker. Although, whether the players sweating on that surface at this very moment would thank him for that is another matter. Nevertheless, this was followed in 1986, by the official switching on ceremony of the club's new floodlights, performed by Lou Macari, who was then manager of Swindon Town.

The most recent improvement came in 1995, when a complete revamp of the changing rooms saw them become the impressive facility they are today. 1996 saw a boardroom change, when colourful, local businessman and football fanatic Malcolm Lyus checked in and presided over the ongoing progress. Lyus installed Tommy Saunders as manager in February 1998, bringing him in from local rivals Calne Town upon the departure of none other than Vic Flippance, whose Odd Down side were put to the sword earlier in our journey. This has all culminated in Chippenham's highest league finish for forty years, when they ended up third in the Western League Premier Division last season.

Chippenham are also one of the few clubs at this level, with support organised enough to produce a fanzine. While still in its embryonic stages, early projections indicate that the publication may sell as well as the club programme and there are endless volunteers for contribution and editing duties.

And the club's ambition has been underlined by the fact that they have taken another rare step at this level, in appointing a full time commercial manager, in the form of Geoff Snell, who, having heard our low-down on the past is more than willing to discuss the future: "Basically, it's a ten year plan for the Conference."

(A further three promotions, through the Non-League structure are required for this, bearing out the theory that Chippenham seem to have greater aspirations than Mangotsfield and for that matter, most other Western League outfits).

"But the ten year aspect is important," warns Geoff. "We know it's a long way to go, and we're trying to do things properly. We're not taking anything for granted, but if we get promotion, we're determined to give Tommy an appropriate budget for the Southern League and obviously to remain solvent at the same time. Going up's one thing, but staying up's another!

In need of some recovery time ourselves, the sharp-end staff begin to drift in. Steve Lodge is first up the stairs. Once assistant physio at Oxford United is his claim to fame, but he now makes his living through the nearby Steve Lodge Sports Clinic. And he goes by the nickname 'Fizz.' Surely a shortened version of 'physio?'

Steve claims otherwise: "It's all about my incredible turn of speed, when I run on to the pitch with my bucket!"

31 year old Lee Burns is the captain and on-pitch leader. A will-seller by trade, he is a tall, well-set man, with short, dark, slightly thinning hair, a friendly smile and vice-like handshake. And in spite of his gentle demeanour, a masterful performance against Mangotsfield and the reaction to him of the home crowd, have made it abundantly clear that he is a veritable rock on the pitch. By now, most of the players are sitting with us and when Burns comments that they should have beaten Taunton this results in numerous nods of approval. Like any good leader, his confidence is infectious and if he says the business can be done, then it can be done.

The players are joined by boss man, Tommy Saunders, and he explains that the club is on the verge of delivering the promised land. "You want to know what makes us tick? We don't have any Prima Donnas. A player does well to keep his shirt here and I don't think there's one who hasn't been dropped at least once this season. I'll tell you something else as well, we've got a really strong squad, with good players waiting in the wings, through injury or suspension or whatever. 'Cuts' (Mark Cutler) is a good example. I signed him in the summer. He's been prolific for Tivvy (Tiverton) and Taunton and I expect him to do the business for us as well." But he's still suspended, which is a bit of a 'pisser' really 'cos we could really do with him against Worthing!"

Too many of the players at this level to mention have had some association with their local professional clubs and Cutler is no exception. High hopes were held for him when he was with Bristol City, but he never made a first team appearance. He is however, a highly respected figure on the local circuit and indeed, a prolific scorer at Western League level. In fact the flamboyant, 25 year old estate agent has a good pedigree in recent knock out tournaments, particularly the FA Vase, in which he was top scorer in 1997–98, including goals in the quarter and semi-finals, whilst playing for Taunton. (Unfortunately, he did not make it to Wembley as Taunton fell at that final hurdle – to Tiverton). It is clear that a lot of players who make youth football with a pro club know they are likely to have a fallback position in the semi-pro ranks. Not that anything less than star gazing is appropriate at that stage of life.

Saunders meanwhile, has not finished: "I've signed a lot of players who've been doing well in the Southern League. And they only agreed to come here because I sold the club to them so well. We've got seven contract players on board now! And when we start to gel we're gonna be a force to be reckoned with. That result against Taunton goes some way to proving that. And you watch us go on Saturday for a start!"

Saturday 2 October, Hardenhuish Park. 1pm

This is going to be a big day. Cars containing those clad in the red and white of Worthing FC are rolling up already and amongst the slamming doors, the Sussex accents somehow augment the ambience.

A quick jaunt up the old stairs reveals the (we have learned) traditional combination of Chippenham players; tea, toast and Football Focus.

"Yeah it's been going on for a few weeks," explains Burns. "We had tea and toast for the first time before a game, while we were watching the football on the telly, and we ended up doing really well, won the match and the habit stuck because we decided it brought us luck!"

It is not long before we catch up with Mr Saunders and once again he is confident:

"We've got a strong squad, which means we can cope with players that are out, just like we did against Mangotsfield. And don't forget about the ones waiting in the wings. For example, I've got Steve Brown, who got back from the States 36 hours ago and he'll be on the bench. And don't worry about jet-lag, we'll let him sleep through the first half and then he'll be fit as a fiddle!"

1.30pm

Saunders' confidence has been cut from beneath him. Chippenham keeper Ian Jones has called on the mobile to advise that he is stuck in gruelling, gridlock on his way to the game, and it is showing no sign of moving an inch. That would be a major blow and Tommy's face shows it. He goes into silent reflection, which is disturbed by blessed relief at 1.35 when Jones calls back to say that the traffic has loosened up, after the source of the problem, a minor smash on the dual carriageway, has been passed and he is now only five minutes away.

"So," says a more relaxed Saunders, "I suppose you wanna know how I think it will go today?"

"Yep", but a difficult one I think

"No. My scout tells me they're a good side but beatable and we've got every chance. And that's good enough for me. We'll let them worry about us today and we'll worry about them if there's a replay.

"I was 75% certain of beating Mangotsfield and I'm 65% certain that we'll beat Worthing. Mind you, I reckon we've got about a 0.1% chance of beating Dover!" Hmmm, realism.

Back outside, there is a strong population of red and white mingling with the usual blue and the air is thick with semi-cockney speak. But nowhere is there the slightest hint of any trouble. Unfortunately however, the kick off is delayed, as an elderly Worthing fan in the crowd has apparently suffered a stroke. An ambulance is called, which arrives in no time and drives across the pitch to the front of the main stand, whereupon the patient is whisked into the vehicle and given emergency treatment, before being taken away.

The game gets under way amid a reasonably kind offering from the weather. The conditions in actual fact come under the category that Trevor Brooking delights in describing as "a perfect day for a football match," the qualifications for which are a cool Autumn afternoon and 'skiddy' surface.

The off is some twenty minutes late, but it takes only a further two for Ben Carrington in the all red strip of Worthing, to break down the right at high speed, dreadlocks flowing behind him. He sends over a high cross, which striker Mark Rice brings down well. He shoots, but the shot is charged down by Nick Tiley. The ball breaks for Worthing's Mark Knee and he forces it home from close range. Many of the Worthing faithful have barely had a chance to taste the hot dogs, but this does not stop a reasonably audible cheer from the sprinkling of red and white around the cricket field end of the ground.

And for the next ten minutes it is purely one–way traffic as the Sussex men really turn it on, with Simon Funnell and Simon James both hitting the woodwork. But Chippenham gradually become accustomed to the pace of their visitors and step it up themselves. Accordingly, on about twenty minutes, a half chance is created for Tony Bennett, but he fires it straight into a Worthing stomach. Then Bennett and Steve Tweddle force consecutive goal line clearances as Chippenham begin to look the part, making nonsense of the class distinction between the sides, and bringing Saunders to his feet:

"That's more like it. Now let's have some more!" He screams.

If Mr Brooking is known to become breathless during the aforementioned favourite circumstances whilst watching a Premiership clash, some of the passing on view today may well leave him with a considerably greater supply of Oxygen. But it is nonetheless becoming an absorbing contest, with a degree of skill way above the perception of the uninitiated.

Still holding their own, Chippenham win a corner on the half-hour after a good run from Tiley. Worthing keeper Lee Bray punches clear, but only as far as that man Tiley, who sends in a cross from the right. Supplementing the attack, Burns connects around about the penalty spot with a glancing header, which flies just inside the far post, under the bar and into the net for the equaliser.

Burns goes berserk along with the Chippenham crowd.

Chippenham keeper Ian Jones foils Worthing raid

And it's all Chippenham now as Ministry of Defence worker Tiley adds weight to the attack and gets on the end of a Tweddle cross, but his bullet header goes just wide. Then the roles are reversed as Tiley provides Tweddle with the ammunition, but the striker's shot is saved. We learn that Tweddle has just left the army after nine years and signed a Chippenham contract and it becomes clear why he and Tiley combine so well.

On the stroke of half time, Chippenham keeper Ian Jones sends a long punt downfield, and a slip by Worthing right back Miles Rutherford puts Tweddle through. Tweddle advances and slides a square ball to the better-positioned Lee Collier, who has made an excellent run from midfield into a great position. He collects, looks up, picks his spot, and strokes the ball…just wide.

Today's referee, Mr Palmer of Radstock brings the half to a close, and Chippenham receive a generous welcome, as they deservedly leave the field on level terms.

The second half starts with more Chip pressure as Tiley and Tweddle continue to feed each other and both go close with respective efforts. Having soaked up their fair share of assaults, Worthing begin to show again, with university lecturer,

Carrington looking really impressive up front. Before long, Burns has rescued Chip with a typical never-say-die tackle on Funnell, who was clean through courtesy of a great ball over the top from Carrington. Then Ian Jones is in the action again as he makes great saves from Mark Knee and Paul Thomas. Inside the last

Carrington in full flow - but he misses this one to the relief of Chippenham

twenty and Carrington turns receiver of an over-the-top ball from the classy Rice. And Carrington is clean through with only Jones to beat. Jones charges off his line. Carrington goes for the lob. It hits Jones in the chest.

That was a golden opportunity and substantial abuse is duly handed out from the blue portion of the crowd. Carrington is not popular today, as he has been making his presence felt through a fine selection of whole-hearted challenges. But in truth, whilst competitive, he is by no means a malicious player and part of the stick he has received may well be down to the awesome pace and ability that becomes apparent whenever he gets the ball.

Five minutes later Funnell puts Carrington through again, but it is not going in for the dreadlocked striker today. In spite of this however, one gets the distinct impression, that one way or another, we have not seen the last of him yet!

All in all, Worthing have had the better of the second half, and with two minutes to go, a comedy of errors in the Chippenham goalmouth, lets Mark Rice in for the kill. But he rounds off the mini pantomime with a badly sliced shot that almost goes out for a throw in.

As we go into the last minute, Tiley breaks down the left for Chippenham. The cross is good, right on Bennett's head in fact. He could be the hero, just like against Mangotsfield. The header is on target. But straight at keeper Lee Bray. Bennett has been particularly unimpressive today. His mobility is not great at the best of times, and his aerial ability has now let him down when most needed. And we will enjoy telling him.

The whistle goes with honours even. They will have to do it all again in Worthing next Tuesday. Saunders shakes hands with his opposite number, Brian Donnelly and marches off to the changing rooms. Just before entering the tunnel, he catches sight of us and shouts over: "We're alright!"

That is a statement that will be put to the test.

7

Who ate all the Pies?

THIRD QUALIFYING ROUND - REPLAY

WORTHING

V

CHIPPENHAM TOWN

TUESDAY 5 OCTOBER 1999

@ WOODSIDE ROAD, WORTHING, WEST SUSSEX

ATTENDANCE 349

Tuesday 5 October, Hardenhuish Park, 2.15pm

Autumn's unpredictability has allocated a glorious afternoon and the wheels of the Chippenham entourage are beginning to crunch across the golden leaves in the Hardenhuish car park. A 130 mile trip to Worthing is too far to risk disjointing the players with separate vehicles and will therefore be made by coach, which will carry players, management, just about every supporter who is going tonight and the authors. The committee, however, have elected to travel independently in the chairman's car. Elitists!

The coach is too big to manoeuvre around the car park, which is hewn away from the foliage at the foot of the steps that lead to the stadium and is therefore stationed just outside, on the main road. Saunders and Bush are humping the club gear on board and track-suited players stand chatting, in groups of three or four. Mark Cutler and Tony Bennett turn up in Cutler's red BMW, the reward for many long hours managing a Bristol estate agency.

At 2.40 Tommy reads the roll call while the driver, worryingly, is engrossed in a map. All are present and correct and the driver is confident he understands his grid references. And we're away.

We recognise many of the supporters now, including the current holder of Chippenham's 'clubman of the year' award, eighty-seven year old Bill Arnold. We spend the first part of the journey listening to how he came to Chippenham just after the war, adopted the Bluebirds as his team and hasn't looked back since. After this, Bill inexplicably takes a seat elsewhere. Clubman of the

Tommy Saunders and Bill Arnold on the coach to Worthing

year at most parks clubs ends up annually with the man who has done the most dirty work in the last 12 months. This concept is not far removed at Western League level.

We stop in Melksham and Devizes to pick up players and the trip to Sussex, easily our longest on the road to Wembley so far, begins in earnest. The background noise constantly comprises of Tommy's voice in motivational mode, the ringing of his mobile (via which questions about this evening's proceedings are being asked by various committeemen) and howls of laughter from some supporters, and particularly PR woman, Jessica. A player starts to smoke and Saunders tells him to stop. He finishes the cigarette but does not have another for the whole journey.

Next up, it's time for some video entertainment and calls for Jerry Springer are ignored as Saunders gets out a copy of Chippenham's latest pre-season friendly against Swindon Town. After about twenty minutes this becomes tedious, as the participants are clearly just going through the motions and the mundane commentary reflects this in no uncertain terms.

Then the commentator declares: "The roof of the stand's blocking the camera angle, so every time the ball's in that corner you'll see fuck all!" Brian Moore this is not. This inspires those of us who were dozing off, to pay attention again and we are treated to a string of expletives and piss takes for the rest of the match. The reporter is apparently some local wag, who it must be said sounded quite plausible at the start of the match.

And maybe more by luck than judgement, he produces a piece of stinging social comment as an unknown ginger Swindon player is substituted:

"Ginger's off, but he'll pick up his grand at the end of the week and he won't be bothered. We'll be at work tomorrow and he'll do two hours training and piss off to the races!" Many a true word. Bitterness, certainly but who can blame them.

Next up is a recording of last night's Sky match, Southampton v Derby and Saunders is in sheer wonderment over the goal by Marian Pahars which squared the match for Saints. "How about that for goal of the season," he drools.

The coach seems strangely quiet after a while and it is not until we stop at a service station on the M25, that many of the playing staff and Saunders himself are revealed to be feeling totally nauseous. Strangely enough, ten minutes in the fresh air seems to cure the sufferers and the cause of the ailment remains a mystery. Pre-match diet is then settled. Chicken and beans for Alan Shearer it may be, but here it's Sandwiches and Chocolate all round!

Back on the coach, Tommy joins us at the front: "I've felt terrible for the last hour, don't know what it was. Some of the lads weren't too clever either, but everyone seems ok now. But anyway, I s'pose you wanna know about tonight do you? OK first of all, I know it was unfortunate, but that delay to the start ruined our routine a bit last time. And I must admit that if the ref had offered to blow the final whistle after 10 minutes, I'd have taken it. But having said that, we should have been 3-2 up at half time. And it was the first time this season that we've gone behind and not lost, so that's progress. This time we'll be better prepared and if we take the lead tonight, I think we've got a chance of winning!

"Obviously their front men, Rice and that Carrington will be a problem, but we coped with them reasonably well last time. I don't like my line-ups to be influenced by the opposition, but I think we'll go man to man on Rice tonight and that Carrington's a bit bloody useful, so depending on how they play him, I might tweak a couple of things to take care of him. I want to be there by 6.30 to have a look at the pitch." Says Tom unabated.

"If it's narrow we'll play 4-4-2 and if it's wide we'll play 3-1-4-2." He proceeds to draw tactical diagrams on our pads to reveal roles of individual players in both scenarios. "And yes, although these journeys take it out of you, I think we're in with a shout! And I'll tell you now that one of our attacking ploys'll be high balls in for Benno. I've heard Worthing's centre half on Saturday wasn't their first choice and that the regular one's back tonight, but I still reckon they're susceptible in the air."

Saunders continues to elaborate on tactical options, but clearly knows they are up against it. This is given away with the old "I'd rather beat Bridgwater on Saturday". The league, the league. Priorities, priorities.

Incessant ringing of Saunders' mobile eventually leads him back to his seat. Among the callers is Chairman Malcolm Lyus, who is making sure of the team's whereabouts at regular intervals. There is a minor panic as we hit heavy traffic just outside Worthing, but this loosens up as we get past the cause, a broken down school football team bus. And we arrive at a sedate, suburban Woodside Road in plenty of time. Oh, for the luxury of a trip the day before, and a night in a luxury hotel. "Oh, for the money", bristles Chairman Lyus, of the Elvis look-alike locks.

As we arrive, we clock the leafy suburban surroundings of sunny Worthing.

Certainly the step up in class football-wise is immediately obvious. This stadium is the best we have seen on our journey so far, with a capacity of 4,500 and a main stand fit to grace the Conference, although probably no higher a standard. There is also a high proportion of proper terracing as opposed to mere hard standing. But the remainder of Woodside Road is a little more typical of the Non-League scene, with a 'standing only' shed along the remaining touchline, supplemented by two uncovered ends and a section of grass 'terracing' known ambitiously as the 'North Bank.' And the houses that surround the ground are fully visible from inside it.

Tonight's referee, Mr Hammick from Romsey has also just arrived and is complimenting a Worthing official on his directions to the ground. In normal circumstances, FA Cup replays should be refereed by the same official as that

Worthing programme sellers

of the first encounter, but this has not been possible as Mr Palmer has become indisposed and Mr Hammick is the last-minute replacement.

We end up conversing with him about the previous Saturday's QPR v Blackburn match, which he proudly tells us was officiated by him. And as we walk around the pitch together he asks:

Is there likely to be any 'afters' lads, y'know, from the first game? It's always useful to know about that kind of thing when you're called in at the last moment like this. And you'd be surprised how often players go into replays with the express intention of nailing someone, because of something that happened first time round."

We assure him that his duties will not be complicated by any such issues. None that we are aware of anyway.

The changing rooms are situated directly beneath the main stand and upon moving in closer as the hazy sun gives way to dusk, the sound of bang-up-to-date dance music can be heard pumping from a ghetto-blaster in the Worthing camp. Closer inspection indicates the sound of Moloko "singing it back".

As the slim, greying, mature figure of Worthing boss Brian Donnelly passes, we decide to make his acquaintance. We explain our business and he agrees to help us out should Worthing win through tonight: "If for no other reason, than I just love the FA Cup! I think it's a great competition and it's certainly the only way that sides like Chippenham and ourselves could ever have a crack against the real big boys.

Last time? Well I thought we didn't play to our potential, although it has to be said that Chippenham did very well. But I didn't have a go at the lads, because that's not my way. I'm very mild mannered and I believe only in encouragement and helping players along. Any other way is negative and detrimental to the cause. But if I think anybody's taking the piss, that's a different matter. A different side of my personality comes out. You see, although my name's Brian, most people call me Sammy, and some say that's quite appropriate, because they think I've got two names and two attitudes.

"Tonight? Well hopefully we've done the hard part. And we've got Paul Kennett back from suspension and Lee Cox back from holiday. They're first team regulars that were missing on Saturday, so that should stand us in good stead. But either way, there'll be no bollockings!

"I reckon Chippenham'll play it safe tonight, probably with one up front. They probably won't want to take any risks. So it'll be a case of whether we can break them down. I believe in entertaining our supporters and we'll do our best to do that as usual, but if Chippenham put the shutters up it may be a bit of a dour affair.

Having checked out the main stand and the shed, Jessica and co are still having trouble with the decision over which is the superior vantagepoint. Eventually they decide upon the left side of the shed, as it will be right behind Tommy's dugout, resulting in maximum concentration of the vocal encouragement. They take their places accordingly and Jessica unfurls her trusty Union Jack over the wall, revealing allegiance to 'Chippenham Town FC.'

Somebody has done a head count and the official amount of souls that have made the trip from Wiltshire is eighteen. The flag acts as a rallying point and pretty soon all of them are ensconced behind it.

As kick off time looms, the Worthing fans pump up the volume. The small crowd takes up a reasonable proportion of the stadium, and in this segment, the atmosphere is electric.

Early Chippenham attacks keep Saunders on his feet right from the start and the Rutherford twins of Worthing are forced into respective, desperate clearances. This gives rise to blasts of Chippenham air horns, causing Saunders to turn round and suggest:

"you should get behind their goal with those, it'll put the keeper off."

Worthing again have the early pressure, without penetration. Saunders is warned to stay in the technical area as he effuses out of control. "Oi, 'Jamer', pick up nine will you, and push on when we get it", he spills out before retreating.

As Chippenham get back in it, some classic end to end stuff ensues, with Burns joining the Chippenham attack at every opportunity and Carrington turning up everywhere for Worthing. And there are heart-stopping moments in both goalmouths.

Worthing keeper Lee Bray saves with his legs, Ray Clemence style, from Bennett. The ball flies out for a corner, which Tiley takes and as the ball comes across, Bray comes off his line to gather, but fumbles the catch. Given how costly such goalkeeping errors can be, luck is on Worthing's side as Kennett beats Bennett to the ball and promptly despatches it behind for another corner. Saunders is up again:

"Put this one right on the keeper - he's flapping - that's two he's dropped now."

Donnelly is busy shouting his own instructions and in doing so has strayed outside his box, which Saunders spots:

"Oi lino! You told me to stay in my box. Well, it works both ways doesn't it?"

"Shut the fuck up," shouts Donnelly.

"What's the matter, under pressure are you?" replies Saunders. "Anyway, you're too old for this!"

The assistant decides to diffuse the situation and has a quiet word with Saunders, but the last word is only ever going to come from one source: "That's OK, let him go outside of his box then. If you're not going to do anything about it that's up to you!"

The corner hits the side netting.

To the great joy of Jessica and co, a Worthing air horn breaks down in the middle of its response:

"One nil to us already," she shouts.

"Fuck of back to where The Wurzels come from,"is the anonymous reply from among the many unsegregated locals that surround us.

But Jessica is unruffled:

"The Wurzels come from Somerset, not Wiltshire,"she (accurately) retorts in the general direction of her unseen rival. But the result is inevitable:

"Well fuck off back to Wiltshire then, you stupid cow!"

Meanwhile back on the pitch, one Worthing player shouts to another, "Fucking wake up will you!"

"Oh, we're shittin' ourselves now number nine," laughs Jessica.

"Ooaar ooaar"is the response from several of the Worthing contingent.

As half time looms, Carrington is causing major problems. Worthing's attacking 3-4-3 formation suits him down to the ground. He looks like Ruud Gullit in the Dutchman's heyday and with a 'licence to thrill' from Donnelly, plays his own brand of Total Football, varying runs and positioning so as to cause maximum problems for those marking him. Half-time is goalless though. And for us 80's memories of being among the plastic palm trees at Tiffany's come flooding back, as 'Papa's Got A Brand New Pigbag' blasts over the tannoy.

The break is also signified by the movements of the Worthing hardcore, as they make the traditional journey to the opposite end of the ground, in order to be behind the goal that their side are attacking in the second half. The majority of Non-League punters, particularly those who are numerous and organised enough to supply a strong choral presence (are allowed) do this on a regular basis. And although Worthing have not served up any real organised chanting as yet, they are certainly top dogs as far as numbers are concerned on our journey so far. At their level of the game, the half-time switch is a regular occurrence and always seems to go smoothly. Perhaps though, it is not suitable for The New Den, or Birmingham v Villa.

Second half, and Mark Rice and Richard Thompson are in the wars, as Rice follows through in a challenge that sets the Chippenham fans baying for his blood. The Worthing front man is clearly another member of the '100% club' and was described by Carrington after the match as "the ideal striking partner." For now though, he has to make do with recognition from the referee as his name goes in the book.

"Thommo - Thommo, just clear it will you!" Such is Saunders' rage that he strays outside the coaching perimeter once again. The Worthing crowd are quick to spot this and there are numerous cries of "get back in your box," some of which are suffixed by "you fat bastard." He does not reply on this occasion.

Worthing are slowly beginning to get on top again and a chance falls to Mark Knee at the far post. He hits it first time and his boot flies off in the process. Both boot and ball end up in the enclosure.

Tempers are beginning to fray now as Burt and Thomas increase the total of today's bookings for the home side. Thomas' foul constitutes an elbow in the face of Lee Burns, who's left writhing on the floor. "That was a forearm smash," shrieks Saunders practically at the point of seizure - "look, he can't bleedin' breathe." Fizz is eventually allowed on to give attention, but not before the referee's assistant has had a quiet word in Saunders' ear and the Worthing fans a louder one with another chorus of "who ate all the pies?." Fortunately Burns' breathing turns out to be OK, but he can't continue. Another major setback for Chippenham. Simon Charity is the replacement. More Worthing pressure follows.

With Chip reduced to playing on the break, Nick Tiley wrestles his way free from the attention of two Worthing midfielders and makes ground down the left. Another Worthing tackle fails to stop him and he is free to get his cross in. It's a low ball into the path of Simon Charity, who has steamed through from the midfield with fresh legs. Charity connects with the cross by the penalty spot and side foots it first time. into the right hand corner of the net! Chippenham are one up and the small band of travelling support goes berserk - A speck of rippling blue amongst a sea of red and white - Saunders turns to the blue portion to milk the applause, then playfully squirts water from a squeezy drinks container at the baying home fans. The water falls short of them. Chippenham are half an hour from glory! And against the run of play.

Virtually from the restart, the ball is fed to Carrington at an awkward height, but he brings it down well, advances and shoots from distance straight into the arms of Jones. Back to the other end Bennett wins more aerial ball in the Worthing box from a free kick, someone needs to get on the end of it to virtually seal the tie but the Worthing defence are there first - Pulsating stuff!

It's been like The Somme for Thompson tonight and he's in trouble again as a fifty-fifty challenge leaves him writhing like a fish on dry land. The way things are going for him, it will be a relief tomorrow morning, when he's back at Weston Super Mare Comprehensive School, where he is head of the First Year. Mind you, that's probably good practice for a night like this.

Worthing are now pushing hard, but Tiley again breaks free down the left. The cross comes in for Bennett, who brings it down well, but he's tackled before he can shoot. Then back to business as usual for Worthing with more pressure resulting in appeals for a penalty as Iain Murphy seems to pull down Carrington on the left of the box. Mr Hammick consults his assistant, but the answer is no! Boos ring around the ground. Twenty minutes to go and Chippenham are still hanging in there. They have been lying deeper since the goal, which is only serving to invite more pressure, although they are right up for every tackle and still grimly digging in.

There is activity on the home bench. A sliced clearance from Chippenham's Iain Murphy leads to a corner and before it can be taken Worthing make a double substitution. It is a major gamble as midfielder, Paul Thomas and star man, Mark Rice are removed from the equation. They are replaced by a wealth of experience, in the form of thirty eight year old Adie Miles as a straight swap for Rice up front and Lee Cox, only three years younger and just back from holiday, slotting into the defence to release Paul Kennett into Thomas' midfield berth. The corner bears no fruit.

Fifteen minutes from glory for the visitors, and despite more pressure, no sign of an equaliser, at least, not until Carrington breaks again, this time down the right. He crosses, Paul Kennett is unchallenged on the left of the box as he races from the midfield. He meets the ball powerfully with his head and Chippenham's world comes crashing down around them as the ball flies past the despairing arm of Jones and into the net.

Kennett is mobbed by players in the all red strip and the corresponding portion of the crowd lets out a mighty cheer that smacks as much of relief as joy. Saunders' head is in his hands. The Worthing bench are leaping about all over the place and their physio crouches down, curls his nose up on one side and sticks a single, central finger up at the Chippenham dugout. "You fat bastard," he shouts at Saunders. Mindful that the job is far from done, Donnelly pulls him back.

The repelling of constant attacks is visibly wearing the Chippenham players down and they're beginning to lose an alarmingly high rate of challenges. But Ian Jones is standing firm between the sticks and makes a string of vital saves to keep them in it.

With four minutes to go, yet another Worthing cross comes in and is nodded down for Mark Burt who has time to look up and pick his spot. He side foots it calmly into the corner of the net and the place erupts. Cue more gesticulation from the Worthing dugout towards their counterparts and even Donnelly cannot resist a comment that is unfortunately, swallowed by the noise of the crowd. This is classic cup-tie stuff.

But the writing appears to be on the wall for Chippenham. For some time now they've been reduced to hopeful punts upfield, which result in only one thing - Worthing coming straight back at them with interest!

Into injury time and more Worthing chances go begging, as Jones in the Chippenham goal saves Funnell's daisy cutter with ease and then parries a harder Carrington effort. But the ball rebounds out to Simon Funnell, who knocks it back into the box and substitute Adie Miles gets on the end of the cross and smashes it home to make it three one.

"Now you lot can fuck off back to Wiltshire," shouts an overjoyed Worthing fan at the Chip army. A high-pitched chant from a very young Sussex lad sums it up: "It's all gone quiet over there."

Chippenham's run is over and despite winding each other up all night, Donnelly and Saunders shake hands like the best of friends. Both sets of players acknowledge the efforts of their respective support and there are emotional scenes among the faithful eighteen as their heroes come over to applaud them to the sound of copious reciprocation.

As we amble around the ground towards the exit, a group of local kids barely in their teens indulge in some serious winding up of Jessica and co. which goes over the top and narrowly avoids a more serious confrontation involving others. Given the disappointing result, this has reduced Jessica to tears and sundry family and friends are trying to comfort her. Friends, Danielle and Kirsty remind her that the lads in question are "only a bunch of wankers." She soon comes round and before long loudly declares that 'The Full Monty' is her choice of video for the journey back.

As we continue to shuffle along the terraces, there are mutterings in West Country burr of "bloody bad man-management" and "We should never have sat back on that lead!"

The post-mortem on tonight's defeat is put on hold as Saunders phones the local hospital and the players sit in sober silence as the ashen faced Bradley Andrews can barely contain his pain, following a late injury. Eventually, the second ambulance of the tie arrives and, the by now, semi-conscious, Andrews is stretchered on board. Saunders hops in the back with him and the ambulance heads back across the pitch and disappears into the night. And the night is overshadowed by concern.

But as the freshly showered players drift out, the conversation eventually moves on to the match itself and Lea James sums up the Chippenham players' consensus of opinion: "We'd been doing well and scored a goal by attacking them. Why all of a sudden did we lie deep and invite them to come at us?"

Next up is captain courageous Lee Burns and he's sick at the defeat:

"It was a tough game, to be fair. Although, we were a bit unlucky with injuries and maybe we could have nicked it if we'd been a bit smarter when we were in front. But at the end of the day, we had them on the ropes for so long. And twelve minutes from glory (he shakes his head) it makes you sick doesn't it?"

We catch up with an extremely complimentary Donnelly in the bar: "Chippenham are very well organised," he says between sips of bottled Bud. "Once they went ahead I knew they'd be difficult to break down and we had to work very hard to get back into it."

One-nil down. Twelve minutes left? Did he think he was on his way out of the FA Cup?

"Well their manager thought so didn't he?" he laughs. "But I think my double substitution did the trick. I could see they had it sewn up at that point and we needed a change, so I replaced our main striker Mark Rice with Adie Miles and pushed the centre half Paul Kennett into midfield, 'cos he's a bit of a utility man and he likes to get forward. Then they both scored!"

No prizes for guessing that the coach is very, very quiet on the way back, particularly in the absence of Saunders who is still with Shane Andrews. And The Full Monty isn't an option. Lee Burns pleads with the driver to stop somewhere so the players can get something to eat, but to no avail: "I've done way over my shift mate and takeaways aren't allowed in the coach anyway!"

But eventually, to the relief of us all, he relents and we stop somewhere on the outskirts of Worthing and pile into a Macdonalds. In allowing this, the driver has also let himself in for a right royal wait as we take the staff by surprise with around forty orders. And on top of that we have to finish our food before we are allowed back on the coach. But after about an hour we are on our way again and news comes through on a mobile that lightens the mood considerably – Andrews is OK.

We arrive back in Chippenham at around two thirty, virtually asleep on our feet. And as we disembark, Benno groans: "It's gonna be a nightmare going to work tomorrow." Indeed, most of these players will be sharing that experience before many hours have passed.

Malcolm Lyus rolls up with Saunders and Andrews as passengers, the committee having agreed to create room by coming back on the coach. Numerous questions are fired regarding the latter, whose problem fortunately seems to centre only around his hamstring, hence his discharge from hospital and current state of relatively pain-free sleep. As we trudge back to the car, we bid our second set of fond farewells en route to Wembley and drive home to Bristol.

On Wednesday 6 October, having tucked the result away in back page corners, the national press remains blissfully unaware of last night's blood and thunder, meaning unfortunately that punters up and down the country must do the same.

That evening Saunders phones an author's house, apologises for being tied up during our emotional goodbyes and explains:

"We lost it because the team was knocked out of shape by injuries to key players and I'm disappointed, because I know Worthing are a decent side, but the task on the night was by no means insurmountable. Anyway, I'm off now to give the baby a cuddle before bed and then it's time for the X-Files."

8

Ben Cartwright - thanks very much

FOURTH QUALIFYING ROUND

WORTHING

V

DOVER ATHLETIC

SATURDAY 16 OCTOBER 1999

@ WOODSIDE ROAD, WORTHING

ATTENDANCE 1,010

The big match atmosphere is apparent all around the maze of houses that surround Woodside Road, as countless cars snap up the dwindling parking spaces. Parking here is not normally a problem with ample street room available for all. Today it will be different. And there are red and white colours everywhere, although the black and white of Dover Athletic is well represented.

Neither manager needs reminding, that the prize for victory today, is potentially massive, as the winners of this tie will go into the random draw for the First Round Proper. Don Reid, a Worthing club official of some forty years sums the feeling up nicely:

"We want to be sitting in front of the telly tonight, waiting for our name to come out of that funny machine."

The fact that the draw can be seen live on *Sky Sports* not long after the final whistle has added to the drama.

Unsurprisingly, Sammy – a café owner (Sammy's Diner) by trade - is totally upbeat and revels in telling us of how he signs many a player over a fry-up. He also remains eternally optimistic that Worthing will be in the 'hat' tonight, in spite of the fact that since beating Chippenham their form has been inconsistent, with a 5-1 home victory over Fleet Town in the F.A trophy and a 2-0 league defeat away to lowly Yeading as the yardstick.

"First of all this is a great day for the club," he enthuses, "and it could be an even greater one if we get through. But this is a tough one. And that's natural the further you progress the harder it gets. But we're really excited about this today and personally I just love the FA. Cup. "I've got no special plans either. We'll play our usual 3-4-3 formation, which we do in virtually every game, and inflict ourselves upon them. And yes, I appreciate there might be a gap in class today, but this is the FA. Cup!"

With that he notices his number two Jason Rutherford beckoning and is off under the main stand, back to the Worthing dressing room, where again the music is pumping like it was Ayia Napa.

This will indeed be a tough test. In spite of the step up in class we have taken

The 'terraces' at Worthing before the Dover tie

in joining the Sussex men, Nationwide League experience in the team is virtually non-existent, whereas the majority of the Dover side have seen professional action. This plus the daylight between the sides due to the respective levels at which they compete, should make Dover's indifferent start to the season an irrelevance tonight, which is a view shared by many Worthing fans.

A look around the ground reveals the stands and terraces filling up with followers of both persuasions and the atmosphere really mounting up. The Dover team are out warming up and their outspoken manager Bill Williams is available for comment as usual:

"Confident? Yes I'm always confident, but we'll only know if I'm justified after the game won't we? We can only prepare and motivate as best we can. And the thing with these games is you sometimes need the rub of the green to get through them. Worthing have got some good solid players and we will need to play today as though it's a Conference game."

"But we've had seven players who've been injured since the start of the season and they've only just started to make their comebacks, mainly around the last three or four games, so match fitness could be a problem. I've had a lot of journalists phone up to ask if we will win today and what I think about the next round, but the truth is I don't know do I? And I'll only talk about the next round if we beat Worthing. Tell you one thing though, I know Worthing will be up for it and there'll be plenty of snot and blood out there today!"

In amongst the reams of Dover fans on the terraces, the attitude is strangely guarded and conversation with them in the bar reveals why:

"We always lose to teams from lower divisions than us in the FA cup, so we always blow the chance of playing a league team. But the law of averages surely says it won't happen to us again and we will get through this time. We certainly bloody deserve to."

At kick off time, Woodside road is well populated and the usually empty grass verges in one corner are fully populated by fans bedecked in red and white. As the teams come out from under the main stand, the Dover fans at both ends of the ground release masses of white confetti, Argentina '78 style. At one end, we see a banner denoting the existence of the 'Maidstone crew,' who, following the demise of their League side have taken to following Dover instead. The presence of a certain Mr Williams at the helm may also go some way to explaining the attraction, as it was he who steered Maidstone United to their Conference Championship success and subsequent Football League status.

The sun-soaked stadium is a mass of colour and the game kicks off to a wall of expectant sound. Worthing sport their traditional all-red strip and Dover their usual white shirts, black shorts and black and white socks.

Dover signify intentions from the off as they pile forward and a chance falls to striker Mark Hynes, distinguishable by his white boots. Alan Ball however, he is not. Hynes is positioned centrally, just inside the Worthing box. But unfortunately for him the boots look a lot better than the goal attempt, as he drags the shot well wide of the left hand post.

Dover dominate the opening exchanges but Worthing soon warm to the task and Marc Rice, a man upon whom many hopes are pinned today, sends a long range volley screaming over the Dover bar. The home fans are galvanised into the first real organised chant of our journey: "If you all hate Dover clap your hands." Not particularly original, but a chant all the same.

The subsequent clapping of hands receives numerous responses in the form of gestures involving only two fingers.

Then Mark Knee makes inroads for the home side as he charges down the left and a dangerous cross is flicked just wide by Carrington. No doubt the Dover

Travelling Dover faithful

90

hand pulling his dreadlocks during the aerial duel played it's part in ensuring the header missed the target. But the fact that Knee had the time and space to get the cross in, is clearly unacceptable to Dover's Jake Leberl as he comes out with a string of expletives that would make Liam Gallagher blush. "Oi, cut the language out," is the response from the red and white clad guardians of morality within earshot behind the perimeter wall.

After twenty minutes of battle, Worthing, cheered on by some frenetic support, have the edge. Half the town must be here today. And the scene is fantastic. A sea of red flanked by two sections of white. All in shirtsleeves and bathed in sunshine. And Carrington is using his licence to thrill to its fullest extent.

As we approach the half hour, it is still nip and tuck out there and the closest we have come to a break in the deadlock is a good, conventional goalmouth scramble in Dover territory, with the danger being eventually cleared. On the half-hour, a Worthing free kick from a central position just outside the enemy box is slid forward for that man Carrington, who turns on a proverbial sixpence and unleashes a superb shot, which screams past the right hand upright. The Dover bench are yelling instructions and one of the recipients, Steve Brown, is not impressed with his coach's perception:

"Fuckin' watch the game!" is the response. Would Sir Alex put up with such openness?

Now Carrington's tireless running is beginning to pay dividends. It takes a good man to keep up with him in this heat and he is winning free kicks and corners for a pastime. On the stroke of half time, a flurry of activity sees Worthing's Marc Rice pay a price for 100% commitment as today's referee, Bernard Baker of Andover, decides the striker's challenge is worthy of a yellow card. From the resultant free kick, Worthing defender Miles Rutherford puts home fans hearts in their mouths as he shapes up to make a hefty clearance but slices it and sends the ball flying just over his own bar. The whistle goes amid massive, ironic cheers from the black and white contingent. No score and Worthing are in with a major shout of pulling off a shock.

In keeping with tradition, the two armies of support change ends and the main body of Dover faithful join up with the Maidstone Crew behind the goalmouth in which they hope all the second half action will be taking place. Accordingly, the home support makes room for them by going in the opposite direction. Again, there are no incidents as the two sets of support pass each other.

Dover come out fighting in the second half. A few minutes in, they come close to tying the game as Clarke turns supplier and Wormull arrives in the opposition box right on time to connect with the cross. But Worthing left wing back Mark Knee saves the day as he rises to take the ball off his head.

Worthing are still chasing everything as effort competes with greater ability. This is typified on the hour by Mark Burt as he shows great determination to keep the ball in play, when most would have resigned themselves to an opposition throw. He comes away with it and feeds Carrington who hares down the right and sends in a low cross to Rice, but once again Hyde is quick to spot the danger and saves at Rice's feet. Williams and co. on the Dover bench are going ballistic over the time and space that the Worthing players are being allowed and reams of orders are relayed to the players. Rice and Carrington combine well again and again in true Toshack and Keegan fashion.

Then at last, Dover seem shocked into life as a long ball from defence falls invitingly for striker Steve Brown. But in spite of launching himself into a dive he cannot quite get his head to the ball for a contact that may well have left Bray with little chance of preventing the visitors taking the lead. The Dover fans behind Bray are driven into song:

"White Army, White Army."
"Dad's Army, Dad's Army!" comes the response.

Unusually for Woodside Road, most of the talking is coming from the visiting bench. Donnelly and co. are clearly happy with the way things are going, which cannot be said for their counterparts who are constantly pointing and shouting corrective instructions.

Activity on the Dover bench sees a straight swap substitution, as Scott Daniels, veteran of some two hundred odd league matches for Northampton, Exeter and Colchester, is replaced by Stuart Munday, who is one of many ex-Brighton players in the Dover side, each of whom of course, are instantly recognisable to the faction of home fans that supplement their support for the Seagulls with visits to Woodside Road. Brighton fans may well remember Munday scoring a memorable goal for them at Leicester City in the League Cup.

"Tone, get warmed up son" says Donnelly and twenty seven year old Tony Holden climbs out of the dugout and begins sprinting up and down the line in time honoured fashion not unknown to parks players everywhere.

But first of all it is another substitution for Dover and another straight swap. This time Steve Brown makes his exit. He was signed from Macclesfield earlier this season and has also played for Southend, Colchester, Gillingham and Lincoln. His replacement is a big name on the national Non-League circuit - Joff Vansittart - a big, powerful striker who was signed from Sutton United in 1998. This is clearly a popular move among the Dover contingent as they give Vansittart a rapturous welcome.

Into the last fifteen and Clarke's second half resurgence costs him a yellow card. In spite of this, his new found verve seems to have helped Dover to look the part and over the last twenty minutes or so, they have been putting some dangerous moves together. The Worthing fans try to rouse their heroes with chants of "come on you rebels." But it is Dover who are in the ascendancy now as ex- Tottenham, Peterborough and Great Britain (in the World Student Games) man, Neil Le Bihan gets a cross in from the right, which is headed behind for a corner by the ever-reliable left midfielder cum wingback, Mark Knee.

A further ex-Brighton man, twenty three-year-old Simon Wormull goes to take the corner. He too can boast impressive credentials, having also turned out for Brentford and been a Tottenham apprentice as well as being recently selected for the England Non-League squad, making his debut against Italy last February. This Dover side simply oozes quality (at this level) and they are gradually stamping their authority on this game.

Wormull swings the corner in and midfielder Jake Leberl is waiting unmarked, on the right of the six-yard box. He meets it with a thunderous header that gives Bray no chance. The white portion of the crowd, now all at one end erupts and the Dover players celebrate in that 'it had to come eventually' kind of way.

Within a minute, a Dover corner finds Wormull, who strikes a powerful shot from the left edge of the box, but this time Bray is there to prevent further damage as Worthing look fit to collapse.

Donnelly then decides that Tony Holden is ready to make his entrance in a straight swap up front, with Simon Funnell. In contrast to the credentials of some of the Dover squad, these two were signed from Shoreham. This has all the makings of another inspired Donnelly substitution as a period of renewed Worthing pressure follows, but with time ticking away, the all-important goal is not forthcoming.

The desperation of the Dover players to defend this lead and get into the First Round Proper is plain to see. This would be the first time that has happened since the rebirth of the club in 1983, following the demise of the old Dover FC and all at the club are determined to bring such glory on board.

Donnelly decides it is time to play another card and takes a gamble on replacing experienced midfielder Mark Burt, with twenty year old local lad, Lee Weston, who can play up front or midfield. He slots straight into a striking position and Worthing are set to play four up front in a last bid to rescue something. "Shit or bust," is the thoughtful attacking strategy, as Donnelly described it afterwards.

One minute left now and Worthing are reduced to a hopeful punt upfield. Holden latches on to it and sends a high cross over. It is asking a lot of Carrington to win the ball in the air against the giant Dover defence, but somehow he does, and the ball tees up nicely in front of him just inside the box. He spins round - hits it first time - and it's there! Worthing have rescued it. The stadium becomes a red and white frenzy and Carrington is mobbed by his teammates. The Dover fans stand in silence, their players mirroring those actions, hands on hips, heads down, totally incredulous. One minute from breaking their First Round duck and they blow it again! The expressions on the faces of the Dover players and fans is a testament to just how sickening this moment really is. Losing your house, getting the sack – all terrible life moments, but an equaliser against you in the dying moments – in the Cup. Real tragedy.

Mr Baker plays five minutes of injury time, but despite some late Worthing chances, it will all be done again.

Post match however, Donnelly is ebullient as ever: "That four up front did the trick didn't it?" he asks rhetorically. "But we were well worth that result. Dover's passing was a bit crisper to be fair, but they could only hurt us from set pieces. Tuesday? Yeah that will be a tough one. They've got a good home record and they'll be determined to put this right, so it'll be difficult for us. And Ben's still nursing his knock, so I hope he'll be OK. We're always a better side when he's around. And what about his goal? Fantastic! He had no right to win that challenge in the air, but he did it through sheer determination. Still it's good for us financially and although I'm sure their camp are quite confident, knowing we're in the draw could give my lads that extra bit on the night.

We enter the bar just in time to see Ben Carrington receive his man of the match award, which consists of a bottle of champagne. The award is accompanied by rousing cheers and quips from the club officials such as "don't let that out of your sight when the lads are around" and "until you scored it was going to Coxy."

Carrington does the round of interviews with local press, as the local hero. The 'Tim, Nice But Dim' of the media world comes forward microphone at the ready, and he commences recording material for a local radio station:

"OK, I'm here with Ben Cartwright."

"Carrington," shout many of us in unison.

He carries on regardless:

"Sorry, Carrington. And I must say you looked very much the hero out there Ben, with your braids flowing."

"Thank you," replies Ben but erm well they're dreadlocks actually."

"Sorry," says the journo, "dreadlocks."

Carrington is extremely eloquent in all interviews as befits a Sociology lecturer at Brighton University. With this, five thirty is fast approaching and Frank Mclintock and Alan Mullery are shaping up to kick off the draw on TV. The suits come out of the Worthing boardroom in readiness. And our journo friend, still recording, proceeds alarmingly: "Yes, there's Frank Mclintock and he's a Wembley loser of course." This causes a number of raised eyebrows and one or two mentions of Arsenal's FA Cup success in 1971. Unperturbed, he presses on and asks Ben of his preference for opposition in the next round:

"Brighton would be nice," says Ben, realising that he's lumbered with this interview for the whole draw, but maintaining a stoic politeness. "But we're not going to be scared of any Third or Fourth Division sides. I've played for Guiseley against Carlisle in the First Round Proper and I know what to expect. And I think we should be confident if we end up playing a league side. But let's get through the replay first!"

The volume of the TV goes up, the packed bar goes silent and David Davies is ready to facilitate the draw. He rightfully mentions that hundreds of teams are already out, introduces Mclintock and Mullery and gets the balls rolling. "We're number sixty," shouts someone at the back of the bar.

The draw wears on. But ball number sixty remains within the lottery-like contraption. Sixty-one comes out to a big "ooh" from the gathered, almost like seeing a shot hitting the bar. Fifty-nine comes out soon after and raises a laugh, as the draw seems to be teasing us. Bristol City come and go, disappointing the authors for obvious reasons, but two balls later the place erupts into a massive cheer. The winners on Tuesday night will be away to Rotherham!

Our hapless friend with the microphone asks for the obvious "delighted" response and then wraps it up: "Ben Cartwright - thanks very much.". We were never sure whether he thought he was at The Ponderosa.

The fact that Ben himself is too young to remember Bonanza also explains why he has not been nicknamed Hoss, in the dressing room. Young man's game this.

We make our way across the terraces into the general (second) clubhouse, where many fans of both persuasions and the Worthing players are merrily ligging and swigging together. All Dover staff however, are conspicuous by their absence and word up is that the visitors' dressing room door is still tightly shut. Indeed by all accounts, none of them know that Rotherham await the winners of the replay. A few minutes later Carrington walks in and an almighty cheer goes up from the table at which most of the Worthing players are sitting. "Good evening Mr Cartwright," they shout as one.

Time to 'buzz off' - Dover leave Worthing under somewhat ignominious circumstances

9

River Deep, Mountain High

FOURTH QUALIFYING ROUND - REPLAY

DOVER ATHLETIC

V

WORTHING

TUESDAY 19 OCTOBER

@ THE CRABBLE ATHLETIC GROUND, DOVER

ATTENDANCE 1,027

Having passed the various rail networks that lead into Dover and having resisted the temptation of a quick trip to France via Euro-tunnel, we come to the final few picturesque miles and descend into the town from the hills, as the sea appears before us, glinting in the distance.

The Crabble ground, is set at the top of an exceptionally steep hill on the outskirts of an area called 'River'.

A winding driveway leads from the main road up to the stadium at an incredible gradient, necessitating a drop to second gear, in order to reach the car park at the summit. But from the top, the panoramic view of the town is truly spectacular and can be savoured by any player taking a throw in on that side of the pitch. With the remaining three and a half sides of the ground surrounded by picturesque woodland, this must rank as one of the most scenic soccer venues in the country.

The stadium itself is small and neat, but surprisingly for a club in the

Conference, lacks a large main stand and all the sides of the stadium are low level, not that anybody could see from the road, hundreds of feet below.

The solitary steward on duty at this early stage in tonight's proceedings is in charge of making sure the car parking side of things runs smoothly. This includes making sure that the Worthing coach drops everybody off at the bottom of the hill and does not try to use the car park. We playfully ask whether this is a ploy to wear out the opposition before the game has even started. He laughs, but explains:

"The car park's not bloody wide enough for coaches to turn round in it. And it's bloody impossible to reverse a coach back down the hill. So if they get up this far, it's disaster." His role also includes ensuring the limited car parking space is set aside for the designated users, which sadly involves ousting the authors down to the roadside. Our early arrival has resulted in prime choice of the ample street parking that is available at the foot of the hill, which is great, but the walk back up to the top is enough to kill off all but the most capable of athletes. The only ones fit enough to make it are the players and they get to drive up and park right outside the changing rooms!

Puffing and panting, we get to the top and discover the devastating news that caffeine injections are not yet available as the 'Centre spot' bar and clubhouse is not quite ready for the off.

He tells us about "his club", starting with assistant coach Clive Walker (not *that* Clive Walker) and his reputation for shouting from the bench at maximum volume. Having seen him in action at Worthing, this does not surprise us. A young lad is busy signing Dover schoolboy forms on a car bonnet in front of us and the steward goes on:

"He's even like it with lads like that in the Under-thirteens. And he smokes loads of fags during a game, but never inhales!" Must base his lifestyle on Bill Clinton, we presume.

During an account of how not long ago, the car park would have been full of Daihatsus as each player was given one by the firm as part of their sponsorship deal with the club, Bill Williams appears from the office and approaches us:

"That AA car's in one of our benefactor's spaces," he barks.

"I know but....." Williams interjects, "We get ten grand a year from the bloke that uses that space - get it out!" And he storms back into his office.

"As I said," quips the steward, "the parking's very organised here."

With impeccable timing, the Worthing coach has arrived and the steward hasn't received any warning to enable him to prevent its ascension of the hill. You need to be ready at the bottom to do this because the hill is so steep, winding and bushy, that any vehicle can virtually be at the top before you know of its presence. And even if you saw it coming up the main road, you would need to be Linford Christie to get to the bottom in time. Accordingly, the coach appears around the final bend at the entrance to the car park to really ruin the steward's day. Looking at the sheer panic on his face, we leave him to it.

With kick off about an hour away, copious amounts of Worthing support begin to arrive (around 200 in all) supplemented by a fair scattering of their local media. And we find ourselves acknowledging several familiar faces, including "Hospital Radio Rich" and Gareth the kit man, in his shorts again, proving beyond all doubt with the temperature rapidly dropping, that he really never does wear long trousers.

As we approach warm up time for the players, Sammy is out and about and he reveals his special plans for tonight:

"I've tinkered with the usual line up," he confides, "tonight we'll have three centre halves with a sweeper, three in midfield and three up front. Ben (Carrington) and Simon (Funnell) are carrying injuries but we'll play them, it's no good waiting to bring them on, when it may be too late. As for how it'll go,

Dover Athletic - a spectacular view

I think Dover obviously didn't play to their potential on Saturday and they'll start like a train in this one. But if we can keep a clean sheet until half time and deal with set-pieces, it may take the sting out of their tail and we could be in business!"

With both sides out warming up, Clive Walker is on the pitch and optimistic:

"It won't be possible for eleven players to collectively play as badly again." And he also confirms that significant changes from Saturday's team have been made, mainly in the front two striking positions in which Mark Hynes and Steve Brown were so ineffective. "We've dropped them and they'll be subs today," confirms Walker "and we've brought in (Joff) Vansittard and (Matt) Carruthers to do the business. Joff's recovered from his broken nose now, so he's ready for a full comeback anyway."

With kick off of this eagerly awaited contest almost upon us, Dover lose the toss. Mark Burt elects to change ends, which the players do accordingly, followed closely by the fans. The players kick off as opposing fans nod to each other in passing.

Both teams are obviously fired right up for this one and as if to confirm that we are in for a full blooded, British encounter, Worthing keeper Lee Bray clatters Matt Carruthers as he bears down upon goal. Carruthers has no doubt endured worse during a stint with the 3rd Paras and does not complain, whereas the Dover fans do. Tonight's official, Mr Penton decides a free kick is sufficient and must then endure a little tune from the home support, based upon the fact that it is very likely he masturbates!

After ten minutes the challenges are still flying in and Dover captain, right wing back Joe Dunne, crumples into a heap after an innocuous looking tackle just in front of the dugouts. Dunne shouts in pain as he goes down and Worthing physio Alan Robertson thinks this is designed to get someone booked or sent off. He shouts this out to Dunne accordingly.

"Fuck off wanker!" supplements Donnelly:

"What's the matter son, lost your ringpiece? Want some toilet paper? What's the matter (number) two, don't fancy it?"

Back on his feet Dunne makes the mistake of getting involved:

"How many times have you been to Wembley mate?" Donnelly knows he has won the day and responds for sport only:

"None how about you?"

"Two mate, two!" (Gillingham and Colchester) comes the reply.

Knowing the job is done, at least for the moment, Donnelly leaves it there.

Next up Carrington breaks for Worthing and sends a cross flashing across the face of the goal, it looks as though it only needs a touch from Mark Burt, but he hits the post.

Worthing's Simon Funnell is next in the action as he lobs the advancing Dover keeper, but the ball goes just wide of the left-hand post. This gets the Worthing fans going again. They have been really noisy tonight, getting right behind the players. Then a foul on Marc Rice goes unpunished and Donnelly is incensed: "I must be watching a different game lino, or have the rules changed?"

With his mind in overdrive, Donnelly is constantly looking for issues to address and this time picks up on the fact that Dave Clarke has been really putting himself about. Time for a wind up then: "What's the matter seven, got no brains up there?"

As Worthing surge forward again and Funnell crosses, Dover come close to disaster as Jake Leberl scoops a strange clearance just wide of his own post for a corner. And as the corner comes over, Miles Rutherford unleashes a powerful shot, straight into the face of Lee Shearer. The ball bounces clear for a throw and the dazed defender is cheered on by shouts of "Shearer, Shearer," in the same fashion as that of his more illustrious namesake.

Worthing chances come and go. A neat Dover move ends in a decent shot from Leberl, which flies just over the bar. As we enter the last five minutes of the half, it's Wormull again, this time down the left and he gets another cross in, which Bray just manages to palm away from he head of Carruthers. Robertson shouts from the bench for someone to get closer to him, but Donnelly has known for some time that the danger lies with Wormull's supply line, right back, Joe Dunne. Hence his earlier remarks to Dunne, designed for no other purpose than to put him off his game and interfere with Dover's heartbeat.

The Dover pressure continues and Bray is being kept busy in the Worthing goal, particularly from crosses, usually sent over by Wormull. But he deals with the danger well on every occasion and the match remains scoreless and nicely poised. In beating away Wormull's latest delivery, Bray is fouled by Clarke, which in turn re-animates Donnelly:

"What's the matter seven, no brains in your head - eh – sawdust is it? The assistant referee feels obliges to step in and although smiling, requests "no personal abuse please."

Half time provides a nil nil scoreline and relief from the rapidly dipping tem-

Centrespot Bar - Dover Athletic

peratures. The players and fans change ends and we're off again.

Wormull and Dunne stand out and are causing problems for Worthing. Carrington, meanwhile, is the main threat for the Rebels and the tension on the benches and in the crowd can be tasted.

Into the last twenty minutes and Mr Penton's assistant gives an offside against Carrington, who in fairness had timed his run perfectly and was clearly on side. Sammy was in a perfect position to spot this and is going absolutely mental. Throwing any semblance of caution to the wind he shouts at the top of his voice: "Now I know you're cheating, Lino!"

A 50 year old bloke in a beanie is equally annoyed: "Sit down, wanker - you don't have to put up with that, linesman!" Not content with this, he walks along to the barrier right behind the Worthing dugout and continues: "If you carry on influencing the linesman, I'll report you to the FA. This match is being video'd you know!"

No response from Donnelly, but having talked himself into a frenzy, the bloke has not yet had enough: "Your team are a very poor standard, it's so poor, rubbish football."

This is enough to arouse Sammy's curiosity and he turns around to investigate. Seeing his attacker he laughs out loud and declares:

"Is that tea cosy keeping your head warm son."

Now the bloke is really starting to lose it and waving an arm all over the place as he shrieks: "Right that's it, in the car park, I'll see you in the car park after the match."

"But I'll be in the bar," laughs Donnelly.

"Right in the bar then," the bloke replies, his head a deep red colour, not entirely caused by the biting wind.

"Ok - and bring the video," retorts Sammy over his shoulder, watching events on the pitch at the same time as swatting away the comments of somebody who is clearly of no more consequence to him than an annoying fly.

But more shrieking results: "Ok in the bar, in the bar and I'll have you, you bastard." Playing with his quarry, Donnelly simply retorts over his shoulder, from the corner of his mouth, "ooh I'm scared." Seemingly content that he has arranged vindication, the bloke goes back to his place on the terrace and leaves it at that. What Eric Cantona would have made of it, nobody can say.

Meanwhile, back on the pitch, Dave Clarke is growing in stature and he and Simon Wormull are making powerful runs into Worthing territory. With ten minutes to go Wormull again bursts through from the midfield. He takes the ball to the edge of the Worthing box and lets fly. On target. The Dover fans behind the goal leap into the air, but the ball hits the post, square-on and is hoofed away. Sick at the fact that that there has been no breakthrough, one teenager shouts, "I've seen better football in the Sunday league down the park!" Having played lots of football with Sunday morning hangovers, we doubt the accuracy of the statement.

Into the last minute of normal time and Wormull is still going strong for Dover. Right on the ninety minutes he gets another chance, but uncharacteristically skies it. Williams takes Le Bihan off and replaces him with Steve Norman. And as soon as play restarts Worthing mount an attack that culminates in a great cross for Carrington who is waiting in the six-yard box. But Shearer does just enough to put him off and he cannot quite get on the end of it, when the merest glance would have done. The last action of normal time sees a good opportunity go begging courtesy of Matt Carruthers, who has supposedly been brought in today to prevent such wastage.

With no score at the whistle, the two tired sides must now endure extra time and then penalties if necessary.

The players remain on the pitch, huddled in their two groups, receiving animated instructions from respective superiors. With the short break over, battle commences again, but without Mr Carruthers, whose previous effort constituted the last straw for Williams. He has been replaced by one of those in disgrace from Saturday, the man with the amnesty being Mark Hynes. Dover start the brighter of the two with good old Wormull pulling the strings. After about five minutes he sends another cross into the Worthing box and Paul Tomas mis-hits a clearance which goes up in a completely vertical direction after smashing in to the head of one of his own defenders. Shortly after, Burt hits the side netting for Worthing, but this is an oasis in a desert of Dover pressure. And Vansittard is next to break for the home side. He plays a good crossfield ball to Carruthers, but Le Bihan was screaming for it in a much better position. Nevertheless, Carruthers has the chance to make amends for last time...But shoots wide.

But before long Carruthers has another clear chance, but Bray gets a hand to the shot and the ball skims against the apex of the bar and post and out for a corner. Bray duly collects the ensuing delivery and Worthing can breathe again. Just before the break, a chance falls to Dover and this time Hynes can make a name for himself, but he hits the side netting.

The fans changing ends struggle to get to their places on time as the teams turn around and kick off without delay. And Worthing are getting back into it with a chance for sub Paul Thomas. But Hyde is equal to it. What follows is a dose of good old proverbial end to end stuff as Hynes is guilty of wasting another good chance for Dover and Worthing sub Adie Miles tries Mark Burt's trick from the first game, of shooting from the halfway line, with only fractionally greater success.

Holden is brought on upfront for Worthing, and one minute later he is clean through - it's a one on one with the keeper – he calmly waits for the advancing Hyde to commit himself and lobs the ball over his diving body...into the net. And he has done it! The perennial substitute has put Worthing in front. Holden immediately disappears under a mound of red strips. Those who have made the trip from Sussex are happy too and invade the corner of the pitch nearest to their vantage points to celebrate with the players.

A bout of further desperate, Dover pressure ending in Bray gathering the ball safely, leaves Sammy telling his men to "slow the game down." But Bray's drop kick only results in another Dover attack and with two minutes to go, Wormull finds himself with another chance. He has crack from just outside the box but again shoots well high and well wide. As the Worthing faithful cheer the miss, it proves the final straw for many Dover fans and they begin to stream out of the ground. While at the opposite end, the party starts tentatively. Many people leave games early, but this is somewhat strange. Their side are only a goal away from squaring the match, and then the penalty shoot-out drama would unfold. Why people want to pay their money, watch a 0-0 game and then exit, while the game is still alive is extremely strange, and yet happens at grounds all over the country at all levels.

With a minute to go, Carrington is through and could wrap it up, but Hyde is off his line to save Dover further embarrassment. Then there is a chance for Dover to silence the celebrating red and white corner, as a cross bounces out for Wormull, but yet again he skies it out of the stadium and into the forest. His shooting has not matched his skill and industry in other areas tonight.

"Ref - Oi – ref, your clock stopped has it?" Donnelly is industrious again. Then it's tactics again as he tells Carrington to "drop back inside," followed by the classic time-wasting ploy:

"Get the ball out to the corners."

But there is no need, the whistle goes and Worthing have done it! And anybody with anything to do with them goes completely mental. Their fans are back on the pitch and players and management team alike are hugging each other and jumping about all over the place. The Sussex press rush on to capture the moment for posterity and the team pose for a group photo. Then they go over to the fans that have remained on the terracing, for a multitude of handshakes and hugs.

In contrast, the Dover players leave the pitch, heads down to a chorus of boos from the home fans that have bothered to stay behind. We later found out that many of those who left early did so because the eventual result had become immaterial due to the ineptitude of their team's performance. A special reception consisting of some particularly unsavoury remarks is set aside for Bill Williams as he leaves the arena:

"You are fucking shit, Bill. Fuck off and resign!"

So Worthing have the stage to themselves and as they eventually leave the pitch, they come off to applause from Dover fans that have especially stayed behind in order to offer their congratulations. "It was all under control," says Lee Bray with a smile to a camera crew.

Boots and socks now removed, Holden is gradually working his way through the journos and edging closer to the showers, but he is not bothered in the least and looks as though he would be happy to stay out there until next week as he confirms his joy to yet another microphone:

"I just can't believe it," he says, sporting a major grin, "I think it was my first touch...I don't think I'll ever get over this. It sat up nicely...I don't remember too much...I didn't fancy taking a penalty in a shoot out, that's why I scored! We deserved to win... there was no difference between the teams...Rotherham will be a great day out. "Do I fancy my chances of scoring against them? I don't know if I'll be in the team. I don't even know whether I'll be playing against Bromley on Saturday!"

In the Centre Spot bar, Sammy is sipping his customary post match bottle of Bud and celebrating with the Worthing fans, who treat him to their famous and surreal ditty in his honour:

"There's only one Sammy Donnelly. His only wish is to go down on Fish in Sussex by the sea."

The party's going on all over the place and the sounds of Worthing songs ring around the bar. Then, all goes quiet, like in a Western saloon, as the doors swing open. The Dover fan in the beanie has arrived to keep his appointment. He walks towards Donnelly. The few of us in the know watch with trepidation. He stops directly front of Sammy, about a foot away:

"Sorry mate," he says stretching out a hand of friendship. "I was out of order there. Well-played. Your lot deserved to win."

'Rotherham here we come!' Sammy Donelly celebrates success against Dover

IO

Thou've got a team to be proud of there son

FIRST ROUND PROPER

ROTHERHAM UNITED

V

WORTHING

29 OCTOBER 1999

@ MILLMOOR GROUND, ROTHERHAM

ATTENDANCE 3,716

The build up to Worthing's big day has not been promising. Their one league encounter since the win at Dover resulted in a 2-0 home reverse at the hands of mid-table Bromley. And a certain Ronnie Moore among the crowd confirmed that he saw "one or two weaknesses," which his Rotherham side could exploit.

Pre-Cup collywobbles or not however, Worthing's biggest home attendance of the season so far witnessed this game, demonstrating the growing enthusiasm brought about by the exploits of Sammy's Rebels.

Indeed, In accordance with the onset of the competition proper and in direct contrast to Old Trafford, from where confirmation of Manchester United's non-participation has at last been announced, Cup Fever has now broken out big-time in Worthing-on-Sea. The unmistakable buzz created by allegedly, our nation's favourite competition, has provided a rude, but rather pleasurable awakening to the Sussex folk and in true Football Focus tradition, countless good luck messages and trinkets adorn the local shops and pubs. The conversation on every street corner seems to centre on how somebody or other is getting to Millmoor and the number one topic of discussion in Sammy's diner? You don't need a degree in rocket science to work that one out!

The local media have cottoned-on of course. They have been milking it all week with rabble-rousing, 'Rebels Take Yorkshire'- style headlines, while the club themselves have sold so much merchandise, that emergency supplies of replica tops and polo shirts have been drafted in to satisfy demand.

Only one piece of bad news spoils the party: Marc Rice found out after the Dover replay that he would miss the big game through suspension. A major personal blow for Rice and significant tactical pain in the backside for Donnelly.

Friday 29 October 1999, 3pm

Outside the ground, at the end of what is officially, the sunniest October since 1959, a fair-sized crowd of local journos and well-wishers are gathered, as the Worthing entourage board the coach. Sammy has arranged cover for the Diner, Physio Fish has delegated all his maritime duties and the players with day jobs have managed to get time off, to enable them to spend tonight in style at the Rotherham Swallow Hotel.

Hospital Radio Rich, and a number of local media hacks will be travelling independently this afternoon and making their own accommodation arrangements. And safe in the knowledge that it will supply far better copy than yet another chip pan fire, they will join Sammy and the players in the hotel tonight. The main body of support, which is estimated at around a thousand, will of course leave tomorrow morning, to form a convoy of red and white, no doubt stretching half way up the M1.

Arrival at the Swallow creates reaction of excitement in players who aren't used to this big time treatment. Sammy's job is to keep the players level headed and calm. They stay in the hotel, where they mingle with the players from Enfield, who face a similar job at Chesterfield tomorrow. Sammy calls the players together for a brief talk about the game, and then sends them to bed early.

Saturday 30 October, 10am

Sammy has the players in a totally private team meeting. This is followed by an equally private session of light training and equally light, but somewhat less clandestine lunch, which is digested during the ubiquitous pre-match delights of Sky Sports. The advantage here is this is far better preparation than sandwiches and chocolate, Chippenham style.

12.30pm

Predictably, the harsh, industrial ambience of Rotherham is in complete contrast to the genteel, cultured character of Worthing, but today, the difference does not end there. The Sussex town is awash with the FA Cup and the great achievement of their team in battling through seven matches to reach this stage. But round and about in Rotherham, you would not know there was a match on, which on the face of it, is understandable, as they have not so much as kicked a ball in this season's competition. And for them, today's encounter will simply be the equivalent of Worthing's humble, Preliminary Qualifying Round tie, away to Epsom and Ewell back in August.

Making our own way to Millmoor, we pass a selection of run down shops in a fairly built up part of the town near the railway station. The area before us opens up and the floodlights become visible. It is sparse, and maybe the kind of place you would expect to see a 'B&Q' or 'Great Mills'. However, all that is on offer is the fairly sizeable, 'Zone Nightclub,' no doubt to be populated around 10 hours hence, by a fine selection of pastel coloured shirts, button down collars and gelled hair combed forward. And the female equivalent.

As we come upon Millmoor itself, we see that three sides of the ground are taken up by a scrapyard and from outside, the stadium looks deceivingly run-down. Inside however, it is a neat, tidy and compact arena, decorated in red and white, with a lush playing surface, and it becomes clear why Dover assistant manager, Clive Walker declared it to be a "positive pleasure to visit and play there!"

With what appears to be a main gate wide open, we make our way inside. Ten or so staff are buzzing around doing their pre-match thing and before long an old boy, whose precise job description is never made clear, challenges us, but a quick flash of the old press passes is enough to send him on his way. "Never mind him luv," says a kindly middle-aged tea lady, "he's a bit of a jobsworth is that one!"

At the corner of the Railway End, is the newly decorated mortuary. This is immediately behind the first aid post that is somewhat worrying. Other than this the ground is impressive, with numerous adverts for Pukka Pies.

We work our way around into the largely wooden, main stand. The club has understandably been extremely cautious since the Bradford City disaster and smoking is consequently, now banned, anywhere in the main stand area. We then go under the structure and take in the changing rooms, boardroom and hospitality areas. Coming back out onto the pitch we meet head groundsman Bill Corby, who, like the pies, is an award winner and boldly claims:

"I'm 'best groundsman in t'bloody league me!" "Look at t' pitch, it's like bloody velvet is that."

Talking to supporters of Rotherham is a mixed experience. They appreciate the monies put into the club by the Chairman but question his ability at PR. They say that Leo Fortune West and Darren Garner will score today but moan about their lack of consistency. Hard to please, Northerners.

1.30pm

Word up is that the Worthing team coach has arrived. As the entourage disembarks, Donnelly and Carrington are immediately collared by the Sussex press and amenable to the last, they give their comments, while the Rotherham stewards usher the rest of the team under the main stand and into the changing rooms. The security here is noticeably higher than anything we have experienced in our journey so far and for all the quality in the upper echelons of the Non-League hierarchy, the moment you go above Conference standard, you enter a different world.

With Donnelly and Carrington still bogged down by the press we end up talking to Gareth the kit man, but not before we have been treated for shock! No Bermuda shorts! In fact he is fully suited up! Shirt, tie - the lot! Gareth is quick to explain that the club 'strongly suggested' he may wish to break the habit of a lifetime for this special occasion and maintains, in spite of our relentless piss-taking, that he is actually quite happy to oblige, on a one-off basis of

110

course. Naturally this is nowhere near enough to stop us and whilst we continue to think how hilarious we are, Gary is getting visibly hacked off.

We also decide to leave Sammy and Ben to enjoy the limelight. We will catch up with them soon enough. Anyway, we have been invited in to see Millers boss and ex-Liverpool player, Ronnie Moore and this seems like a good moment to take up the invitation. So we make our way behind the Tivoli End and up the iron steps and into the modest admin block. In keeping with the different world of league football, into which we have been thrown kicking and screaming, there is no way we can get near Ronnie's office without permission in letters of blood, in triplicate. We advise a suitable staff member of our appointment and, after checking with his boss, lets us deeper into the labyrinth of red tape. The corridors are buzzing with bodies in a hurry and Ronnie's one of them, but to his credit he has made time for us

"Alright lads," he says in a mild Scouse accent and shakes our hands. Although noticeably busy, as you would expect on a matchday, Ronnie is not having to cope with the kind of media attention being heaped upon his Worthing counterpart. If the Millers were to win through today, a big Third Round draw would however, probably remedy that situation.

Ronnie is a tall, tanned, fit-looking man. It is difficult to determine the colour of his hair as blond or white, but he retains a youthful appearance and commands respect immediately. Pondering upon the day's events, his comments are refreshingly honest:

"There's not much I can say, that hasn't been said thousands of times before is there?" He smiles. "You know, we'll try not to underestimate them and all that. But we've gotta be confident really, especially with the home draw. It'd be very different if we were at their place mind. A lot of Non-League clubs playing league teams at home today will have taken heart from Rushden's win last night. No one in my kind of position needed that result! But the trick is to get it right mentally. We've prepared for this as though it was a Third Division promotion clash and I've told the lads to treat it that way on the pitch. They know there may be a storm to weather over the first fifteen minutes or so and they'll be ready to dig in. And I've told them they'll need to be patient before the first break comes their way. But the important thing, is that we don't give them anything at all to celebrate, especially early on, which I'm optimistic about to be honest, as we've only let in one goal here all season!

We decide it's high time to let Ronnie go back about his business and thank him for taking time-out with us.

"OK lads, no problem. See you after the game. And maybe in the next round eh!"

So it's back down the steps and time to find Sammy and co. with a minor detour to see whether a Rotherham fanzine is anywhere to be found. Having had no luck, one of us asks a young lad selling programmes if he can point us in the right direction. About 13 years old, football crazy, he is bound to know:

"What's a fanzine?" is the response, in front of a dozen or so assorted punters.

But a semi-cockney cavalry comes to the rescue, as a couple of Worthing fans enlighten the lad appropriately: "A fanzine's written by the fans and tells the truth (he holds up his newly-purchased Rotherham programme and points to it)...Not like this!" The young lad however, is unimpressed and carries on, still seemingly in blissful ignorance of the additional reading material that he could obtain, relating to his favourite team. We exchange smiles and shrugs with the Worthing fans and make our way back into the stadium.

Meanwhile, the first elements of support are beginning to trickle in to the stadium. So, by choosing a more sensible helper, we soon establish, that Rotherham do in fact have a very good fanzine, that goes by the handle of 'Moulin Rouge', and with which Ronnie Moore and his number two John Breckin are the first Millers management team to have a meaningful relationship. We are advised that Moore is very guarded however and that Breckin takes all the flak on his behalf.

Having at last escaped the press, Donnelly and Carrington join their colleagues in the changing rooms. And before long, the players begin to emerge for the warm-up, in new tracksuits especially purchased by the club for the occasion. Why is it that non-league clubs only ever get new trackwear when they manage a cup run. Who cares about the bonuses, get a cup run and get a trackie out of the club. Sammy follows them onto the pitch, encouraging and instructing, coat collar turned up and chin dug deep into his chest as the rain begins to thicken. "I'd love to do this today for them", he says, pointing to the fans milling in the away end.

Tactics? "Well it seems they'll probably start with a 3-5-2 formation, which I think we'll match, with Paul Kennett playing deep in midfield. That's in preference to Adie Miles who can't really play deep, so he's a sub today. It's a shame about Ricey mind, but there we go. Anyway, we'll be very organised, especially

I hope, against set-pieces which will be a danger. And I hope I've geed them up enough, because we'll need to compete one hundred percent all the way through. If you do that it brings dividends. And I hope I've instilled enough confidence in them to show composure on the ball. If they don't, we'll be punished. The main thing is that we play to the plan. If we do we'll have our moments, which of course will need to be seized. But you know what? Above all, I want us to come away from here with some respect!"

In the background, Chewy Raistrick is now doing the rounds as Dusty the Miller Man and having mock fights with the Rotherham players.

The crowd is thickening up inside the stadium, and the Worthing numbers behind the Railway End goal are swelling. And the rain is relentless. Before long, both sets of players are back inside for their final briefs before crossing the Rubicon. With tactics already boxed-off, Donnelly's got one thing on his mind. Motivation!:

"Compete with them, don't be in awe. They've each got two legs and two arms just like you! Remember a Non-League team will cause an upset somewhere today – let's make it us!"

With that, it's ShowTime and the Worthing players, with their all-new, all-blue, away kit making its debut, work their way down the tunnel amid the sounds of clicking studs and shouts of "come aaan." Then it's into the arena with a quick sprint, to be greeted by, what transpires to be a smaller than anticipated army of support. The Worthing fans gathered behind the goal are an island of red and white, surrounded by empty spaces and once again things are put into perspective. There are plenty of gaps in the home areas too and although this is Rotherham's highest home gate of the season, the stadium is, in terms of its capacity of 11,500, only just over a third full. This is definitely not a big game for The Millers.

We are joined in the stand by Radio Rich, who has abandoned the main body of support, in favour of this vantage point, which will enable him to get a better view of the action for his match report. The only thing is, he has taken his life in his hands by wearing a Worthing top, which hasn't gone unnoticed among the locals in the stand:

"Ah'm not bein' funny mate, but what league are thou in? Is it t'Unibond or what?" As is often the case when league clubs meet Non-League, the atmosphere is friendly and while our Yorkshire friend was a fraction condescending and looked to have indulged in one too many pre-match beverages, Rich looks to be safe.

Mr Hill signals the start of the competition proper and we are away, amid shouts of encouragement for Leo-Fortune West, "come on Leo" and abuse for Ben Carrington, "is it a bleedin' woman playin' centre forward?" Dreads are not big in deepest Yorkshire.

Early doors (thanks Ron) Rotherham press and win a corner, which they take in Euro '88 style, where the ball is cut straight back to a runner for the shot. The runner is midfielder Kevin Watson and the shot sails over the bar. With Rotherham's strong start it takes around ten minutes for Worthing to settle, but having weathered the early storm they begin to knock the ball about confidently.

Ben Cartwright spurns a brace of opportunities, and this is followed by a trio of chances for Rotherham's star midfielder Darren Garner. One goes wide and two over the bar, one of which clips the horizontal, from a delicate close range chip.

Meanwhile, Rich's earlier tormentor (seemingly, the self-appointed resident wit) has clearly been reading his programme and picked up on the fact that Donnelly runs a café:

"Hey Sammy, bekkon and egg sandwich to go, please. Sammeh, chip butty and a cup of tea please mate."

Leaning on the side of the dugout, Donnelly is far too engrossed in the game to respond, if indeed he can hear. Dover, this is not.

Fortune-West misses opportunities, which include stubbing his toe with a shot within the box. Rotherham take control of the game, though and pressure mounts. Unperturbed by the pressure, Carrington and Funnell continue to combine well and appear to be Worthing's best hope of doing any damage. Approaching the half-hour mark, this combination works together as Funnell puts Carrington through with a clever back-heel. Carrington lets fly from a central position around twenty yards out. It's clearly bound for the bottom left hand corner of the net and the Millers fans in the Tivoli End behind the net look on in disbelief. Keeper Pollitt gets a hand to it and turns it round for a corner. The corner is cleared.

Those of sound hearing could detect a ripple of applause for Carrington from the home support, but less astute aural skills are required to hear the abuse:

"Eee, they've got a lass at centre forward."

On the half-hour, target-man Fortune-West breaks down the left and puts over a cross, which Worthing half-clear. It falls to ex-Bolton playmaker Steve Thompson, who loops a shot in from 20 yard to the far right-hand corner of the net and Rotherham are one-up. The home fans explode in relief.

More Millers pressure follows, with forward Paul Warne getting increasingly in on the act, but there is no further breakthrough. Worthing are 1-0 down at half time, but they are showing enough to build on.

During the break the nightmare of the wit continues, as we get a full run down of how he and his mates put two mattresses in a van and headed for Wembley in 1996, because you couldn't get a minibus anywhere. And then how he has never seen a sea of red and white as spectacular as that day, including the time he had watched Liverpool in an FA Cup final."

As the second half starts Worthing seem distinctly rejuvenated. Carrington's still popping up everywhere and Garner's desire to stop him results in a foul and yellow card. As Rotherham get back on the attack, they win a corner, in front of their fans at the Tivoli End and in a resulting challenge, Paul Dillon goes down after a sickening blow to the head. With Dillon sparked out, the Yorkshire wit claims he cannot see what is going on because Donnelly is standing in his way:

"Sammy, sit down mate, I can't see, seriously Sammy I can't see bugger all." Donnelly edges into the dugout. Dillon is carried off, now conscious, but puking his guts up over the side of the stretcher.

"That's travel sickness is that."

A flurry of Rotherham corners are defended sternly. The wit strikes again: "Two more bacon sandwiches, Sammeh!" Unable to contain himself any further, Donnelly turns around: OK mate, that'll be two pound fifty!" Only a beanie hat missing now.

Meanwhile, from the Railway end we can barely hear the strains of: "His only wish is to go down on Fish, in Sussex by the Sea."

Unsurprisingly, there is no home response to this.

While Rotherham are still seeing a fair amount of the ball, they do not seem that adventurous and frustration is creeping into the crowd: "This is t' worst match I've seen all year, sitting back on a bloody one-nil lead." Exclaims an alternative Yorkshire voice this time.

But to be fair, adrenaline-fired Worthing are playing out of their skins and closing them down well, which is typified by Carrington. With twenty minutes left on the clock, he is still running strongly and can be found helping out in defence as well as attack.

Donnelly orders Adic Miles on in a classic striker for defender substitution. The departing Lee Cox salutes the applauding Rotherham fans.

Into the last fifteen and Worthing are giving it their all, but they look less like scoring now and it is beginning to look as though Carrington's early misses could prove fatal. Meanwhile the Worthing fans are at their loudest, desperately trying to cheer the lads on to one final effort. And the players respond with a period of desperate pressure. Every attack sees the red and white in the railway end bubbling with excitement, their volume directly proportional to the proximity of the ball to the Rotherham goal. A half-chance and then a corner come and go, but still no equaliser and the minutes are ticking away. Mark Knee adds to the agony by smashing a volley straight at Pollitt.

Into the last ten and Rotherham break from the Worthing pressure. Steve Thompson gets to the by-line on the left and sends a cross over. Darren Garner gets on the end of it on the left apex of the six-yard box. His glancing header is inch-perfect, past Bray's despairing arm, into the top right hand corner and it's 2-0. Worthing have again paid the price for giving Thompson space and as a result their dream is all but over. Thompson and Garner are indeed a class above and have inflicted a mortal wound this time.

The game is over, and the Rotherham fans are cheering Carrington's every touch. Indeed they out-boo the Worthing contingent when he gets booked with three minutes to go. The inexplicable friendliness that emanates from many league clubs towards their Non-League counterparts has struck again. Note: This only applies when the league side are winning.

The score moves to 3-0 with a disputed penalty, slotted home by sub Gary Martindale. Game over, and the whistle confirms the fact.

The Yorkshire wit leans over to Radio Rich: "Thou've got a team to be proud of there son!"

Back in the Worthing changing room, there is no argument, no apportion of blame, only congratulations all round. They know they have given their all and earned the respect with which Sammy wanted to leave Millmoor. Meanwhile, rumours abound that Ronnie Moore is so impressed with Carrington's contribution that he is actually toying with the idea of offering him a trial. This may be the stuff of dreams for Burt however, but Ben's attitude paints a very different picture:

"It wouldn't be worth it," he explains. "I've got a decent job - for life hopefully – and my football with Worthing supplements that nicely. For me, professional football would be too big a risk for too short a career!" Once again, the picture of football being every man's dream becomes distorted.

The traditional Donnelly interview ensues: "Every player played their part," he exclaims. "To go in only one-nil down at half-time was great and that was against the run of play. In fact their manager's just told me he would have settled for that at the time. And who's to say what would have happened, if one of Ben's shots had gone in? I really thought we were in with a shout of a replay at half time. "And I thought if we had a go at them second half we could have gone away with something, but it wasn't to be. Although we did have a go and Ben and Simon caused them all sorts of problems. We could have settled for losing one-nil, but I like to win games and I put on an extra striker in the second half to try and do just that and to entertain our supporters who paid good money to come up here. And I think we did entertain them. Tell you what, I've always respected my players, but to see them put up a performance like that against a side second in Division Three was tremendous. Three-nil definitely flattered Rotherham. And as for the penalty that was a joke!"

As we say our goodbyes to Sammy, Ben and Radio Rich, the stark realisation sets in, that we are about to leave behind the warm, comfort-zone of the Non-League scene and our friends from Sussex. And Donnelly puts a fitting epitaph on Worthing's involvement in our journey: "I'm very proud of the club, but completely choked to be out of this wonderful competition!"

On top of their round by round prize money however, Worthing will pick up a share of the furthest non exempted club award worth £1,600, making their income in prize and potential grant monies alone around the £18K mark. They also received a plaque for the South East performance of the Round, awarded for the victory at Dover, to brighten the trophy cabinet. Hopefully these dividends will provide significant consolation.

But for us, the competition goes on and our allegiance switches to Ronnie Moore's Rotherham United. Accordingly, this is a good time to catch up with him: "We've drawn Barnet or Burnley away," he says the moment he sees us – they're playing tomorrow so you'll have to wait and see where you're off to."

The draw hadn't been a particularly massive occasion for Rotherham. The biggest fish would only be a top Division Two side after all. If they were to get past that hurdle however, and into the hat with the big boys for the Third Round Proper, that would be a different matter. But for now, relative indifference will reign, as away to Burnley would provide a stiff, but unglamorous task, although the prospect of visiting fellow Division 3 high-flyers Barnet, has induced a minor incidence of drooling amongst the Millmoor punters.

Of today's encounter, Moore brings us down to earth: "We're pleased with the result, but not the performance," he says, in far more serious mode than pre-match. "Although we were never actually in trouble, they were really bright up front and we weren't comfortable with that for the whole ninety minutes, which means something's not right. But our first goal came at the right time, because we could easily have been one down by then. And the second was important as it came just when they'd started pushing hard for an equaliser.

"The Penalty. Swan Lake, I'm afraid".

II

What, No tickets?

SECOND ROUND PROPER

BURNLEY

V

ROTHERHAM

SATURDAY 20 NOVEMBER

@ TURF MOOR, BURNLEY

ATTENDANCE 8,110

For some reason, arguments over Rotherham's debut performance in our FA Cup odyssey raged, in pubs, clubs and Internet chatrooms alike. Supporters were moaning at the performance, despite a clear victory.

Fanzine Editor Steve Exley was amazed and commented: "Ask any Direshites fan how they're feeling." (The much-hated 'Spirerites' of Second Division Chesterfield had gone down 2-1 at home to Enfield, from the Ryman League Premier Division. The Rotherham Swallow had clearly proved a luckier base for them than our friends from Sussex).

'I'm almost speechless. People are MOANING????? Are they completely out of their minds? Are they stark raving bonkers, or been to Butlins on Pluto?? We are second in the league. We have the best goal difference in the whole country. We have won our last four home games by eleven to nil. Eight out of fourteen league matches have ended in clean sheets. The press and opposing fans say we play good football, and we do. Now call me a blind, stumbling, ridiculous optimist, but I think this is good, yes, on balance I think this is a good thing. I think we can smile occasionally, clap the team a little maybe, perhaps even offer verbal support to our heroes individually for their efforts, quietly of course to avoid embarrassment".

Saturday 20 November – Turf Moor

This is a different world. A massive stadium, plush reception area with uniformed women behind the desk, two decent club shops and a 'Centre Spot' Restaurant in a different class to the one at Dover Athletic. This is truly the big-time. For all the talk of sleeping giants, we simply had no idea that Burnley were such a big club. Only one problem. Despite a thorough search by one of the nice women in claret and blue they have no trace of our press passes anywhere, and they do not care if we are writing a book or not, we will

Vertigo at Turf Moor

120

not be coming in without them. This of course presents a problem. Turf Moor is not exactly like Worthing or even Rotherham for that matter, where you could demand to 'see the manager' in order to sort it out. This is the big time.

So what to do?

We retire to the car, get out the mobile and stick on the blagging boots. Our methodology must of course remain classified, but suffice to say that upon return to the lush carpets of reception, two passes are waiting for us and we are back in business. Retrospectively, Teamtalk magazine owe the club a belated fax, and the "man from the FA" who made the call from our car asking for a favour can go back to London to relax.

The Press room at Burnley is very impressive, and buffet and coffee are freely available. We understand why many reporters appear to analyse matches from a safe distance when we realise this is the level of hospitality. The food is great, so we tuck in like there's no tomorrow. Having carried out the standard procedure - particularly where *gratis comestibles* are concerned – we have eaten until we feel completely sick. But to be fair we need it to protect ourselves from the cold. Winter has truly set in and the weather begins the build up for the traditional decimation of the Third Round - albeit shifted from January to December for this season's competition, much to the disgust of many institutionalised punters.

Pre-match, 35 year-old, Steve Thompson is on hand to discuss Rotherham's chances of overturning the team he left in 1997. And he confirms what the surroundings suggest:

"This is a massive set up. Burnley are probably one of a handful of sleeping giants. But we were looking forward to coming here. On our day, we've got nothing to fear in the Second Division, but Burnley are a strong side and we'll need to be at our best to come away with anything. They've strengthened since we were last here and it'll be a different game today from that one on Sky. I'm glad Stan's turned it around for them and I'm looking forward to seeing some of the lads like Paul Weller, Chris Brass and Andy Cooke. My prediction? Well it'll be difficult for us, but I just hope we enjoy it and it'll be a good yardstick of our progress. That's as much as I'm saying!"

The stakes are high today, not least of all financially. And having defeated Burnley 3-0, in their last FA Cup meeting here, two years ago in front of a Sky audience, The Millers can at least claim the psychological advantage if nothing else. But the Clarets have come a long way since those dark days of Mr Waddle's control - when there was a distinct lack of Diamond Lights – and the only survivor in today's Clarets line-up is Andy Cooke. Indeed, Burnley are now favourites for promotion to Division 1 and are up with the leaders.

Although, Burnley boss Stan Ternent is taking nothing for granted: "It'll be a tough match," he admits, "obviously Barnet are in a similar position and they were no pushover. And I know Rotherham are a good side. But we've got dangerous players that they'll have to be aware of." He continues, "This is a nice change from League action and a big day, with a big prize. It's an important competition and the object of the exercise is to get into the hat with the big boys. But we'll see how it goes!"

Stan is a genuinely nice geezer, albeit one with a great inside knowledge of the game and bags of experience, and yet it is not difficult to assess he has a hard edge.

The spacious stadium is not packed to the rafters by any means, but Rotherham have brought a fair sized crew of around 1500 and as kick-off time looms, they are making some decent noise. The teams line up ready for the off, Burnley in claret shirts, white shorts and white socks with claret and blue trims and Rotherham in their changed kit of white shirts, black shorts and black socks. We take our places way up in the press box at the back of the James Hargreaves stand, and are treated to a sumptuous view. This however, does not consist of the archetypal, northern, industrial landscape, but centres on the edge of town, where only one or two sizeable chimneys give way to rolling countryside. The top of this stand is incredibly high, and incredibly steep. There is no doubt that the view of the game allows for easy tactical assessment, but vertigo as a definite worry.

Today's referee, Graham Laws from Whitley Bay - a detective by trade, cue several obvious jests – then gets things under way and Burnley start like they've overdosed on Red Bull. And Rotherham, visibly shocked by the Clarets' momentum, are on the back foot straightaway: "Let's hope we bloody well carry on like it," is one Lancashire aspiration. And the perpetrator is not disappointed.

Before long, central defender, Steve Davis gets on the end of a Glen Little corner on the edge of the six-yard box and fires in a header which Mike Pollitt brilliantly tips over the bar, for the first of a series of fine saves which even set the Claret faithful purring. And there are copious comments referring to him as "pure class" and "putting Seaman and Schmeichel to shame," as well as a shout or two of "sign him up Stan." This is complemented by another Burnley fan who yells, "good save Mike Pillock." And he is clearly impressed with his own material, as the phrase is repeated several times in the first half, interspersed by loud laughter (his own).

In a superb Burnley move, striker Andy Payton back heels to left midfielder Glen Little, who sends over a great cross for Paul Cook arriving from the central midfield. But Cook curls his shot wide. Showing courage under fire, Rotherham hit back through Darren Garner who powers in a shot, but it's high and wide. Then a good low ball into the Burnley box finds Trevor Berry arriving from the left. He turns sharply and smashes in a close range shot, only for Paul Crichton to pull off an excellent save at the near-post. But this is a rare attack for the Millers and they are being overrun by superior strength and skill.

Although restricted to counter-attacks, Rotherham push forward whenever possible and striking partners Fortune-West and Warne both get shots in. But neither has the power, pace or guile to beat Crichton. After twenty minutes they have pushed too far and leave themselves exposed at the back, resulting in Andy Payton exploiting the space and getting into the Millers box. He clashes with Big Pol and falls to the ground, although he still gets the shot in, but John Varty clears it off the line. As Pollitt shapes up to take the goal kick, he of the sharp Pollitt related wit is quick off the mark again:

"Come on you bender, hurry up."

In spite of their side being under the cosh, the Millers fans grouped in the Cricketfield stand can still raise a chant, "Burnley, Burnley give us a song" rings out to no reply from a strangely subdued home support. But as Payton turns his man in the box and lashes in a superb shot, the Clarets fans are on their feet celebrating a goal - until Pollitt somehow intervenes again and the ball is kept out of the net. Burnley though are displaying bundles of slick passing and the gap between the two sides is apparent.

Rotherham attacks are a rare commodity now and Millers fans hopes are up when Kevin Watson has time to line up a shot on the edge of the box, but hits a poor effort way over the bar. Then normal service is resumed as Steve Davis makes another foray from the back for Burnley. Forward Andy Cooke shows great skill on the right flank to send over a pinpoint cross and Davis jumps way above his marker to produce a classic, attacking downward header, but Big Pol's on hand to deflect it away again.

Hard-working Burnley midfielder Mickey Mellon gets into the Rotherham box and he is set up by forward Andy Payton. Mellon is tackled at the point of shooting and performs a dive that must have required an equity card. Like a true detective, Mr Laws is not fooled and waves play on. Those who have crossed the Pennines are not fooled either and cue the chants of "cheat, cheat, cheat."

Next up, Stan Ternent orders Glen Little to switch flanks, which he does and promptly shows his skill down the left as he beats three Millers defenders to get a cross in and from the resultant second phase play Mullin sends a shot crashing against the bar. Rotherham had planned to get forward via wing-backs Rob Scott and Trevor Berry today, but they are constantly pegged-back by Little and Mullin pushing up, as well as Burnley's relentless running and endless possession.

But still it will not go in for Burnley and Rotherham hold on until the break.

With no score at half time and the amount of pressure the Millers have absorbed with no resulting damage, Rotherham fans could be excused for believing that this is one of those days where you are destined to win by the odd breakaway goal.

We descend from the nosebleed-inducing heights of the (nevertheless impressive and well-equipped) press box at the back of the James Hargreaves stand, and with appetites back in full effect, make a beeline for the pressroom.

The second half kicks-off with a rejuvenated Rotherham enjoying a few minutes of pressure. This raises the spirits of the travelling Yorkshirefolk and the Clarets support who have truly found their voice now, respond accordingly to make for a much better atmosphere. Before long Burnley are back on top and midfielder Paul Cook is through for a one-on-one with Big Pol but with the home fans on their feet in celebration, Pol does just enough yet again and Cook puts it wide:

Cue: "Ee Ay ee ay ee ay o, up the Football League we go," from the Millers masses and more Rotherham pressure. The Burnley fans respond with "Stan Ternent's claret and blue army." Burnley's second smallest crowd of the season is becoming their loudest. And on the pitch the pendulum swings back to Ternent's men as they ride the Rotherham pressure and get back in the driving seat. Club skipper and left-back Gordon Armstrong heads against the bar from another Little cross and the Turf Moor faithful are beginning to mumble about whether it is to be their day. If it is, much will be down to Armstrong who has played a real captain's innings today.

But with around twenty minutes to go, the mumblings of frustration are getting louder and many Clarets fans are getting that awful gut feeling - just waiting for the fateful Rotherham break. Although for the neutral, it is difficult to see from where it will come. Garner and Thompson are being rendered ineffective in midfield and Mitchell Thomas - who has seen it all before in the 1987 final with Spurs - is dealing with the physical threat posed by Fortune-West with consummate ease.

But as Burnley chalk up their 14th corner of the match, the ball is cleared only as far as Paul Cook. The former Coventry and Wolves man unleashes a left-foot shot from 30 yards and it swerves around the outstretched arms of Pollitt and into the net. Three quarters of the ground explodes in relief and when the cheers eventually die down, "you're not singing anymore," rings out from all around as Clarets everywhere thrust their pointing fingers at the silent Millers fans. Having scored his first ever FA Cup goal at Barnet in the previous round, Cook seems to have developed an appetite. But neither he nor anybody else ever discovered whether the dramatic swerve on the ball was created by his cultured boot or a deflection from an unfortunate defender.

A short period of Rotherham pressure follows, resulting in a save from the under-employed Paul Crichton and right-back Dean West clearing a subsequent shot off the line. The storm having been weathered, Burnley wide-man John Mullin, who earlier switched with Glen Little and is now on the right gets on the end of right-back Dean West's throw into the danger area. The former Sunderland man has been troubling the Millers with his pace all day and does not hang about as he moves to connect on the half volley, with the outside of the right boot. And the ball smashes into the top corner of the net to give Burnley a two-goal cushion. Rotherham seem dead and buried and surely Mullin has booked Burnley's passage into the Third Round wonderland. They say that 2-0 is a dangerous lead. And there is still a quarter of an hour to go, but any comeback seems the stuff of fantasy now as Burnley are cruising.

The goal has really sparked the Clarets fans into life and choruses of "bring on the Bastards" ring out. The aforementioned being of course the much-hated Blackburn Rovers, whom Clarets fans confirm to us they would dearly love to draw at home and despatch accordingly in the next round.

There is discontent among the Rotherham faithful as one shouts an invitation to the Burnley support to meet him outside, presumably not for dinner in the Centre Spot restaurant. Then, in sheer frustration, a couple have a pop at the stewards and a whole host of fluorescent jackets are there like a shot, just in time to prevent a major 'off.'

Ternent brings Cook off to rapturous applause and Ronnie Jepson gets a run in his place. In the dying seconds Andy Payton almost gets in on the act for Burnley with another top-corner bound effort, but Pollitt claws it away. And not to be outdone, Crichton pulls off a carbon copy at the other end from Paul Warne.

Soon after Mr Laws blows his whistle and ends our association with the Millers before it has had a chance to blossom. So now our focus must shift to Stan Ternent's promotion chasing Second Division outfit. And from what we have seen here already, surely Burnley are destined for better things. The set up is purely Premiership, that's for sure and today they've despatched a decent Rotherham side, virtually without batting an eyelid. Also inescapable, is the fact that we have left behind any semblance of cosiness and entered the competition proper in a big way. Even if we come across a small club at home in the next couple of rounds, the stakes will be so high that homeliness will go out of the window. Things will be a lot different from here on in.

Post-match, Paul Cook plays down the plaudits:

"As I've said before, it doesn't matter who scores. Our priority was to get through. And it's nice for the club to be in the Third Round for the first time in a while."

Ever-willing to credit his colleagues, he continues, "All the lads are enjoying it at the moment and there's a will to win. The likes of Andy Cooke and Andy Payton worked ever so hard. People might say for no reward, but the reward is that the club is in the next round!"

In the well decked-out pressroom, we are busy gorging ourselves again on the free buffet, which now consists of dessert, as Ternent walks in, stony-faced as though his team had lost 10-0. But he is as dry as ever: "Come on then, fire away, I've got to get to bed tonight."

But he goes on to say that it was a good competitive match with the right result and that "the players showed admirable patience and got their just rewards in the end." And he continues:

"I thought Andy Cooke and Andy Payton worked their socks off today. They didn't get a break in front of goal but they caused untold problems for the Rotherham defenders. But we've got players who can score from positions all over the pitch and I think we showed that."

"Hopefully we can put a Cup run together now. It'll be good for the club both morale-wise and financially. Especially after last year, which was a transitional time for us and possibly the hardest I've faced in twenty years of football. But now everything in the garden's rosy!"

The real worry about these press conferences however, is the questions. The managers come in, sit at a top table, flanked by the club's press minders and look set for a detailed analysis of tactics and strategy. Then, the assembled low level journos ask them "how they saw the match, were they happy with the result, how is important is the cup compared with the league", and such drivel. To be honest, the conferences look interesting but never are. We have been really excited at getting "inside" the workings of the media and the real football men, but it just never happens. The Conferences are a damp squib, and the managers look wholly bored. Judging by the standard of the questions, they have every right to be. And whenever a criticism levels its head, the manager gets aggressive and the journo drops the point and retires behind the media scrum. Each conference just seems to be haggard. A tired reporter trying to wring a printable quote from a tired manager, before each can clear off home having done their job.

There are no complaints from the Millers faithful about the result, although criticism is apparent for Dillon and Fortune-West, who both struggled today and were substituted accordingly, with Dillon described as "trying to give Burnley a goal." That said, most Millers fans accept that honours have been settled and that there is possibly a long way to go before they can really compete with the likes of Burnley. And to quote Steve Exley:

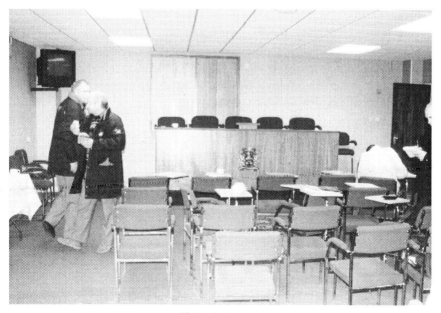

The Burnley press room

"If that's Second Division football, how the hell are we going to survive if we get promotion?" He goes on to express concern that the whole Rotherham team cost only £100K, while one Burnley player is worth almost a million. His assessment is accurate. There is no doubt that gaps are emerging between each division, probably with the best 10 teams in each division creating a mini-division in each one. The facts are that Burnley will probably go up and survive in Division 1, Rotherham may do the same in Division 2, but their prospects of going any further diminish year on year. In spite of those statistics, Ronnie Moore is bitterly disappointed and leaves Chief Executive Phil Henson to do the talking:

"Overall the best side won on the day," says the totally, up-front Henson, "although we were in with a shout in the first-half. I thought Mike Pollitt played well and we looked dangerous on the break, but Burnley looked a really decent side in the second half and it was no disgrace to go out." Nobody can fully explain Moore's absence and it's unheard of for him not to turn up like this. But the reason was never given.

But incredibly, all is not lost for Rotherham. With this already becoming the most unusual FA Cup competition of contemporary times, another 'bombshell' has been dropped. The FA have masterminded the revolutionary 'AXA Wildcard' slot, designed to reinstate one losing team from the Second Round, in order to fill the gap left in the Third by Manchester United's eventual withdrawal.

It is indeed hoped that this innovation bearing the sponsor's name, will go some way to assuaging their apparent unease over the non-involvement of the top attractions and current holders. Some reports suggest however, that AXA; some 18 months into the £25 million contract in question, are absolutely furious that United cannot somehow be embodied into the tournament and may well claim compensation as a result. This would be likely to take the form of either hard cash, or ticket-draining corporate packages, but a complete pullout is not envisaged.

At this stage it hits us that we have a selection problem. If Rotherham are drawn as the wildcard, whom will we follow then? The Millers on the basis that they are still in the tournament, or Burnley as their conquerors? After examining all arguments in their entirety and using this predicament as an excuse for a protracted discussion in the pub, an executive decision is made and we are unanimous. The concept of our odyssey is based on allegiance until a side is no longer in the competition – so if Rotherham come back out, we go back to them! Or maybe, we move on to Burnley. Alcohol fuelled debates, eh...

12

Jim Smith is like Santa after every game - red cheeks, red nose and giving goals away as presents!

THIRD ROUND PROPER

DERBY COUNTY

V

BURNLEY

SATURDAY 11 DECEMBER

@ PRIDE PARK, DERBY

ATTENDANCE 23,400

On Sunday 21 November, all those who love the Claret and Blues are huddled excitedly around TV sets and radios as the draw for the Third Round is made. And a fair number of Millers retain a passing interest, on the off chance that they may become involved again as the AXA Wildcard entry. Today's draw will contain 63 balls instead of the usual 64 and the final team out will be at home to the Wildcard side. But the identity of those lucky losers will not be known until all 20 Second Round ties, including replays, have been concluded – which is scheduled to be the case on Tuesday 30 November. On Wednesday 1 December, the 20 losing teams will go into their own draw with one pulled out and reinstated in the competition accordingly.

Plenty of cheers go up in the Turf Moor vicinity as Burnley, one of the last balls left in the machine, are eventually drawn away to Premiership strugglers

Derby County. A big game, a big day out and in the view of many Claret connections, including Mr Ternent, by no means an insurmountable task. "I'd have preferred a home draw like anybody else, but I think we have a fighting chance of making something of it," is his initial reaction "and financially, it's great news!" Initial projections were indeed to indicate Burnley's share of the receipts to be a six-figure sum.

Meanwhile, Aston Villa are the latest club to make history in the competition as they will be the first ever opponents of a pre-determined wildcard entry.

In the meantime, apart from the devastating news of our departure in the event of Rotherham's reinstatement, a little more of the gloss has been wiped from Burnley's Second Round success. The club had estimated a trading loss of almost a million pounds, which was to be announced at the AGM on 16 December, but the accounts have now revealed the overall deficit for the financial year ending May 1999 to be almost twice that of the original estimate. And having lost money on general trading, they have also spent a million pounds plus on transfers and increased their wage bill into the bargain. Chairman Barry Kilby however, refuses to be downhearted. He has invested three million quid into the club since coming on board a year ago and makes his two-part strategy crystal-clear:

"Initially it was to spend money to avoid relegation, and then to lay the foundations for a promotion challenge, which is now unfolding. We're making strides on the income side and investing in the playing side too, which is showing through and will hopefully help us achieve our short-term goal of promotion to Division One. But not many teams can do that with a players' wage bill of less than two million. And we can't stand around waiting to get lucky!"

Wednesday 24 November sees the Clarets play badly and still get a 0-0 draw in a league match at Reading, but Royals boss Alan Pardew is not impressed, accusing Burnley of being a physical side and making it "an ugly game." This however, is no doubt offset by a compliment from no less than The Prime Minister, as in an interview for the forthcoming Burnley video, Rhapsody in Claret And Blue, Mr Blair describes the Clarets as "probably better supported than most of the Premiership clubs." To clarify, he means on a home crowds versus town population ratio. No doubt another comment influenced by well known claret, Alastair Campbell.

Saturday 27 November, sees the first of two away clashes at Wigan. And the Clarets come away with a respectable 1-1 draw and valuable league point. But the game is marred by crowd trouble, reportedly due in no small way to the JJB Stadium's seating arrangements, which result in rival supporters sitting together. This leads to poor attempts at moving the Clarets fans into the unoccupied Adidas Stand, frayed tempers, some over-zealous stewarding and the eventual, some say unnecessary, arrival of the riot police. Reports are then forthcoming of crushes on the way out of the ground and appalling traffic control outside. This is not an enjoyable jaunt for some, but a good performance plus Andy Payton's first goal since mid-October does redress the balance.

Wednesday 1 December sees the dawn of the big draw for Rotherham and clarification of which path we will take to Wembley is shortly to arrive. At 11am the twenty balls are put in the hat and drawn out live on Sky Sports News. But for the Millers it ends in disappointment. Darlington will be the ones to make history as the first club to be knocked out in the Second Round and still appear in the Third. They will take on Aston Villa, at Villa Park.

And Rotherham, still riding high in the Second Division, can now fully concentrate on the proverbial league. Opinions are many and varied over the merits of the Wildcard slot and some of the most cynical perceptions are based on

The Clarets in fine voice at Pride Park

the fact that Darlo could conceivably go on to greater things in the Cup than their conquerors, Gillingham. The FA stand firm however. They insist that the scheme is guaranteed to help a smaller club and put another interesting angle on the competition, and deny that it is a desperate measure to appease AXA, who have not been happy bunnies since the biggest attractions of the competition were allowed to pull out. Meanwhile colourful Darlo Chairman George Reynolds says he is delighted and will be "buying Sir Alex a prawn cocktail and T-bone steak!" And as if this is not history enough, Villa and Darlington have never met before!

On Saturday 4 December, in another under-par performance, Burnley scrape the three points courtesy of a 1-0 win with Payton on target again. But a Wycombe penalty hits the post in the process.

Next up is the Auto Windscreens tie at Wigan on 7 December, but Ternent makes a number of changes to maximise the availability of key players for Saturday's clash with Derby and Armstrong, Mellon, Cooke and Cook are rested accordingly. One of the replacements, Alan Lee, puts them one-up, but Wigan equalise and go on to win 2-1 via the 'Golden Goal.' Having already been knocked out of the Worthington Cup by Manchester City, our odyssey is now their only remaining route to Wembley and the Clarets faithful begin to look forward to the trip to Pride Park as the countdown begins. Always up for a laugh, various Clarets supporters groups are trying to get as many travelling fans as possible to dress up as Santas and take balloons, confetti or even flashing reindeer antlers! Anything to make it a special occasion whatever the outcome. All five thousand away tickets have been sold and the organisers are putting the word about that they are looking for a sea of red and white to complement the claret and blue. And it is predicted that many will go along with the request. The message is: "forget the Christmas 'do' – use the money on the party at the Park instead!"

Pre-match, the media interest in the competition has noticeably increased with the entry of the big boys (well, all but one anyway) in the Third Round and the papers are full of it. And this tie is seen as a potential banana skin for Jim Smith's Derby team, especially given their poor home record and Burnley's impressive away form. Ternent meanwhile is relishing every moment and declares:

"We are going to a fantastic stadium to play against a Premiership team full of international players and it'll be interesting to see how we respond." And he reckons Burnley can do the business, "OK we go there as complete underdogs, but I feel we've got some class players and all the onus will be on Derby. So if we get a break or two, who knows what could happen?" His face cracks a smile for once. "It's not beyond the bounds of possibility that we could go down there and get a result if we play our own way and we have no hang ups or fear factor, because our players are more than capable and a lot of them have played at that level. There will be total respect but no fear!" as he concludes, the stony face returns.

For all the talk of Cup upsets and Derby's lowly league position, their team sheet will contain barely an English name on Saturday and they will be fielding a selection of the cream of Europe and beyond, including around half a dozen internationals. Not to mention the fact that they play top-class opposition every week. In stark contrast, Burnley can point only to four men with Premiership experience; Thomas, Armstrong, Cook and Mullin and one who has performed at the top level in Scotland, in the form of Payton at Celtic. Indeed on paper it looks unlikely that Burnley can add to their one Fourth Round appearance since 1983.

As well as their own away record, Burnley can take heart from Derby's abysmal recent form of 9 defeats in 12 matches, incorporating 8 defeats in their last 11 home games and the fact that County come in to this tie having lost two on the bounce at Pride Park. But the hard facts centre on one issue, what will be done to prevent County's pedigree players from running riot? Ternent accepts that experience will play a part, but refuses to worry about the track record of the big names his men will be facing, like recent arrivals Craig Burley (coached by Ternent whilst at Chelsea) and Georgi Kinkladze.

Smith has signed the two from Celtic and Rangers respectively since the Third Round Draw was made, in a bid to bolster County's season amid promises of "further Christmas shopping." But Burley's move was almost scuppered by the player's impromptu pay demand of 15 grand a week, after John Barnes had agreed a selling price. Burley was also unimpressed at being asked to take a 20% pay cut should Derby be relegated, which ultimately deterred Colin Hendry from accompanying him to Pride Park.

But Ternent says only, "If you set your stall out to stop this one or that one from playing, you lose track of what you're doing yourself!" But he does confess to having had "a bit of a chat about Kinkladze with Paul Cook and Micky Mellon."

As for the supporters' build up, with the onset of technology, they are now able to trade insults long before their sides meet and Derby and Burnley supporters have been taking the piss out of each other on the Internet all week. These include the seasonal

"Watch out Sheep Shaggers, the Santa Clarets are going to wipe the floor with you", and "Jim Smith is like Santa after every game - red cheeks, red nose and giving goals away as presents - now all he needs is the sack!"

Matchday is upon us!

Wow, what a press room, what a buffet, and wine too. This is absolutely out of this world hospitality, and just for some tired old hacks. What must they get in the boardroom? Hot quality turkey and cranberrry pie – home cooked not mass produced, toast, soup, rolls with real meat in, carved off the bone. Absolute luxury. Well, this is the Premiership, and so we presume, this must be premiership treatment. Our overwhelming desire now is to get a job as a Premiership journalist. Who cares about the football with treatment like this.

The Derby press room is sumptuous, elegant with big screen TV and comfortable chairs. This is the big time. However, one author has to go and get a

The Burnley Santas in full song at Derby

photographer's pass, so he is forced to leave the journalistic scramble for food. Directed to the photographers' room, he is met with a stony cupboard, a yellow bib, and a cuppa in a polystyrene mug. Who determined that photographers are scum whilst writers are God?

Anyway, we digress, but that buffet... Getting back to the real world, as we approached Pride Park we saw that it is one of the new breed of 'out of town' stadia, which go hand in hand with the new breed of out of town shopping centre, DIY store, cinema complex and so on. And like its aforementioned counterparts, it is bright, shiny and comfortable if maybe a little soul-less and in the middle of a sparse, industrio-retail wasteland. But quite frankly, who gives a toss about soul? Who needs the shrine of their favourite club to be moulded into a maze of streets? At Pride Park there is ample parking for starters and even a free minibus service across the sprawling concrete plains to the stadium for goodness sakes.

As the stadium looms before us it is revealed to be an impressive, space-age construction, with cheery ambience so much better than the numerous decaying, uncomfortable relics that serve only to dampen the spirit. Outside the ground, fans of both persuasions are milling about with no hint of trouble. And the odd Santa can be seen. Centre of attention is the players carpark, where young lean men in suits are playing Mr Nice Guy and signing autographs for lots of little people and the odd bigger person with obligatory anorak, and fur covered autograph book.

On the inside, it is light years away from the Baseball Ground, with row upon row of shiny black seats and an unbroken space-age oval roof providing all round cover.

As a point of interest, Derby have not completely abandoned their old home as it is still used for training and reserve matches.

The 5,000 travelling Clarets will be housed at one end of the stadium in the Mansfield Bitter Stand. Looking straight ahead to the opposite end, they will see the McDonalds Community stand with it's unorthodox tower of executive boxes in the left hand corner, giving the ground a continental feel. The Toyota West Stand to the left is two-tiered with a horizontal row of executive boxes. And it is higher than the rest of the stadium, necessitating a downward slope of the roof at the points adjoining either end. If you are a symmetry freak this could spoil the ambience for you.

To the right is the East Stand, which houses some of the more animated Derby support, unsurprisingly, in the corner adjoining the away end.

Some Burnley fans are criticising the structure and describing it as "Meccano," or "a computer-generated scene from Star Wars." But in a good-natured debate with them, we say, so what! It is covered, comfortable, not so big that you cannot see from one end to the other and the toilets are clean! This is a great place to watch football. Undoubtedly, jealousy plays a part in their opinion.

Further behind the scenes, is a set of extremely plush banqueting areas for club sponsors. An organised tour of the ground is going on simultaneously and the female half of a young couple not far from us notices that one table is set aside for the Derbyshire Building Society. "Where's ours?" she smiles playfully. The male looks at us and clearly feels obliges to explain, "I dawn't think so duck," he smiles, looks at us and elucidates, "we work for Nationwide y'see." He continues, half toward her and half still in our direction. "We'd have to be relegated so's you could have a free dinnah!"

We move on to the relatively compact boardroom, where Lionel Pickering and his gang of four make those important decisions and entertain their visiting counterparts. The room contains a special kick off indicator operated by the referee, so that they do not get too carried away with the hospitality and miss the match. Adjacent to this room is a larger one set aside for directors and their guests.

In the executive boxes, interested parties will need to budget at around £21,000 per season, minimum.

Back outside, just past the well-padded seats of Jim Smith and Lionel Pickering, the excellent and award-winning facilities for disabled spectators come into view. These facilities have reputedly resulted in significantly more disabled fans wanting to attend matches here. Things are a lot better for the disabled Rams supporters these days, not least of all with the formation of their own supporters club.

Moving on down to the dressing rooms, there is a major difference between the home and away facilities. Visiting sides have less space, no clock, and facilities which consist of a rickety old physio bench. Derby however, have more spacious surroundings, a highly equipped physiotherapy room, warm up and warm down areas for pre and post-match activity respectively and a Subbuteo-style pitch and flip chart for tactical purposes. The players' kit is of course already laid out, but since a Paulo Wanchope shirt recently took a walk, every player's shirt is now security-tagged. And there is no communal bath due to the risk of disease transmission through the water.

As you step out of the dressing room, there is a sign, which reads, 'The biggest crime in football is to give the ball to the opposition,' which was initially instigated by a certain Brian Clough and liked so much by Jim Smith, that he had it reintroduced. The only problem now of course, is that with so many foreign players, it is not clear how many of the team can read it. The match officials' dressing rooms are smaller, but very well equipped and there are two identical ones, to cater for the new entity of the female official. With the ladies room still largely unused, it is usually commandeered by 'Rammie' the club mascot, who confirms that he thinks of it as his own because he has only ever had to share it once – with Father Christmas.

Further along the corridor is a crèche for players' children, with walls adorned by the usual – 'A' is for apple - type posters and there is no truth in the rumour that David Beckham uses this room for his own educational purposes. Neither do half the Derby team come here to learn English.

As we near kick-off time the travelling Clarets behind the goal in the Mansfield Bitter end are firing on all cylinders and they really pump up the volume to drown out the announcement of the Derby team over the tannoy. As if to draw the lines of battle, the Derby announcer cranks it up as well and the Clarets respond with a '92 style wall of sound, that outweighs anything he or the Derby fans can come up with. Every Burnley player's name is cheered - loud. This is excellent support. And the entire procedure is repeated when the announcement is made for the second time. And the singing is cranked up again when the Derby song is played.

After this and a couple of verses of "no nay never, no nay never no more," the sides come out to rapturous applause with confetti, streamers and claret and blue balloons from the away end. Derby are in white shirts, black shorts and black socks and Burnley in their famous claret and blue shirts, white shorts and white socks. This is party time.

Today's referee, Mike Riley, from Leeds gets the tie under way in the driving rain, which blows diagonally onto the Burnley support, in spite of the space-age roof. But that is the last thing on their minds. They are too busy getting behind their players and blasting out another chorus of Chim-chimeney-chim chimeney-chim-chim-cheroo. The recipients of this strangely Dick Van Dyke-esque encouragement line up in a 4-4-2 formation, thus dispelling all rumours of a reversion to the five-man defence (with which they started the season) in order to cater for the threat of Dean Sturridge and Giorgi Kinkladze in particular.

And before long it becomes clear that Ternent has set his stall out to come here and win, as Burnley, at full-strength with the return of Cook, Cooke, Mellon and Armstrong, show no fear of getting forward. Indeed after Craig Burley's long-range effort, virtually straight from kick-off, Paul Cook heads a corner just wide, followed by Glen Little's jink through three Derby defenders to lay on a shot for Mellon who smashes the ball into the side netting, getting the Clarets fans behind the goal on their feet. Then a move down the left sees Mellon switch the play to the right with a neat flick, which finds right back, Dean West who sends a twenty-yarder screaming just over the bar. This sign of attacking intent from West, complements the defensive solidity that he and left back Armstrong have already shown with some robust challenges in the opening exchanges, leaving County's thoroughbreds safe in the knowledge that they are in for a game. And lifted by the overwhelming volume of support, it is all Burnley.

A flurry of Claret corners follows, making a total of six to Derby's none. And lifted by overwhelming noise from the Mansfield Bitter End they look well in control. This authority is maintained for around twenty minutes and culminates in a good break by Payton who crosses in towards Cooke. Cooke heads the ball down for Payton to run on to at the edge of the box. Payton sees Poom off his line and executes a delightful chip. But the 6 foot 5 Estonian national keeper (and Devout Benny Hill fan) scrambles back and tips it over for a fruitless corner. With plenty to cheer about, the Claret and Blue Army are still in fine voice and leave their seats in unison as they sing the generic anthem to which you simply attach the fans/team/board member of your choice: "Stand up if you hate Bastards."

Early on the Derby fans were strangely muted, but now they seem to have warmed up. Some chanting comes from the corner of the East Stand, which drifts across the empty seats in the cordoned off section that divides the two armies: "Sit down you tarts, sit down you tarts, sit down you tarts sit down!"

The aforementioned empty seats contain one author, who in his role as photographer today, is sat pitch-side and gets soaked like the other hardy perennial snappers.

But as feared and expected by the Claret and Blue Army, Derby's cultured internationals begin to get their act together with Tony Dorigo beginning to forage down the left flank. Nimni is gradually getting to grips with the game in midfield and is the driving force behind Derby's best moves.

"Stand up if you hate Forest." But the Claret and Blue Army refuse to be outdone and retort with the same song, using the term of endearment set aside for Blackburn Rovers. As if to continue the topic of local rivalry and underline their feelings on the subject, this is followed up with: "Hate Bastard Rovers, we only hate Bastard Rovers etc."

Meantime, with half an hour gone, the Derby onslaught continues as front man Sturridge cuts into the box from the right and lets fly. But Crichton's excellent save typifies the professional way Burnley have been withstanding this pressure. Towards the end of the half, Derby central defender Horacio Carbonari gets further forward and shapes up for a spectacular 20 yarder. But the Argentinian doesn't live up to his nickname of 'Petaco' - which translates to 'Bazooka' - as he scuffs a daisy-cutter straight at Crichton. Carbonari is a truly cosmopolitan player with an Italian passport, as opposed to fellow countryman Esteban Fuertes, who has no passport at all, so decided to get one forged in order to enable a move to Pride Park. Unsurprisingly, the move fell through!

The admirable Crichton makes good saves from Dorigo and Sturridge as Derby dominate the latter exchanges. Both sides defend well and the half is scoreless.

Ternent's halftime talk centres on two things, Nimni and Dorigo. And Payton is ordered deeper to police them accordingly, in what will be a fairly fluid 4-5-1 formation for the second half.

Derby start where they left off as the second half gets under way, as Nimni pulls the strings. Burnley are not without chances and Andy Payton sends a diving header just wide. After an hour the sides are still deadlocked at 0-0. Smith sees that something needs to be done and Mikkel Beck, recalled from the much-hated Nottingham Forest goes on in place of right back Vass Borbokis. Delap moves back to his more familiar right wing back slot to accommodate Beck up front and Seth Johnson replaces the largely ineffective Kinkladze. Smith changes things from 4-3-1-2 to a potentially more solid 4-4-2. And the changes are roundly booed by large sections of the Derby support.

But in truth, the midfield activity of Kinkladze and Burley has been overshadowed today by the industry of Paul Cook and Mickey Mellon. And Ternent's tactic of a deeper lying Andy Payton has worked like a dream on the pre-half time threat of Nimni and Dorigo, which in turn has released Mullin to do more damage down the right in what has been a gargantuan performance from the ex-Sunderland man. His powerful running with the ball and neat passing have constantly pegged County back, leaving plenty of space for Cooke, Payton and Little to worry Derby's constantly nervous defence.

But before the new additions have a chance to find the pace of the game, Burnley get forward again with Little down the left flank. He gets to the dead-ball line and knocks it back to Gordon Armstrong who has surged forward from defence. Armstrong puts in a deep cross. Poom comes to meet it but changes his mind and edges back to his line. Payton rises but the ball is too high. Andy Cooke comes in at the far post having lost his marker and stoops to conquer with a downward header – which glances off central defender Steve Elliott's shoulder and into the net. This results in the total detonation of the claret and blue hoards in the away end. And on the pitch, the Burnley players are all over each other. A deafening rendition follows:

"When he gets the ball he scores a goal, Andy, Andy Cooke (to the tune of Boney M's hooray, hooray it's a holi holiday). This is underpinned by count-less choruses of "Stan Ternent's claret and blue army" and the Derby fans muster

Burnley players acknowledge their incredible support after beating Derby

a response in the form of da da da da – da da da da – you stick your Burnley up your arse (to the tune of - we'll keep the red flag flying). But it is the Lancastrian voices that last the longer.

Derby's new formation cuts no ice as Burnley push on regardless looking for a two goal cushion as Mellon and Armstrong both get forward for goal attempts and Paul Cook just misses the target from 35 yards. In the last ten minutes, Cook and Thomas have gone into Mr Riley's book, accompanied by Armstrong who almost kicked Burley into orbit!

Pride Park looks fairly full, but the official attendance is announced over the tannoy as 23,400, implying around 10,000 empty seats. The tally of away support is given as 4648 of which it later became evident from one of the Yuletide stattos that 174 had dressed as Santas!

It's nip and tuck , in the rain-soaked floodlit arena, but there is still no addition to the score and with five minutes to go the Claret and Blue Army can smell victory and the songs and cheers are relentless. In spite of the lack of time to rescue this tie, Derby seem to show zero urgency and Burnley are cruising. And the noise from the away end is relentless.

Derby fans are left to mutter about losing Steve McLaren to Man United.

With the Burnley fans whistling for time, Cooke misses a good chance to end it all, but then the referee finally produces outright hysteria in the barmy Claret army. Stan Ternent is forcibly led to the army and cheered relentlessly.

Meanwhile Jim Smith has been a trifle over keen to get away and rumour has it that he is already on a plane to check out more foreign talent, (Belgium actually) leaving number two Billy McEwan to carry the can at the press conference. McEwan is small, moody and extremely unhelpful to the assembled hacks, who actually have to try a little to get a genuine quote. Billy Mc appears to be a poor mans Gordon Strachan, and proud of it.

Wet exhausted and ecstatic players are wheeled in and out for rent-a-quote including Mitchell Thomas who despite his Spurs exploits describes this as "one of my greatest FA Cup moments."

The Derby players have been instructed not to comment. Thus the deliberately inarticulate Billy McEwan is the only spokesman to emerge from the defeated dressing room with this comment: "Jim would never leave a game before the end under normal circumstances, but it's important he sees a player to make a final decision as to whether we sign him. And he had to go and see that player tonight. We were beaten by a better team on the day, and it was 'Roy of The Rovers' stuff for them. Their keeper made some great saves".

Ternent emerges from the noisy Burnley dressing room to face the press conference hailing this as "a fantastic day" and adding, "it was a thoroughly deserved victory".

Burnley are further rewarded with another Premiership day out. Coventry City away. The crazier element of supporters retreat to discuss costumes.

The score says it all

13

Half-way up the stairs

FOURTH ROUND PROPER

COVENTRY CITY

V

BURNLEY

SATURDAY, 8 JANUARY

@ HIGHFIELD ROAD STADIUM, COVENTRY

ATTENDANCE 22,774

Fears of a cup hangover abound on Saturday 18 December, as the visit of lowly Cardiff City to Turf Moor signals Burnley's return to the scramble for Second Division points. During the initial warm up, there are mutterings of discontent all around the ground as the announcer barely mentions the great victory of one week ago, with only a couple of hasty asides thrown in, between cheesy Christmas hits of the 80s. This however, does not prevent huge applause for the Clarets when they come ready for the off as the supporters are really up for recapturing the golden moments of Pride Park.

Indeed, there are no special acknowledgements or references to the day at Derby. Players arrive businesslike on the pitch, and get on with their job. This may not be surprising to many football fans, but Burnley followers believed they had contributed to the big result at Pride Park. Punters in their thirties or thereabouts may recall the Fleetwood Mac album, 'Rumours' from the late Seventies (non-possession of which at the time carried risk of arrest by the vinyl police). The track containing the lyrics, "players only love you when they're playing," springs to mind.

One woman in the stand sums up the mood precisely: "Its back to bloody bread and butter land then".

An 'After The Lord Mayor's Show' - type atmosphere, with the subdued Claret and Blue Army out chanted by a very sparse Welsh following is the order of the day. However, despite a sluggish start, Burnley nick the points with a 2-1 win.

The following games see patchy form with a 4-2 drubbing by Bury, a home 3-2 win over Oxford and defeat at Notts County.

Gordon Strachan watched Burnley at Meadow Lane and commented that the Clarets were "well organised despite the result". He added, "when we play them, there's absolutely no way that we can afford for our standards to drop in the slightest." But in truth, on that showing, there has been little to prevent him sleeping soundly in his bed tonight and in the words of one travelling Claret: "He won't exactly be quaking in his boots, will he?"

Burnley boss Stan Ternent is quizzed by pressmen on the eve of the game.

"There's no question about it. Gordon Strachan has really turned it around in the three or four years that he's been there. He's done a fantastic job and has very good players who work very hard for each other. They're a tight unit and we'll give them the utmost respect because they deserve it, but we won't be scared of them. But yes, they are an excellent side and it will be a very difficult game for us, but I would say that if we play to our full potential, we'll give a good account of ourselves. We've got nothing to lose and everything to gain haven't we? So we'll just go there and I'll encourage the lads to enjoy their day and don't forget, anything can happen in the cup. But the main thing is that we don't embarrass ourselves".

And on the crisp morning of Saturday 8 January, under "ominously sky blue skies," the M6 is alive with Burnley colours - in cars, mini buses and coaches, many containing the chosen dress form of Arabs, as another mass exodus to the Midlands gets under way.

Coventry has an ambience more akin to the industrial North than the Midlands and Highfield Road is significantly different to Pride Park in that it could hardly be more Urban. It is like the ground was built first and houses erected tightly against it as an afterthought. Indeed at least one occupier could literally lay claim to being a next-door neighbour. But when you approach the stadium, the big-time ambience is there to be seen - no question.

Inside, there are four stands of equal height, in more traditional than space age style, with chic sky blue seats all around. This is another ground that has seen considerable improvement in the last few years. The large open terrace at one end has been replaced by single tier stand called the Comtel East Stand. The opposite end now has a two-tiered stand. The Burnley supporters will get a side on view today as they will populate just over half of the M&B stand that is set aside for away supporters.

Over the years, Coventry have earned a reputation as a go-ahead club, with perpetually modern facilities in spite of largely modest achievement on the pitch. However, whilst Highfield Road has been revamped into a relatively neat arena, capable of housing 23,000, it still has a slightly worn ambience and the press facilities are appalling compared to the likes of Burnley and Derby. A small, shabby room with no pre-match food, a plate of sandwiches and one cup of tea at half time, and nothing to warm the post-match cockles.

But the Sky Blues have not lost sight of their goals. Having met us at reception, youthful General Manager Neil Bryson, reveals plans to construct a state-of-the-art 45,000 all-seater stadium, with retractable roof and moveable pitch, ready for the 2001–2 season. This will be located at the 'Foleshill' site, just off the M6 and will incorporate a major shopping centre and it's own rail station. It is planned to host other top-line sporting events there too, as well as conferences and trade shows and it is set to become the largest indoor venue for pop concerts in Britain, at four times the size of the NEC!

The Sky Blue Tavern, behind the M&B Stand is packed to the rafters with Burnley support in high spirits and fine voice. All would dearly love to see their beloved side win, but many accept that "lightning isn't gonna strike twice." One female fan actually pledges the rest of her life as a nun if Burnley win today and she seems serious. A steady trickle of fans makes the short trip from the Tavern. The stadium is beginning to fill and the left side of the M&B stand is bristling with claret and Blue, supplemented by about 200 Arab costumes, put together mainly by un-imaginative use of tea towels and bedding material. And sets of dodgy moustaches and glasses abound. Quite how many arabic nations dress in candy striped sheets is somewhat overlooked.

In fact, there has been an element of concern over the potential racial overtones that these outfits could convey and a number of Burnley fans that normally participate in these fancy dress days have refused to join in.

As numbers increase, the Coventry cheerleaders do their thing in front of every stand, some looking a fraction overweight and most barely old enough to make our unsavoury thoughts legal. Sam the Sky Blue Elephant is cheerily patrolling home territory along the perimeter as the (half decent) Coventry song blasts over the tannoy, with the excellent tongue-in-cheek lyrics:

"Every year, the dreaded fear, but we're still here, the Sky Blue Army."

Meanwhile, "Stan Ternent's Claret and Blue Army" echoes from a now, packed, away side in the M&B stand, while the overwhelming numbers in Sky Blue retaliate with the straight-forward "Coventry, Coventry."

The teams line up, Coventry in their traditional all sky blue and Burnley in equally famous claret and blue shirts, white shorts and white socks. Today's referee is the very experienced Stephen Lodge from Barnsley. He was on the FIFA list until 1998 and is no stranger to the unique FA Cup atmosphere, having officiated in the '96 and '98 Semi Finals, which straddled his finest hour in the '97 final. Amid an abundance of swirling Argentina '78 style paper pieces, Mr Lodge duly gets this phase of our journey under way.

The message is clear at Coventry!

After only two minutes the Claret And Blue Army are on their feet as the ball travels to Glen Little in the Coventry six yard box. But countless hands go over wincing faces in dismay, as Little's control lets him down and the chance goes running away. A better first touch would almost certainly have seen Burnley in the lead.

The man standing out however is Coventry's Robbie Keane. He creates a couple of chances and is scaring the Burnley back line to death with his pace and skills. Unlike Derby, Coventry have made an impressive start and stamped their authority right from the off. They look a classy outfit and a nervous Claret chorus of "what a waste of money," greets Keane's every touch.

Still in the first ten, a sky-high ball into the Burnley box is won by Steve Davis, but his clearance is poor and only finds a sky blue shirt, leading to the menacing figure of Keane, probing down the left again. This time he knocks the ball inside to Chippo who plays a 'one two' with skipper Gary Mcallister on the edge of the 'D'. Mcallister's return ball is a neat backheel, which Chippo runs on to at speed and unleashes a shot from a central position, fully 25 yards out. It's an absolute screamer and flies past Crichton's despairing hands, straight into the left hand corner of the net. As a devout Muslim, Chippo has just ended a period of one month's fasting (no food intake between sunrise and sunset) through the holy period of Ramadan and, having re-commenced a full diet last Saturday, is looking visibly refreshed. The Moroccan confirmed post match that his dynamism had suffered a little during the fast, but said that he had "much more energy today than in recent games."

With 80 minutes still remaining, there are resignations in the massed Burnley ranks to the fact that this is a taste of things to come. A little premature maybe, but it has to be said that Coventry look in breathtaking form already and having become the first team to score against Burnley in this season's FA Cup, they look fully capable of getting a few more.

More Coventry chances come and go, with the clarets fearing a rout. Keane and Roussel miss opportunities and Crichton makes at least one good save.

On the right of the Claret engine room, Mullin is beginning to ease in to the pace of the game and gets on the end of a knock down from a long ball out of defence. He then combines well with Payton to get a cross in, but it is well cut out by the rock-like figure of Swedish international, Magnus Hedman in the Coventry goal. Then after an incredible run from Keane, in which he beats four men and lays it off for Hadji, who blasts over from 20 yards, Burnley begin to feature. The midfield of Mullin, Mellon and Cook are back on track and battling it out for control. One or two half chances are created but Hedman is impressive in the City goal and Paul Cook fires their best chance yet over the bar.

They fail to level however, and go in for the break one nil down.

Given the rub of the green, the situation could just about be retrievable for Burnley, so there is still the proverbial 'all to play for' in the second half. But for us it is a rest from the now bitter January air and into the press room for a cup of tea and a scramble for the communal plate of chips that has been placed out.

As the second half develops Coventry look to be in control and playing within themselves. Hadji unbelievably scoops a rebound off the post from Mcallister, over the bar from close range. A better Hadji shot is saved well by Crichton pushing it onto the post and the Roussel shot from the rebound is headed off the line.

"Little, on the right, Little, Little on the right.". is the tactical chant from the Claret army, suggesting to Stan that his playing of the winger on the weaker side is not working.

Down on the side of the pitch however, Ternent is unmoved. Next to him though, the fiery Strachan is up and screaming at his men as they seem incapable of lifting the game another gear and burying the lower opposition.

When Coventry right back, Paul Telfer's long range shot is deflected to Claret captain, Gordon Armstrong in the Burnley box. Armstrong's low pass out of defence is careless and does not find it's intended target of Little. The ball is knocked back inside the penalty area for more Chippo attention. He has his back to goal, but with an amount of time he simply cannot believe, turns, takes a look up and from the right edge of the box, curls a low left footed shot past the claret and blue statues - and Crichton - into the far corner of the net. Some say it took an unfortunate bounce over the keeper's hand, but Crichton was clearly too far off his line to deal with the shot properly. The score is 2-0 and the cue for an explosion of sky blue in over three quarters of the ground.

"You're not singing anymore," is the inevitable chant.

The police in the meantime are busy telling the fired-up Burnley fans to remain in their seats, when the Coventry supporters have barely been in theirs all game. This is pointed out to the constabulary by various Clarets but the observations fall upon predictably deaf ears.

Now Ternent decides to change things. At long last the Claret and Blue Army get their wish as Little switches to the right.

With Burnley desperately trying to push forward, gaps are being left for Coventry to exploit and as Paul Telfer ends another desperate Clarets attack, he begins a move of some 12 passes involving half the Coventry team. Palmer collects and plays it square, along the ground for Whelan on the right edge of the six-yard box. Whelan has got his back to goal and Steve Davis for company, but the first touch of the game for fresh legs leaves tired limbs standing and creates ample space for a shot, albeit from an acute angle. No problem – with his second touch Whelan threads it through the eye of a needle, past Crichton's outstretched arm and into the bottom left hand corner of the net. He had so much time he could have written this book first. 3-0 and Whelan is on his knees with fists clenched, milking the adulation from the stand.

The game winds down and Burnley are out of the Cup.

Having made final gestures of thanks to the Claret And Blue Army, the Burnley players finally run back towards the tunnel, to be greeted by another accolade, this time from hundreds of Coventry fans who have stayed in their seats to acknowledge the performance of worthy opponents. Cheesy moments some would say, but emotional stuff nonetheless.

At the press conference in the cupboard, Gordon Strachan enters sporting that familiar expression, best described as a kind of suppressed smile, which confirms that he is going to be on top form. He descends the steps leading down to the pressroom, stops about halfway and starts taking questions. This is obviously the closest Coventry can offer to a podium.

"I was constantly worried between our first and second goal," he admits and I was relieved to see the second one go in because Burnley were doing very well at the time. In fact, they did well for the last 15 minutes of the first half and the first 15 of the second and you could see them thinking, 'this could be our day' and our players agreeing with them!"

An incredible question comes from a journo who either hasn't been listening or didn't understand Strachan's accent:

"Were you at any time worried today." With barely the batting of an eyelid – he must be used to it – Strachan confirms: "Aye, between the first and second goal."

In the absence of another question, as the journo's shift around clearly frightened by the man's cutting wit he continues, "I asked our players to start well and they did. They dominated for about the first twenty minutes. But after we scored a cracking goal and created other chances, we decided it was time to show the fans how good we were at flicks and all sorts of things and that's not my idea of football. In fact we lost our shape and we tried to entertain without shape, which you can't do. I thought Carlton (Palmer) eased the burden by trying to maintain it and the Moroccans took the pressure off a bit with their contributions. But if we had kept our shape better it would have been easier. Not easy. Easier. Then it was all Burnley until we scored our second".

Seeing his chance a question comes from the floor as to whether Coventry have been over – elaborating in this way all season. "No, just today," comes the response. "Next question?" says Strach conducting affairs.

"So you've kept your record intact of never failing to reach the Fifth Round then?" Strachan puffs his cheeks at regular intervals, as though taking part in a futile exercise and with some of the questions that he has been asked today it is difficult to blame him.

"Is that right, how do you know that then?"

"It was in the programme."

"Is that right, oh well that's fine then, that's good." He is totally taking the piss, but checks himself and carries on regarding today's proceedings:

"We had half an hour, no, forty minutes of good football, the rest was nae great, but it was enough tae get us through on the day and that's all ye can ask the players tae do!"

With Chippo a virtually unanimous choice as man of the match, everyone is raving about the Moroccans, including Strachan, who describes them as "a joy to work with, due to their commendable attitudes." And he confirms that more players from that country are definitely top of his 'New Year wish list':

"If I can get more Moroccans here I will. They're a manager's dream. If all my players were like them my office would be empty and I'd know they'd be out there training every day because they have total respect for our football.

"Chippo and Hadji believe they are ambassadors for their country. If they do anything wrong, they feel they've let their people down. They want to show what African football is all about and their attitude is first class, it couldn't be any better. Because of his religion Chippo doesn't drink, whereas Hadji is allowed a drink if he wants one. But he's a proper player, so he doesn't drink either.

"The only problem has been for Chippo. He's had a bit of trouble coming to terms with the English weather, 'cos last week he skidded off an icy road into a hedge and knackered his club Subaru."

It transpires however, that Strachan will shortly be losing his two stars as they join their national squad for a pre–African Nations Cup workout. But by all accounts, they will be allowed back for Saturday's home game against Wimbledon, which impresses the Coventry boss, leading him to say that this is indicative of his "excellent relationship with the Moroccan authorities, whose commendable attitude reflects that of the players." Unfortunately however, they will not be available for the next round on 29 January, as the African Nations Cup, hosted by Nigeria, will be in full swing:

Strachan departs when he is ready, and Stan takes his position on the stairs. "The main thing is that we didn't embarrass ourselves," he says, clearly confirming to those of us in the know, that this has been his obsession since having Coventry watched for the first time and in the process realising just how good they were.

"Don't get me wrong, I'm disappointed that we lost the game and we aspired to get a result of some sort, but I think the lads played really, really well and if we maintain that level of performance in the league, hopefully we'll end the season with a suitable reward.

"As far as today's concerned, we were bang in it for 70 minutes weren't we? We came close to scoring on two or three occasions, but it just wouldn't go in. And let's face it, goals change games - certainly against Premiership opposition – and if Premiership opposition gets two goals ahead, things become very difficult.

As the players move on and we move out, there is a somewhat depressing air outside the now deserted stadium. Maybe because we now have to move in Premiership circles and being followers of Bristol football anything outside the Second Division is way beyond our comfort zone. But whatever the reason, the freezing, sodium-orange air around Highfield Road signals the end of an era. Something tells us that it would have been nice to build an even stronger rapport with Stan and the Claret and Blue Army, but rules is rules and it just isn't to be.

Meanwhile one or two straggling Arabs clamber into their vehicles, muttering plans for a Viking theme day to keep the season's momentum going. And any striped sheets not relegated to life as dusters will go back into the dark corner of the airing cupboard, to which they were initially consigned in around about 1985.

The pubs are empty, and no Coventry fans can be seen anywhere. A London Claret shouts his opinion: "What is it with these Premiership fans? Do they all go home for their tea, Radio 606 and then a quiet night in with Match of the Day as the highlight?"

Meanwhile the build up to the Pride Park clash begins in earnest.

14

Resign Strachan!

FIFTH ROUND PROPER

COVENTRY CITY

V

CHARLTON ATHLETIC

29 JANUARY 2000

@ HIGHFIELD ROAD COVENTRY

ATTENDANCE 23,400 (Yes, the same as Derby v Burnley)

"Could it be our year?" asks a beaming local reporter, after the Fifth Round balls give Coventry another home draw against Nationwide League opposition. "I dunno," quips Strachan, but it's certainly been our week."

He is responding to the surrounding multitude of media men (and one woman), who believe this "passport to the Quarter Final" in the form of Division 1 high fliers Charlton Athletic. (Note shades of '87). And he continues unabated:

"Yep, we can definitely go further, and sure, I believe we can get to the Final if we play to our full potential - why not?"

His comments are music to the pundits' ears:

"Really?" asks one,

"Yeah really," laughs Strachan. "We can go all the way." The journos can hardly scribble that one down fast enough. And before leaving to join the Moroccan squad, Chippo had earlier fanned the flames by declaring:

"Yes, there is no reason why we should not have a good chance of winning the Cup." And not to be outdone, Hadji had supplied his two penneth:

"I too believe this team is good enough to take us to Wembley."

It's a quote a minute these days at Highfield Road. And the press are lapping it up.

Right now however, Strachan has the relentless, more pressing, overused and proverbial 'bread and butter of the league' to worry about. This comes not least of all in the form of a good old fashioned 'transfer saga,' involving Cedric Roussel's proposed, permanent move from Belgian club Ghent, from which he is currently on loan. On the back of the 21 year old striker's recent successes, Ghent are now messing around over their asking fee, which started off at around £500,000, but has now been hiked to various estimated amounts, some of which go as high as a cool £4 million. Sky Blues chairman Bryan Richardson is handling negotiations and confirms that he is optimistic of finding a "satisfactory solution for all parties."

Roussel meanwhile, has benefited no end from Strachan's undoubted coaching ability including the essential loss of a stone in weight and the honing of his aerial skills. Indeed, Strachan makes it clear that he finds Roussel's new striking partnership - formed with Robbie Keane - to be so impressive, that the soon to be out of contract and now, somewhat unsettled, Noel Whelan has (in spite of his own weight watching success) been consigned to the bench.

But big rumblings are coming from the boardroom as recently re-elected club president, Geoffrey Robinson MP is hitting the headlines for all the wrong reasons. He is known to have a selection of financial ventures on the go which have helped transport him into the millionaire bracket, although it seems that one or two have come back to bite him.

Having many an opinion on the Chairman's business dealings is fanzine "Gary Mabbutt's knee". The 'zine is named after the part of the famous Bristol boy's body that deflected the ball into his own net, whilst playing for Spurs in the 'sacred' 1987 final. And it is laced with 70's and 80's nostalgia, including a most commendable page on bearded Sky Blue players and photos of football cards bearing the likes of Ernie Hunt and Terry Yorath. Those old enough could almost taste the chewing gum. This is complemented by a fair helping of witty repartee and caustic comments, rounded off by a thank you to Vasco De Gama, "for giving Fergie a lesson in football and humility". What can they mean?

By Tuesday 11 January, it is back to business as usual at Highfield Road, as Ghent continue to prevaricate over the Roussel deal, courtesy of the now ubiquitous £4 million price tag. They have got wind of the fact that British soccer pundits are beginning to sing Roussel's praises and other English clubs are beginning to sit up and take notice. So the fear now, even though the player himself has already agreed terms with Coventry, is that someone else will come in with a gazumping offer. And, with the player free to walk away under the Bosman ruling in a year's time, it is unlikely that Mr Richardson will agree with the current valuation and put him alongside Moustapha Hadji as Coventry's second most expensive signing in history.

The following week however, the grin on the face of Strachan disappears as he decides to break his silence over the contents of Sir Alex Ferguson's controversial biography, in which the charm school graduate himself levels criticism at a number of his former players and colleagues. Those under the cosh include Jim Leighton, Brian Kidd and, you guessed it, the current Coventry boss. In the book, Fergie labels Strachan as, "someone you shouldn't turn your back on," and until now, a diplomatic silence has reigned. But following Jim Leighton's response at the weekend, Strachan decides to give an interview to Scottish newspaper, the Daily Record and says:

"His book should have been a celebration of his achievements. It should have been positive. But he chose to use it as something else. He had a different agenda. And like Jim Leighton, I'm very disappointed about his attitude to people who actually helped him when he was a manager at St Mirren and Aberdeen."

In typical Strachan-esque fashion he adds a piece-de-resistance:

"Mind, I'm always civil to Alex when I see him and I always will be. But there's no exchange of Christmas cards."

On Friday 14 January, with preparations for tomorrow's home game against Wimbledon in full flow, the Moroccan FA fail to live up to Strachan's praise. His build up is disrupted at the eleventh hour by announcing that they will not be releasing Chippo or Hadji from African Nations Cup duty after all. This means that the duo could miss up to 5 games and causes uproar among the supporters. But Bryan Richardson takes it all in his stride and although he admits it is a "major blow," refuses "to blast anyone" (no doubt much to the disappointment of sports sub editors everywhere). Instead, he comments that:

"The coach just changed his mind and said that he didn't want to let them go at this stage. And it's certainly not the boys' fault because I know they wanted to come back for this game, but these things happen and we have to live with them I'm afraid. But we've got a good squad and the lads will be replaced by top quality players.

Meanwhile, over in Nigeria, Hadji tries to explain: "It is very difficult, this situation. The team manager changed his mind after training this afternoon and he wants to do more work with us. It's not an ideal situation, but at Coventry we do have some really good players and a good squad and hopefully they will do well at the weekend in our absence. I wish the manager and the team luck for the game!"

So on Saturday 15 January, Strachan's re-shuffled side are left to deal with a tricky little number at Highfield Road, against the perennially unpredictable SW19 Crew, who are breathing down Coventry's necks, with the two sides coupled just below halfway down the Premiership. Strachan is not available for comment and is revealed by sources at the club to be "a little bit angry about the Moroccan situation." But he needn't have worried, the shout after the game is "who needs the Moroccans," (how quickly the milk turns sour) as Coventry cruise to a 2-0 victory courtesy of a great performance from McAllister, who nets a penalty to bag his 100th league goal and sets up Keane's killer second.

Noel Whelan is understandably upbeat after turning in a half decent display and explains that his return to form coincides with a "return to his fighting weight after 3 months on the sidelines with an ankle injury." And he admits:

"Because I couldn't train while I was injured I put on loads of weight, but I've been watching what I eat and now I'm down to 13 stone 2, which is bang on for me. My sharpness is back and I feel really good and I couldn't wait to get off the bench against Burnley. I even felt that if I could get hold of the ball and shoot I would score. Fortunately my first touch was good, the shot was on target and the rest is history. Now I just need to get my first Premiership goal of the season and win my place back."

Noel has settled in well at Coventry and describes his relationship with some of the players. "Well I've known Carlton Palmer a bit and he's a smashing lad – in small doses. He's great to have around the dressing room and the club in general, but if you didn't know him you'd think, 'what on earth is this guy all about!' Oh and you won't catch me staring into his eyes in Café Rouge either, not like Hadji and Chippo."

"Cedric Roussel lives in the flat below me and when we've got a hangover we go straight to the physio next door. Cedric was a bit shy when he arrived, but he's not shy now at eight o'clock in the morning when he sticks his Backstreet Boys CD on when I'm still in bed. I think the couple below him have told him to keep it down. Good job too!"

"I love being back though, I'm not the best person to be injured because I'm hyperactive at the best of times. Not being able to play football was taking a massive chunk out of my life. The physio was on overtime keeping me occupied in the gym, but that got a little bit tedious, so I ended up nicking the aerials and hubcaps off the lads cars and burning Carlton Palmer's tracksuits, y'know the kind of thing."

"I'm not sure whether the physio enjoys living next door to me. It's maybe a little too close for his comfort. I think he's had to buy a few extra car aerials y'know. But he's a nice fella and when you're injured you put your trust in his hands. He kept my spirits up well when I was missing the banter with the lads. I find it difficult to be a spectator and I must admit I didn't come to all the games when I was injured. I get too involved in the stand, I end up pushing the person next to me when someone goes in for a tackle."

Meanwhile, Hadji grabs the only goal in a warm up game against Trinidad and Tobago and although the Moroccan coach rotates the players ad infinitum, both Coventry men play the full 90 minutes.

Wednesday 19 January, sees contractual hassles as improvements are worked on a deal which will prolong the stay of Magnus Hedman. Sources within the club reveal that his stature as one of the best keepers in the Premiership could secure an extension to his existing contract worth three times its original value. Negotiations opened a month ago, but Richardson still insists there is no rush to tie Sweden's in-form 'number one' to Highfield Road with a long term contract:

"We're continuing to meet with his agents on a regular basis. We'll keep talking until we agree something or fail to agree anything. But I'm very hopeful that we'll agree something" is his quote for the press.

Meanwhile, Paul Williams and Gary McAllister have contracts that run out at the end of the season and Williams has already rejected the club's 'final' offer through his agent Struan Marshall, meaning the potential loss of yet another defender. More importantly as far as the fans are concerned, is the fact that McAllister claims he has not even received an offer yet! Having turned 35 on

Christmas day, the skipper is enjoying a real Indian Summer and nobody wants to see him go. Consequently, appeals for the offer of a one year extension and/or some kind coaching role are in abundance. Such are the problems facing a premiership club.

The following day sees The Mail lose a number friends in the Warwickshire area with a front page article on why Gordon Strachan should be the next manager of Manchester United, although this was undoubtedly offset by a proportional increase in circulation.

Roussel is still pleading with his old club to let him go at a sensible price, but Richardson insists that saga is almost over and that he is "fairly confident of a result." He shouldn't have been so modest, because by Thursday 20 January it is done and dusted, with the damage minimised at a mere £1.2 million for a 5-year deal. Coventry fans are widely delighted, not least at seeing off competition from Spurs and Liverpool. Such success helps the belief that the Sky Blues are a genuine Premiership outfit.

But the papers meanwhile are using the Roussel signing story as an indication of Keane's imminent departure to the San Siro, on the basis that his replacement has now been secured. And the Italian press is catching on as well. Now, whilst this would make sound, short term financial sense, Coventry spokespersons (those mystery people who only appear in the Press) are quick to point out to us that Roussel and Keane work as a partnership, which was demonstrated to good effect during the victory against Burnley.

Another eve of another match brings another bombshell on Friday 21 January but this time the news is good and the sports journos have something else, upon which to focus their Coventry – related attention. Thanks to a scouting deal with Argentina's '78 World Cup winner, Rene Houseman, an estimated fee of £1.5 million has been splashed out for Peruvian internationals Walter Zevallos and Ysrael Zuniga. Our Gordon however scoffs at such a price.

The big advantage for the club is that the players much needed crash course in English wont cost a penny. Zuniga's wife is a qualified English teacher.

Turning to tomorrow's game, in answer to the question of whether Derby's poor home form equates to Coventry's first away win of the season, Strachan reckons that the elusive victory is "just around the corner". Clearly this is managerial speak for 'we should put one over Derby, because they are crap.'

However, the planned first away win of the season goes awry. Saturday 22 January brings only disappointment in a scrappy 0-0 stalemate at Pride Park, in which Coventry's first away trip of the new Millennium fails to ring any changes.

This time the flair and industry of the Moroccans was sorely missed (slices of humble pie all round after the post Wimbledon comments) and in the post-Derby press conference, Strachan admits:

"If you took those two away from any Premiership side it would be a problem and it's a problem to us. So, we have to move the team about. But you never know, sometimes you discover some gems when you're under pressure."

Back in bread and butter land, Sheffield Wednesday's victory at Tottenham means that Coventry are now the only side in the Premiership without an away win this season, a situation shared solely by Cambridge United and Clydebank in the rest of the English and Scottish Leagues put together. But in a bizarre set of statistics for this season, Coventry can boast the best defensive record away from home in the Premiership, with only 10 goals conceded, compared to Liverpool on 12 and Arsenal and West Ham on 13.

The next opportunity to break their duck will be provided at no less an arena than Old Trafford itself, where the hosts have not lost at home for over a year

After the visit to the Theatre of Dreams, Coventry will take on Sunderland, Tottenham, Leeds and Aston Villa, all of whom also reside in the top half of the table, which, although still beckoning invitingly, cannot realistically be entered without good results against current occupants. These matches will of course be interspersed by their Fifth Round FA Cup tie and a subsequent Quarter Final appearance if they get past Charlton. Stimulating times for the Highfield Road faithful and the next 6 weeks or so could well make or break their season, as victories in those Cup games would book a Semi Final place, and a good spell in the league could see them sitting pretty in the Premiership.

Conversely however, an ignominious FA Cup exit would be most unwelcome, particularly on their own turf next Saturday.

Monday 24 January, sees tickets for the Charlton match go on general sale. Our contact in the ticket office reveals that business is brisk and Coventry fans are warned to get in there quick to avoid proverbial disappointment. Charlton meanwhile, have already snapped up their allocation and projections now indicate a complete sell out and bumper pay-day for City.

As the build up to the big game gathers momentum, there is a heart-warming moment for all Coventry fans on Tuesday January 25, as ex Sky Blues defender and current Youth Community Officer David Busst, becomes the new manager of Southern (Dr Martens) League outfit, Solihull Borough. And in doing so, he pays tribute to a trio of City bosses:

"When I was at Coventry, Gordon and Ron (Atkinson) were great around the dressing room and it was Phil Neal that got me into the first team. I'll take bits from all of them and add my own views."

Busst is taking over from another former Highfield Road defender, Paul Dyson, some 3 years after sustaining one of the most horrific injuries in the history of the game - a leg broken so severely against Manchester United, that a host of seasoned professionals could barely look. And he still walks with a limp to this day. Busst was promoted from youth team coach at Solihull and will combine his new (part time) role with existing Sky Blue youth team duties.

On the contractual front, Magnus Hedman now looks set to snub the interest of some Premiership big boys, in favour of a lucrative extension to his existing contract. Agent Claes Elefalk confirms his client's happiness at Coventry and the fact that the deal should soon be finalised, with pen going to paper next month, to end some 7 weeks of negotiations. Hedman's proposed salary is estimated to be in the region of £800,000 per annum.

"We'll take a thorough look," says Elefalk and in February we will come to a conclusion, most likely that Magnus will sign. Otherwise we will take time out and resume talks after the European Championships."

The proud possessor of a new nickname - 'clean-sheet'- after recent top-notch performances, Hedman confirms to the press:

"I am very interested in prolonging my contract at Coventry. The club are showing that they are willing to work hard to keep me and my family are happy here, and that's a big argument for staying!" So is £15 grand a week presumably.

And many Sky Blue hearts are gladdened on Friday 28 January, by the content of a message from afar. In an interview, on this, the eve of immense matches for both his teams, Hadji reveals that he is homesick, not for Morocco, but Highfield Road:

"I'm missing Coventry and watch for their results all the time. It's difficult for Youssef and myself because five weeks is a long time to be away." Aaaah.

Meanwhile the scene is being set for tomorrow's clash, as both managers face endless questions about the twin towers. For someone new to the managerial game, Strachan deals with the press remarkably well and he is fielding questions today like an old hand. This time with serious head on, he explains:

"My players think they can win the game, but they'd think that if it was Arsenal, Charlton or whoever. And if they can do it tomorrow it becomes a different ball game, because I think when you get to the Quarter Finals, Wembley becomes a reality. But at the moment we're focussing on tomorrow!"

"Apart from the World Cup, it's still the best knockout competition in the world. It's the most prestigious, most glamorous, most historic. Everybody in the world (!) wants to see the FA Cup Final, so it's always an ambition to get there and a great day out if you make it". Well, there goes another view in defence of the old woman.

Meanwhile, for anyone who fancies watching tomorrow's proceedings in style, there are still a few hospitality packages left, starting at £45+VAT per person. And the club's adventures could be watched by many more fans in the comfort of their own home, if talk of a new TV consortium comes to fruition. The press have dug up some info to the effect that Coventry are 1 of 6 Midlands clubs planning a joint venture to set up their own digital TV channel. The deal is reportedly in the process of development with Carlton TV and is most likely to be based upon a pay-per-view idea. The other clubs involved are Wolves, Leicester, Birmingham City and Aston Villa.

Matchday, Saturday 29 January arrives and by about 1.30 there is an electric feel about Highfield Road. Having again failed miserably to blag a parking space to go with our press passes, we cruise the maze of small, surrounding roads looking for somewhere to park. There was no problem last time, but this is a different story and in the end there is no option but to do business with a couple of local 'entrepreneurs,' who are renting out various dodgy back street nooks and crannies. We look on in dismay as what seems to be the final place is taken, but the older of the two, a bloke of about 35, calls over to his teenage protégé:

"Oi, Jimmy, move them two wheelie bins will ya."

The apprentice does as he is told and a barely sufficient gap is created in what can only be the back of someone else's garden. Still, desperate problems (like getting up late) call for desperate solutions. Clearly still on a learning curve with regard to the noble art of extortion, young Jimmy curls up in embarrassment as he asks for the requisite payment.

And £5 lighter in the wallet department after a reasonably successful negotiation, we join the steady streams of Sky Blue regalia leading to Highfield Road from every direction, while significant quantities of Charlton colours add contrast and Cockney accents to the proceedings.

For the first time on our journey, everyone is truly up for the Cup and whilst it is not yet time for the local shops in Coventry or SE7 to bear good luck trinkets and messages, today's winners will not be far from such rituals. The Cup has started in earnest, with the doomed twin towers visible in the distance.

Having earlier visited the nearest retail emporia we could find to the ground, there was no sign of any interest in the football match taking place about half a mile up the road. Seemingly for all they cared, the nearby titanic FA Cup struggle could be taking place on Pluto! But there again, why should there be? As even for Coventry, this is by no stretch of the imagination uncharted territory.

When inside Highfield Road, having again moaned like mad about the lack of free food in the media room, we console ourselves with the lush pasties at the back of the main stand and walk through to the press box suitably bloated. As we take our places, the journos are having convulsions: Something has disturbed the talk about Geoffrey Robinson. Shock, horror! Noel Whelan is not in the squad! His place has been taken by the untried Runar Normann! Explanations have already been sought and an 11th hour calf injury is being blamed. But there is no pulling the wool over the eyes of the wizened hacks and talk of Whelan being withdrawn so as not to jeopardise an impending transfer is rife. Fees of between 2 and 3 million are mentioned along with a selection of destinations, the most popular of which are Everton and Bradford City.

But the speculation dies down with the onset of play. On pitch, the match is preceded by fireworks (the FA obviously believe that we are far enough into the tournament to spice each tie up with that 'special occasion' feel). Also the cheerleaders and Sam the Elephant are doing their thing. This provokes an overdue question from those sad enough to care (us): Why an elephant?

Investigations are in order and between them, the hacks and fans provide a wealth of information, stretching far beyond our original enquiry:

The club badge consists of an elephant with a castle on it's back and a red and white cross on it's side, this being a traditional symbol of St George and a more elaborate version of the English flag. St George was believed to have lived in the Coventry area, resulting in the City adopting the elephant and castle as its logo sometime during the 19th Century. Coventry Cathedral apparently displays a corresponding brass. When the club changed their name from 'Singers FC' (after the local bicycle works) to Coventry City in 1898, the logo was included as the centrepiece of the club crest and although the significance of St George has declined, the Sky Blues still hold their symbol in high regard.

The cheerleaders take up position by the tunnel, signifying that it's virtually ShowTime. Enter players stage right, both sets in their traditional kits. Cue the requisite, dominant explosion of Sky blue and the corresponding red and white balloons and tickertape in the M&B Stand directly facing us. Charlton have sold their quota of tickets and numerically, they will be as well supported today as Burnley were in the previous round. Whether they will match up vocally is yet to be seen, but they are off to a good start.

Battling against a raging wind and a pitch littered with paper, balloons and firework debris, Keane wins a corner almost immediately, from Charlton central defender Steve Brown. McAllister takes the kick and a neat little routine sees Eustace sell a dummy and the ball ending up with Telfer, who puts a decent cross over, but Palmer's header lands harmlessly on the roof of the net. This sets the Highfield Road faithful's adrenaline running and their support is deafening. Charlton retaliate soon after, as John Robinson holds off Breen's challenge and gets his shot in. Hedman saves with his legs and this proves to an isolated attack for Charlton, as Coventry run around like they have been on a concoction of Lucozade and Red Bull and dominate the opening exchanges.

Another Charlton break ends with dreadlocked, Swedish striker Martin Pringle getting on the end of a knock down from Andy Hunt and hitting a volley from 12 yards, which his compatriot blocks well in the Coventry goal. And then it's back to situation normal as the Sky Blues pour forward again. The ball comes to Normann on the left and the debutant heads it inside Shields and into the path of Roussel, who consummates his marriage to Coventry from about 15 yards out, by flicking the ball with the outside of his boot, over the head of the advancing keeper Kiely.

"Just as well Normann can go forward," laughs one Coventry hack as the cheers die down, "cos he can't fuckin' tackle or defend."

City continue to press. Forcing two saves from Kiely. After about 20 minutes, Paul Williams hits a superb, long ball out of defence to McAllister, who plays a neat one-two with Keane and races into the penalty area unchallenged through the inside left channel. He takes one touch to control and sends over a cross that swings away from Kiely. It's inch-perfect and presents Roussel with a simple header, which he despatches like a bullet from around the penalty spot 2-0.

"You're not singing any more," booms from the chief wind-up merchants on the West Terrace, which is the end to the right of the Charlton fans, and Roussel and co. celebrate accordingly. With McAllister pulling all the strings and Keane buzzing around everywhere, this looks like a complete doddle for Coventry and will surely only be a question of how many they will get."

On the half hour, Hedman is forced into an easy save from a rare Charlton attack as a Robinson header lacks direction.

10 minutes from half time Mark Kinsella knocks another free kick to Newton, who this time is forced wide, but still manages to deliver a cross. Hedman appears to have it covered, but Andy Hunt intercepts and presents Robinson with an excellent chance from about 10 yards out. But Breen charges down the shot. Froggatt and Normann keep thrusting down the left, but Newton begins to revel in the extra space this gives him down the Charlton right. Intent on going in at the break with some reward for their increasingly potent efforts, Charlton surge forward again and win a free kick on the left. Powell floats it over to central defender Richard Rufus, who has arrived as a target on the right side of the box. The ball bounces harmlessly off Rufus' head and flies well wide of the Coventry net. But Newton prevents the goal kick by somehow reaching it with an acrobatic overhead kick, to send the ball back across the box to Robinson and he throws himself forward to head in to the far corner of the net from close range. Charlton have nicked one back. The ground falls silent, with the notable exception of a red and white explosion in the opposite stand. In fairness they deserve it as well.

But before things can get under way again, there is a blow to Charlton's chances as influential midfielder Mark Kinsella (a Republic of Ireland man rated as a threat by Breen and Keane) is replaced by Andy Todd. According to the press box men in the know, Kinsella has been suffering from a gastric bug all week and should not really have started.

As the first half edges into stoppage time, we have a complete role reversal on our hands and Coventry fans are begging for the whistle as Strachan goes frantic by his dugout. It has taken Charlton about half an hour to adjust to the pace, but they are right in there with a chance now, while anyone connected with Coventry will be grateful if they are still in the lead at half time.

Meanwhile play goes on and Greg Shields hits in a free kick to Andy Todd whose pass finds John Robinson at the edge of the City area. Robinson's shot is parried away by Hedman, but a pack of marauding red shirts are following in and a few fans in the main stand cover their eyes. Newton gets there first on the right and slams the equaliser, under the feet of Pringle (who leaps in the air to get out of the way) past the despairing foot of Breen and into the net. Just reward for his labours and confirmation of the worst fears of those who dared not look.

A string of expletives fly from the Main Stand. Strachan has a seizure of Graham

Taylor v Holland proportions and the Charlton fans go mental. Dermot Gallagher blows his whistle and two contrasting half time talks are about to be delivered.

But by far the most serious issue of the day occurs when no chips show up in the media room.

Tea however, is available and hits the spot nicely, as does another pasty in spite of the fact that it must be bought and paid for in the snack shop. What kind of treatment is this. Next year we're following Derby at home.

It seems that Alan Curbishley has delivered the more effective pep-talk, as Charlton start the second half where they left off and any hope of Coventry re-finding their early rhythm seems a million miles away.

Andy Hunt spurns an early chance. Strachan's headaches then increase, as – still suffering from a knock received in the first half – Paul Williams limps off to be replaced by Richard Shaw. Shortly after, Keane's frustration boils over as he gets involved in a touchline tussle with Newton, claiming that Newton had deliberately blocked his path. Mr Gallagher goes into Henry Kissinger mode and play continues.

McAllister then hits a long-range shot, which Kiely cannot hold, but is cleared by the quickest man in the box, Rufus. The game dissolves into a scrappy, long ball affair as the struggle for supremacy hots up. Strachan makes changes as the manager most desperate to win first time. These include the introduction of Laurent Delorge, who is making his debut at long last.

As the game wears on, there is still very little in it, but Strachan's substitutions have injected a little get up and go into Coventry and they look most likely to break the deadlock. But in spite of three successive corners, all they can achieve is a couple of goalmouth scrambles.

A penalty appeal by Cedric Roussel is denied by Mr Gallagher, and Charlton try to make the most of their luck. As Brown sets about dispossessing Keane, everybody in the press box is busy pencilling the replay date into their diaries and various groups of fans in the Main Stand begin talk of half days and best routes to South London. The red and white masses however, clearly do not see the necessity of hosting such a game and generate a sound of Burnley-esque proportions no doubt sensing the potential to make this occasion a 'one stop shop' for their team. Brown meanwhile has played the ball forward for Pringle on the left wing and a route to the corner flag to waste a few more seconds is available. However, conscious of Charlton roars from the M&B Stand Pringle holds it up on the edge of the box and knocks it back to left back Chris Powell. Powell despatches a cross, which ricochets off Andy Todd and falls for Hunt on the right, who shoots and somehow squeezes the ball past Froggatt and Hedman at the near post.

Unbelievable. It's gone in! It's a sucker punch of gargantuan proportions but the stuff of fairy tales for the Addicks.

2-3 and half the M&B stand simply erupts into a volcano of red and white as the South London boys go utterly ballistic. And the chant (to the tune of 'Bread of Heaven') is "Coventry, Coventry, can we play you every week, can we play you every week!"

A steady stream of Sky Blue heads towards the exits. And Strachan will need a straight jacket if he does not calm down. In direct contrast, Alan Curbishley – with much less to lose - has retained an air of relative calm and his next move is a somewhat inevitable, time-wasting, double substitution as former Coventry man John Salako and Paul Konchesky come on for Graham Stuart and John Robinson. To their eternal credit, City's heads are still not down and Delorge has a shot blocked on the line by Robinson. Then out of nothing, Palmer is faced with a really good chance to equalise...But he sends his header onto the top of the bar as he did in the first half.

And so ends Coventry's participation in our road to Wembley. "Fuckin'

"We've Done it!" - Charlton celebrate the winner

shite!" "Crap!" "Resign Strachan!" "Worse than Villa!" is ringing in our ears.

As a breathless, muddy, Andy Hunt returns from Charlton's prolonged post match celebration, he is as high as a kite:

"It was a fantastic performance wasn't it? If we carry on playing like that there's no reason why we can't get to Wembley, none at all. But we're not getting carried away with the Cup. Promotion is still our number one priority. But I'll tell you what, this side never knows when it's beaten!"

Back in the media cupboard, Alan Curbishley is first to arrive at the customary interview position half way down the stairs. He's clearly happy, but demonstrates his usual ability to understate for England:

"At two-nil down, I was sat there thinking, 'we don't want to get a walloping here' but we did really well to get back in it and it was a great performance in the second half."

Remaining equally calm before the microphones that are being thrust up the stairs, he continues:

"I wasn't surprised that the second half turned out to be 'end to end stuff' and I was a lot more optimistic then, because I know we'll always create chances. And we did. Andy Hunt had a few and he put the most difficult one away!

"It was nice to see three different players get on the scoresheet as well. And it was especially good that Andy Hunt got one. He works really hard and is excellent at bringing players into the game, but he needs to keep scoring. He didn't get enough goals last season, although he's got more this year. But Andy played really well today and if he carries on with that sort of performance, week in week out, I'll be happy."

Cue the inevitable question of who Curbishley fancies in the Quarter Final:

"We'll just wait and see what the FA Cup throws up. God knows when the draw is, but we just want a home draw. Last time we got to the Quarter Final we were away to Man United. Well that can't happen this time can it." Cue murmurs of laughter from the assembled journos.

Then he is back up the steps and out of the door. But before long Strachan arrives for the post-mortem, amid a deathly hush. As always, Gordon is treated as the prodigal son, and all assembled cower down before the great man. Just for safety, most take a step back.

"What do I think? I can't think, I'm still in shock" he gushes almost uninvited. "No, it was an excellent game of football for the neutral. That was demonstrated by the score. I was happy with the start, then we had to re-organise when

Paul (Williams) got hurt and they managed to get right back into it."

"But we can only blame ourselves and also congratulate Charlton on the way they played. If they show that kind of spirit and ability, they could go on to win the FA Cup if they get a decent draw. But that doesn't mean that we're not devastated by this result. Some people thought this was going to be our year, but that's gone now and we'll just have to bounce back."

Yet another inept question flies from the ranks:

"Do you take any positives from this."

"Erm, there weren't too many positives", he retorts, looking stupefied by the question.

But undeterred, the young hack continues:

"Cedric Roussel?"

Even in adversity, Strachan is barely able to restrain a laugh and replies:

"Oh aye, that's the one!" Gordon makes his ascent. His departure cues the usual cowardly journo humour.

"He seemed reasonably relaxed considering".

"Aye, but don't turn your back on him".

Gordon Strachan descends the steps of the Coventry press room to face the post-Charlton music

15

Ey oh skip to my Lou

QUARTER FINAL

BOLTON WANDERERS

V

CHARLTON ATHLETIC

DATE 19 FEBRUARY

@ THE REEBOK STADIUM, BOLTON

ATTENDANCE 20,131

After the news from last Friday's AGM that the recent share issue has raised the targeted £3.5 million and with that, confirmation that Alan Curbishley now has the financial backing to fund another assault on the Premiership, Charlton Athletic PLC chairman Richard Murray is a popular figure. Tin hats were recommended head gear for the meeting, as the gathered masses had set to vehemently oppose the much-maligned move to the Millennium Dome, as part of the 'Sports Dome 2001' consortium. But the proceedings were far more civilised than anticipated, with the state of the Valley meat pies and PA system inducing by far the most aggravation.

On Sunday 30 January, the FA Cup draw does little to diminish Mr Murray's merriment, as the Addicks are presented with an awkward, but eminently winnable tie at Bolton, as a Semi Final appearance waits tantalisingly for the winners. And with both Semis scheduled for Wembley this season (to the eternal annoyance of those who feel it devalues the Final) Curbishley's men are but one step from the Twin Towers.

However, as always seems to be the case on our road to Wembley, once the victory celebrations are over, new pressures soon kick in and Monday 31 January brings more pressing matters accordingly. In this case they take the form of a board meeting, which finally decides that Charlton will not be going to the Dome. Mr Murray officially announces that the club will be withdrawing from the consortium, mainly on the grounds of "cost and the absence of significant grant aid," and he confirms that they will now concentrate on developing the Valley instead.

And he states to the waiting press:

"We are very ambitious for the future of the club, but believe we can realise all our immediate ambitions here. After all the club has gone through, we simply cannot envisage life other than at the Valley. We will continue to build the club in a responsible and financially prudent manner and will concentrate all our efforts on returning this great club to the FA Premier League, where it belongs!"

Stirring stuff, but with the spin boiling down to the fact that it really was not financially viable to move, plans to revamp the Valley are confirmed to be in full swing, starting with the installation of 6,000 seats in the North End of the ground. And the club have been well proactive about this, having secured planning permission from Greenwich Council back in December. When the work is done, the overall capacity will be increased to 26,000 and it has to be said, the gleaming red and white Valley surroundings look pretty splendid already, and are unrecognisable from the derelict area of not so long ago. So it certainly will not be a case of throwing good money after bad.

Getting back to customary post-giant killing procedures, the club's supporters could not be happier; Curbishley and his playing and coaching staff are on top of the world and the local rags produce more 'Happy Valley' headlines than you can shake a stick at. The joy is compounded on Tuesday 1 February, when 'Curbs' is confirmed as the latest, Nationwide First Division, Manager of the Month, Charlton having won all 6 of their matches in January as well as climbing to the top of division 1.

But it is not all good news. Bolton do not expect a capacity crowd at the

Reebok for the Quarter Final and have therefore offered extra seats to Addicks fans. But those plans have today been scuppered by the police. The construction of a 150 room motel is currently limiting the normal away area to 3,142 places, but Wanderers offered to make an additional 1500 seats available along the side of the pitch, plus a possible extra 500 depending on demand. However, the police have deemed the presence of away support in these areas to be too difficult to patrol and therefore an unacceptable risk, so it will not be happening and Bolton have contacted the Valley today to reluctantly withdraw their offer

On Wednesday 2 February, it becomes clear that Charlton are in for a week long celebration as Steve Sutherland, the club's special projects co-ordinator, makes a triumphant debut on the Channel 4 show, 'Fifteen to One' blowing his 14 opponents away with ease. Fans will have to wait until February 22 to see this latest Addicks victory for themselves and one local wag suggests:

"Perhaps they'll put it on wide screen at the Valley, for those who can't make it home from work on time."

By close of office play today, all but 500 or so of Charlton's ticket allocation for the Bolton game have been sold, before they have even been offered beyond the season ticket holders. Whilst this is great news for the club support-wise, Chief Executive Peter Varney expresses his concern that Charlton fans will attempt to buy seats in the Bolton areas of the Reebok Stadium:

"We've still got 14,000 fans eligible to buy tickets," he announces with an anxious look about him. "And unless there is some change in the situation, then I have real fears that our fans will attempt to obtain tickets other than through ourselves.

"I've been in contact with Bolton, and they've confirmed that it won't be a sell out. So tickets in the home areas won't exactly be like gold dust and I've made my concerns known to them, especially as our supporters will be heading up that way on Saturday on their way to Stockport, so it'll only take a small detour for them to apply in person. We're keeping a close eye on the situation.

Saturday 5 February, sees the aforementioned league action at Stockport. No Charlton player had ever scored at Edgeley Park, neither had they bagged a hat trick home and away against the same opposition in the same season, nor had they netted hat tricks in successive league games. But upon the final whistle of this 3-1 Charlton victory, none of the above any longer apply. And not long after the final whistle, a statto confirms that Andy Hunt and co have re-written an even more sizeable chunk of the record book than anticipated, as this is the club's 10th consecutive away game without defeat and 9th consecutive straight win. And nobody can remember them notching 3 goals in 4 consecutive away games before.

Totally separately however, Peter Varney is a much relieved man, as the live beaming of the Bolton game back to a big screen at the Valley has now been arranged, thus discouraging those without tickets from going. The relief is shared by the 400 or so fans that queued up at the Valley ticket office this morning and were turned away an hour before opening time, when it became obvious they were so far down the pecking order so as to be pissing into a Twister. Fans more likely to be successful had their names, addresses and telephone numbers taken, while the dead-certs were issued with vouchers.

Still determined to completely resolve the situation, Varney has now written to the FA offering to pay the extra policing costs. Bolton Chief Executive Des McBain confirms that as things stand, they can only offer 12-13% of the total stadium accommodation to Charlton, "without causing a major headache." FA regulations state that 15% must be offered, but at this point there seems to be no animosity over the issue.

Confirmation that the Bolton game can be watched live on a big screen in front of the West Stand, is proudly announced by Mr Varney, on Thursday 10 February. Admission will damage the wallets of standard punters to the tune of £6, while those entitled to concessions will pay £4. Tickets are ready for sale first thing in the morning and by 10am on Friday 11 February, around 500 seats have been sold.

The following day (Saturday 12 February) the home clash with Wolves takes place in front of a capacity 20,000 crowd - including a couple of small brass bands - who are treated to a continuation of Charlton's amazing run. Second half strikes from Graham Stuart and Steve Brown secure the club's 10th win on the bounce and keep them 4 points clear at the top of Division 1.

The Charlton fans around us, explain that the mindset of the average Addicks punter, is that they will always be let down by their side sooner or later, usually after being taken to the brink of glory. We go some way to consoling the punters by explaining that any frustrations they feel are magnified tenfold by the long suffering supporters of both Bristol clubs.

The countdown to the Quarter Final begins with news on Monday 14th February, that over 3,000 tickets have been sold for the screening of the action live at The Valley. But first on this week's Valley schedule is Nationwide League action on Tuesday 15 February, which turns out to be another record breaking night, as Charlton beat Fulham 1-0 for their 11th consecutive win and 9th straight league victory. The muddy conditions are not conducive to good football and Charlton's performance reflects this, but they are boosted yet again by the contribution of Richard Rufus. Home fans assure us that Rufus has few matches for pace in the entire Nationwide League and Brown certainly no equal when it comes to the 50-50 challenge and tonight they have proved themselves to be a worthy backbone of the side.

The suitably euphoric Charlton fans pour out of the Valley singing to the tune of Mull of Kintyre:

"Valley Floyd Road, oh mist rolling in from the Thames,
My desire, is always to be found at Valley Floyd Road.
Many miles have I travelled, many games have I seen,
Following Charlton, my favourite team,
Many hours have I spent with the Covered End choir,
Singing Valley Floyd Road, my only desire."

But the joy is unfortunately curtailed for some home fans, as they experience the nastiest shock at PC World since Gary Glitter's last visit. After the nightmare parking restrictions imposed due to the opening of the dreaded Dome, an increasing number of supporters have started to risk using the store's car park for home games. But tonight they have returned to find their wheels clamped and a £50 release fee awaiting them. Such is their joy however, that nobody seems bothered in the slightest. And one punter makes things abundantly clear:

"Worth every fackin' penny if we win the chempyanship mayte. Every fackin' penny!"

A week which has seen local journos licking their lips and wetting their pants in anticipation and excitement respectively, builds to it's crescendo and over the last couple of days, Curbs and the players have been surrounded by microphones and notepads. Interestingly, in our bid to get the juiciest stories for this book, we have, to all intents and purposes, become part of that media circus and can actually appreciate the necessity and stimulation of a decent report. This is particularly understandable in the case of the local rag or radio station, who struggle from day to day with stories of garden fetes and supermarket openings and for whom an FA Cup Quarter Final story is manna from Heaven. And keeps another chip pan fire off the front page.

So, as we join the media throng and jostle for position as we have so many times on this journey, first under the cosh is Graham Stuart, perhaps inevitably, as he has already held the Cup aloft in an Everton shirt, following their 1995 win against Manchester Utd. Stuart obliges with plenty of copy fodder, as he explains that his absolute dream would be to lift the trophy again, this time against Everton (who must dispense with Villa at Goodison on Sunday for those aspirations to be maintained) and that no less a person than his mother has already decided that this is Charlton's year:

"My mum keeps telling me that when I won the Cup with Everton, the final was played on May 20th and that this year's final is also on May 20th, so as far as she's concerned our name's on the trophy, although 40,000 Evertonians could claim the same thing.

By Saturday 19 February, the scene is set. Just off the M61 a huge, space age arena that can be seen for miles around looms ahead and as we bear down upon it, pockets and streams of colourful and contrasting allegiance can be seen around the perimeter. Having now given up all hope of getting preferential parking for the rest of the tournament, we have had to take our chances with the masses, but facilities here are excellent with acres of space. We pay a fiver for the privilege but at least nobody has to move any wheelie bins.

After the now traditional travel from pillar to post in order to collect our press passes, we eventually enter the ground via the West Stand reception, which is in the mould of Derby's Pride Park, but on a yet grander scale and is truly sumptuous, like a luxury hotel. There are even state of the art lifts which take you up to your desired area in the stand, each with a recorded voice to advise of which floor you are on.

And our excitement rises as we imagine the magnificent buffet that surely awaits us.

We barge past Mark Lawrenson, who is accusing Ray Stubbs of stealing his pass, and storm into the press room and make a beeline for the munchies. Thick white tablecloths. Yes, good so far. And it's onward, ever onward to the goodies, which consist of …soup. We look around in a panic…more soup. Bloody soup everywhere, supplemented only by the odd roll. What is this all about? Is it the chef's speciality or the only thing he knows how to make. Or is the club now sponsored by Campbell's? Our dreams have died in tandem with our appetites, so much so, that we can only manage a meagre three bowls and four rolls each.

Not a bad ambience here though, as we slurp our freebies next to Lawro, Alan Parry and Lou Macari and enjoy an excellent view of the spectacular Lancashire countryside. And the Reebok facilities, it has to be said, are admirable, despite an obsession with soup!

We make our way up to the press box at the back of the West Stand as the regular punters are treated on TV monitors all round the stadium, to footage of Nat Lofthouse scoring goals at Wembley in the 1950's. One seasoned wag remarks:

"Aye, and the bloody team sheet didn't read like a friggin' Nordic telephone directory then either!"

We enter the stand and look around in awe at the magnificent interior of the Reebok Stadium. This is by far the best we have seen on our great journey and it is a truly unique construction. The four stands completely enclose the stadium. The lower tiers of each stand are all of the traditional rectangular shape, while the upper tiers are semi-circular. Diamond shaped floodlights are supported by a

Big support for Bolton against Charlton at the Reebok

futuristic, tubular steel structure and this is all topped off by a video replay screen at the corner of the South Stand to our right. Only problem is, lumpy, bumpy and brown, the pitch does not measure up to the surroundings.

Our seats are just to one side of the radio commentary box, next to Lou Macari who is doing live commentary. And it's a long way down from here to the pitch, which is possibly more terrifying for those with a fear of heights than the Burnley equivalent. Further feelings of mild panic are therefore induced in one phobia-ridden author.

But this is a nice comfortable little area. You get the feeling of being totally safe. As was predicted, the match is not a sell-out and there are plenty of free seats up here, but no obvious sign of any rogue Charlton fans at this point.

Down on the pitch, the requisite fireworks are in full flow and the atmosphere is building up nicely. There are still no obvious pockets of Charlton support in the home sections, but word up is that there will be a fair few dotted around the ground, although no trouble is planned.

Meanwhile, the legitimate Charlton following is massed away to our right in the South Stand and they are in excellent voice. The home announcer obviously fancies himself as a bit of a rabble-rouser and he is really trying to get the Bolton fans to return the compliment, with some degree of success:

"Come on, let's really get behind the lads today. CUUM AAAN!"

Meanwhile back at the Valley, 5,601 punters in Charlton's West Stand are creating their own atmosphere in front of the big screen. So in SE7 and BL6 the scene is set and it remains only for the teams to enter the proverbial arena.

Both in their traditional colours, the sides come out into the hazy winter sun amid the strains of 633 Squadron on the PA, as showers of confetti rain down from the Charlton support banked up to our right. Red and white balloons are bouncing everywhere in the South stand and the noise is deafening as the Wanderers fans do as they are told by the rabble-rouser, their accents seemingly adding an extra syllable to the word 'Bolton':

"We luv you Bo-well-ton, we do."

The blond haired figure of Eidur Gudjohnsen is first to show after about 30 seconds, as he cuts inside from the right and unleashes a left-footed 20-yarder that skims Dean Kiely's crossbar. A square ball 10 minutes later from Hunt to Pringle presents the Swede with a glorious chance to put Charlton ahead, but he can't direct his effort far enough from Wanderers Finnish keeper, Jussi Jaaskelainen, who parries it away accordingly. And there is nothing in it as both sides go straight into overdrive in a pulsating opening.

Before long, Bolton central midfielder Robbie Elliott begins to make an impression and breaks forward to shoot from 20 yards, but it's a poor effort which sails way to the left of Kiely's goal. Elliott is soon in the action again though, as his midfield partner Alan Johnston battles well down the left to create another opening. Charlton's Richard Rufus is presented with a chance to clear the danger, but succeeds only in knocking the ball into the path of Elliott, who is in space only 6 yards out. He reacts quickly to stab the ball goalwards but sends it crashing against the post. In an attacking frenzy of plentiful midfield involvement, Bolton are soon given another chance, this time for Johnston, but he skies it way over the bar.

It's an open game, but the serious chances are falling to Bolton.

The immensely impressive Claus Jensen hits a volley wide, and right back Dean Holden's shot is headed off the line by Charlton left back Chris Powell. Bob Taylor - a familiar face to both authors and something of a hero to one (when at Bristol City) - is putting himself about up front for Bolton and his work sets up another opportunity for Elliott who blasts it over the bar. And then for Gudjohnsen who smashes it squarely into Steve Brown's face.

Elliott returns the compliment soon afterwards with a cheeky backheel, which puts Taylor through, but he takes the ball too wide and Kiely saves the shot. Gudjohnsen also reciprocates and presents Taylor with another chance, which Todd throws himself in front of as thought his life depended on it. The shot is successfully blocked and Todd has demonstrated how fired up he is for this one, probably helped by the fact that he is getting booed by the Bolton fans every time he touches the ball.

Just before half time, Barness blocks one of Taylor's trademark overhead kicks with his arm, in the box, but highly rated referee Graham Poll awards a corner.

At the back of the stand that we thought was so safe and cosy, we notice a bloke in his mid twenties wandering from seat to seat and shouting encouragement for Bolton. He mainly chooses seats with no punters in the surrounding area, but then sits with another couple of blokes of the same age, which we presume are his mates, all the while effing and blinding at Mr Poll and all things not Bolton. He stays there for about 2 minutes and then comes over to us:

"What a fookin' game, eh lads?"

"Yeah not bad mate," "yeah pretty good" are the responses, with combine harvester accents suitably disguised, so as not to promote any kind of aggression, or worse still, inspire any further conversation. Luckily he goes off again, this time in the direction of Lou Macari.

"Hey, skip to my Lou, why don't you fook off!" He sticks two fingers up at Macari and walks away, fortunately right past us without stopping. Macari looks puzzled and the two blokes we thought were this chap's mates look at us and shrug their shoulders. We return the gesture and look at Macari who does the same. The antagonist walks down the steps of the stand and disappears mercifully into the crowd chanting and punching the air all the way. No doubt thinking "that told em".

Half time arrives with no score, and Charlton - in spite of some inspiring moments and looking the classier outfit - pretty much on the back foot.

Back in the press room, any forlorn hopes of a variation on soup are soon dashed. But the unlimited tea and coffee go down very well and we count our blessings on the basis that things could be a lot worse on the hospitality front. For example we could still be at Highfield Road.

Suitably re-armed against the increasing cold, we make our way back out to the second half action and the rabble-rouser is really bigging it up:

"C'mon, let's bring back the magic of the past to this great club...C'M OOOOONNN!!!"

To be fair though, he is doing his job really well, and, although partially assisted by Bolton's lively first half performance, he has succeeded in working the home crowd up into a frenzy.

And the second half gets under way with the Wanderers fans baying for victory with a wall of sound. The Bolton players look suitably mad for it and when put through by Gudjohnsen on the right, Michael Johansen looks as though he is being fired by rocket fuel. He advances into space and knocks it back to Gudjohnsen, who shoots from a really tight angle. His shot flies past Kiely, bounces off the far post and into the top corner of the net before Charlton can even find their feet. Bolton are one up thanks in no small way to crowd power and pure adrenaline. But nobody could deny that they deserve the lead. Unfortunately, the Sunday papers showed no credit for the goal to the announcer.

This seems to act as a catalyst for the wanker from earlier, who comes bounding up the steps of the stand, makes a bee-line for Macari and points a finger right in his face:

"Whaddya fookin' think of that Lou? Ya fookin' wanker!" Macari is not impressed, but incredibly there is no sign of any security staff and the nutcase is allowed to carry on at his leisure:

"Fookin' one nil Lou, eh? stuff you mate!" Gradually losing patience, Macari now looks as though he is about to get up and deal with this guy himself, in the middle of the live commentary. As we prepare to take over the mike in Harry Carpenter fashion, the nutcase is back off into the crowd.

Back on the pitch, Sam Allardyce immediately orders a more withdrawn role for Johnston, who had been given a licence to thrill on the left of midfield, in a fairly fluid 4-3-3 formation. Johnston's move gives Bolton a more solid 4-4-2 shape that is clearly designed to afford a little more protection to their slender lead and against the inevitable onslaught to come.

30 seconds later, tempers begin to fray as Bolton right back Dean Holden and Charlton's John Robinson tangle once too often and end up on the deck. Robinson grabs Holden by the throat and gives him a friendly tip, along the lines that next time he will not be let off so lightly and rubs his face in the turf. Mr Poll's attentions meanwhile, are firmly placed on the play, which is still going on and Robinson's actions go unseen. After his release, it takes about 10 seconds for Holden to decide that he wants revenge. He chases Robinson for about 30 yards down the pitch and when he catches him, lets fly with a classic head-butt. By now Mr Poll has sussed it and produces the red card without hesitation. So Holden, who has only just returned from suspension, is off on a walk that will lead him to another one and Robinson goes unpunished.

"What the fook did 'e do!" exclaims a rather frustrated, red-faced, pie-eating gentleman in the stand, who looks as though it's going to cause him a burst blood vessel if the cholesterol doesn't kill him first. One or two however, have clocked the incident and are going wild over the fact that Robinson is getting off scott free: "Ref, ref, he fookin' half-strangled him for fook's sake!"

Allardyce reshuffles quicker than a Tory cabinet, and Bob Taylor is replaced by Paul Ritchie. Ritchie slots into central defence alongside Mark Fish, dislodging Gudni Bergsson to the now vacant right back position, resulting in a 4-4-1 formation.

Charlton revive slightly, but despite this Curbs decides that Charlton will not survive this one without a man for the big moment, and brings on Mark Kinsella to a great roar from the Charlton end. Kinsella goes straight into central midfield, and shows genuine class

With 20 minutes to go, Curbs decides he needs to further increase his attacking options from the midfield and brings on John Salako, another ex Bolton man. He replaces Andy Todd, who comes off to a tirade of abuse from the home fans.

Tempers are still flaring up out there as the highly regarded Mr Poll struggles to contain the aggression. And the next victim is Richard Rufus who falls to a vicious Robbie Elliott tackle, resulting in a somewhat lenient yellow card. Rufus limps off to be replaced by Carl Tiler.

In to the last 5 minutes and Bolton begin to break free from the shackles of the previous twenty. Jensen, with a chance to wrap the whole thing up, blasts just over. Jamaican international, Ricardo Gardner fires wide. Determined not to be outdone, Kinsella is growing in strength by the second and blasts another 25-yarder. But Jaaskelainen tips it over the top. A minute later, Kinsella lets fly with a carbon copy effort, which produces another superb save from Jaaskelainen, tipping it this time onto the post. It bounces back out for Robinson who has a clear chance with the keeper sprawling on the ground. He hits Jaaskelainen again and within minutes misses again.

Those were crucial moments that went Bolton's way and as the clock ticks round to 90 the air is filled with Lancastrian victory choruses. Obviously in celebratory mood and presumably feeling he has sufficient ammunition for a further showing, Macari's earlier tormentor surfaces again. And horror of horrors, this time he's brought a friend. And they're both at it:

"Ey oh skip to my Lou."

"Whaddya make of it Lou – eh?"

"We're gonna fookin' win mate."

With Macari this time far too engrossed in climacteric commentary to know or care of his twin tormentors' existence, they walk off into the distance singing Bolton songs, thankfully never to return.

But win they do, as the whistle comes soon enough. Sam Allardyce punches the air and hugs just about everybody in sight and the whole Bolton set-up milk the thunderous applause that echoes around the stadium. Curbs and the Charlton players are inconsolable.

Back among the white tablecloths, the quietly spoken Allardyce is first in: "What an outstanding cup tie," he begins. "Really exciting for the fans I should think. That really was a magnificent performance by both sets of players on a difficult pitch."

"Even though we couldn't score, we were going so well first half, I just didn't want half time to come. And I just hoped we could keep it going after half time.

And what a great strike it was from Eidur. It was just what we needed and it was at the right time. He always scores quality goals. Now he's got four goals in four rounds. Not bad for a young lad. He's only 21.

"But in the end the hero emerges and I thought our goalkeeper was the hero today. He made some wonderful saves when they were really needed. But we should have already put the game to bed by time we scored. We deserved everything we got today!

Another predictable question from the ranks: Can you win the Cup?

"Why not? We could easily have won the Worthington Cup, but we fell at that last hurdle. Today we've shown that we can compete with the best side in this division and deserved to win. We've also shown this season that we can overcome Premiership opponents by beating Derby, Wimbledon and Sheffield Wednesday." A silence descends.

"Alright thanks chaps," says Sam when no more questions are forthcoming and he's off to join the celebrations.

Around 10 minutes later a devastated Curbs walks in and takes a seat at the table right next to us.

"Yeah we're disappointed," he confirms. "It would've been nice to have had a home draw today. Bolton wouldn't have fancied that but there you go."

"I thought we did ok in the first half and we defended well, although we were grateful to get in at half time without being a goal down. We knew Bolton would come at us because they always have a go when they're at home. But if we'd weathered the storm a little longer, the game could have opened up and we could have got a foothold.

"The sending off changed things as well. It was like the last time we were in the Quarter-Final, Schmeichel got sent off and that changed the game. It's not easy playing against 10 men as a lot of sides have found out and it wasn't easy on that pitch either. Even so, their keeper made some great saves and I was a bit disappointed with John's chance at the end - as I know he is - especially as it was a similar scenario to the one he stuck away against Fulham on Tuesday. Given the choice, I'd rather have those three points against Fulham, and I'm grateful that we've come through today without any bookings or injuries. But having said that, we desperately wanted to win this tie and play in the Semi-Final!

"But we wish Bolton all the best and yeah, if they play like they did against us today, then they'll be a match for anyone and maybe they could go all the way, especially in a one-off situation at Wembley.

"Looking to the future though, we're a different club than we were five years ago. We're much better equipped these days. We fell away then after losing that Quarter final to United, but that won't happen this time. We're playing regularly in front of 20,000 sell out crowds and I'll be very disappointed if we fall away now."

Down, but by no means out, Curbs gives a polite smile and leaves. And before long, we all move as one into the adjoining room where Bolton skipper Mike Whitlow and the man himself Gudjohnsen are waiting to be pounced upon. Pointing over to his Icelandic colleague, Whitlow sums it up nicely:

"One of the reasons we did the business today, was because our keeper made some great saves. But see him over there? Different class!"

16

Deano's miss

SEMI-FINAL

BOLTON

V

ASTON VILLA

2 APRIL

@ WEMBLEY STADIUM

ATTENDANCE 62,828

Whitlow's post-match comments in the Bolton pressroom met with generic nods of approval, which is universally reflected in the match reports, with the Mirror's 'Gud News' headline and various references to 'the Ice Man,' giving the general thrust of the copy on Sunday 20 February.

Indeed this victory has drawn much praise from the press, including a declaration that Bolton had proved the romance of the Cup to still be very much alive and in the words of the Sunday People:

'Who Needs Manchester United In the Hat?'

And predictably enough, much is now being made of the fact that Bolton were the first side to win the FA Cup at Wembley in the good old 'White Horse Final' and how fitting it would be if they were also to be the last.

Big Sam Allardyce deals with the increasing media attention slowly and methodically, sporting a constant 'sick dog' type expression behind a moustache that simply cries out to be complemented by a black vest and leather trousers. Slightly stockier than in his youth, Sam, now 46, is still instantly recognisable as Bolton's solid, centre-half of the Seventies (the moustache was still prevalent, although sadly, trendier then).

Sam believes that fate, if not the odds, could be on his side:

"This club won the first FA Cup at Wembley in 1923 and I believe our name could be on the last". "When I took over, this club had lost contact with its supporters," he looks deadly serious, seeming to concentrate on every word: "But I've worked hard on getting the players out to meet the people again and there's nothing like an FA Cup Final appearance to help something like that along. It can bring new players in, bring old fans back and set you up for the following season!"

Meanwhile, Bolton's top scorer (16 strikes in league and cup) and man of the moment, Eidur Gudjohnsen is still very much the darling of the press, as he talks through his priceless goal for the umpteenth time. Having served his media time, the blond 21 year old slings his bag over his shoulder and makes off, leaving the dust to officially settle on the Quarter Final victory and the run in to the Semis to begin. Their opponents on the big day are to be Aston Villa, which by all accounts induces a huge smile on John Gregory's face.

Meanwhile, the FA have decreed the date of Bolton's historic Semi-Final clash to be Sunday 2 April, at 3pm, with Chelsea taking on Newcastle a week later. The official date, upon which the scramble for tickets can start, is still to be announced as the Wanderers admin. staff go into overdrive.

But Allardyce is currently blessed with a reasonably stable period for the club, in which his biggest headaches are the imminent suspensions of resident hothead, Dean Holden and the not always so ice-cool Gudjohnsen. Holden's suspension is likely to be for the duration of 3 games, starting with the home clash against Charlton on 4 March, followed by the encounters with Palace and Fulham. Gudjohnsen's ban starts on Saturday, when Wanderers travel to Barnsley.

But first on this week's Reebok agenda is tomorrow's league match against Portsmouth, for which Allardyce confirms that he will keep faith with the side that beat Charlton. And sporting his usual forlorn face, big Sam explains:

"Saturday's Cup win was proof that the team has now turned the corner after a period of upheaval and transition. People forget that we were disappointed with our Worthington Cup Semi-Final performance against Tranmere, but reaction from the players since that day has been one of character and good performances. But now we've won four out of five and won them comfortably. It's been a great reaction from what was a very big disappointment."

"And," he adds, "decent players provide competition for places don't they, which drives players on. And now I've got that competition all over the pitch, although Allan Johnston's due to be playing his last game for us on Saturday, then he's due back at Sunderland. He's been a fantastic success for us since he came in January. Between you and me, I might just have a crack at getting him for a bit longer. It won't be for much longer though, Glasgow Rangers have got him lined up."

Allardyce has put great store in warning his unchanged side that 'post-Cup hangovers' will not be acceptable for the home game against Portsmouth. But on Tuesday 22 February, 12,672 fans (considerably less than saw the defeat of Charlton) witness a basically dominant Wanderers performance with a 3-0 victory, in an altogether more sedate affair, in terms of both action and atmosphere. However, bad news comes in the form of a hamstring problem for the popular Mark Fish, which forces him to limp off after an hour, and an uncharacteristically quiet display from Johnston, caused partially, perhaps by a switch of wings with Johansen early in the second half. Dean Holdsworth misses an absolute sitter at the end but the day is already won.

Post match, the good news is that Johnston is staying for another month. Reports from the treatment table have also brightened big Sam's demeanour and he is positively on the brink of smiling as he announces that: "The injury which put Mark Fish out of action against Portsmouth isn't serious. It's just a tightening of the hamstring, caused by the fatigue of playing in the African Nations Cup (seemingly the bane of everybody's 1999-2000 FA Cup campaign) the long journey back and the big game against Charlton played so quickly after his return. But he should be fit to play at Oakwell on Saturday."

"On Thursday 24 February, with Saturday's clash at Barnsley looming, Allardyce is back to normal, like he is carrying the weight of the world on his shoulders."

"There's still a problem with Mark Fish's hamstring. It's not cleared up as quickly as we'd have liked. We're going to wait and put him through a fitness test on Saturday morning. That'll decide whether he plays against Barnsley. As you know, I was pleased with Paul Ritchie on Tuesday night and he will deputise if Mark's not fit."

At fellow promotion hopefuls Barnsley, on Saturday 26 February, Holdsworth takes the place of Gudjohnsen as expected, while Fish does get through his early fitness test to make the starting line-up. But Allardyce plumps for Ricardo Gardner in place of Allan Johnston. Bolton only manage a 1-1 draw, and the performance is not Cup winning material.

Monday 28 February, brings no better news as it becomes clear that skipper, Mike Whitlow picked up a groin strain against Barnsley which is getting worse instead of better and Mark Fish's hamstring problem has flared up again. And when you add the fact that Dean Holden's suspension kicks in on Saturday, you have 3 out of Bolton's first choice back 4 missing for a vital game against the top side, who will be hungry for revenge to put it mildly. In short, Bolton have a good, old-fashioned injury crisis.

Meanwhile, the press add fuel to the fire, with gossip concerning an 'end of season sale' at the club, with Gudjohnsen and Jensen top of the list, particularly if a hat-trick of visits to Wembley is not achieved. This, according to the media men, would be a necessary antidote to the club's financial situation, which could only otherwise be addressed by the rewards of Wembley appearances and promotion. (Ah the perils of a new stadium).

The rumours eventually spur club Chairman Phil Gartside into action and he booms to the waiting Paparazzi:

"That's absolute nonsense. There will be no such sale of players as you put it. But like everyone else, if we get an offer we can't refuse, then we'll have to consider it. But that is an entirely different situation, although I am not expecting any offers. Yes of course we have a financial situation to resolve, but we are working on that as a separate issue!"

It is also announced that Wembley tickets will be available from Sunday March 12, with seat prices ranging from £15 to £50, with various Corporate packages also up for grabs.

Wanderers take on Charlton on Saturday 4 March, in front of 13,788 in a far less passionate affair than the previous encounter. Whitlow fails a late fitness test, but despite the eventual inclusion of Mark Fish, Wanderers are unable to recapture the magic of the Quarter-Final. 2-0 for Charlton.

"We'll have to win every match now, to reach the Play- offs," groans Allardyce.

The next pre-Wembley "important" league game is in front of 15,236 at

Selhurst Park. The match is not without incident, the only problem being that Bolton are on the wrong end of it as Mike Whitlow and Gudni Bergsson receive their marching orders, bringing Bolton's red card tally for the season to 9. Whitlow ruins his own comeback and goes off for two yellow cards, while Bergsson stupidly gets involved in a fracas with Palace's Finnish international Striker (on loan from Chelsea) Mickel Forssell.

"That definitely takes all hope of a play off position out of our hands," laments Allardyce. "Mike and Bo should have known better, but the referee was very poor. He was in a different world!"

On Saturday 11 March, Sam is given a shot in the arm by the fact that Mark Fish's 'Jeckyll and Hyde' hamstring is in a Dr Jeckyll phase and he will be fit to face Al Fayed's men. He is then injected with the bigger boost of a 3-1 victory:

"Fate and fortune were with us and we took advantage," confirms a more relieved than delighted Allardyce. He is referring to a debatable penalty decision in Bolton's favour, and his approach to the ref this week is decidedly more philosophical.

Allardyce is particularly complimentary about the contributions down the wings against Fulham of Allan Johnston and Michael Johansen: "I was really pleased with the amount of crosses we put in today. I think Allan put in more crosses than he's done all season." Holdsworth missed another easy chance in this one but insists " I know I've missed a couple of sitters lately, but what the heck!"

Following the game, Bolton appoint a new club Commercial Director, in the shape of 37 year old Gareth Moores, from Acton Bridge in Northwich. Having worked for Reebok in Bolton, Gareth's CV now makes impressive reading and includes the roles of, General Manager at London Monarchs American Football Club (where he carried out pioneering work in bringing American Football to British audiences) European Marketing Manager for Reebok based in London and most recently, Sales and Marketing Manager at Lancashire County Cricket Club.

With a clear confidence and penchant for spin, Gareth announces to the press:

"There is a clear and strong brief to further develop off-field revenue in order to boost the financial benefits flowing onto the pitch. This will help to build a broad-based leisure business, which will be able to take advantage of the new commercial and media opportunities that a club like Bolton is faced with."

In this busiest of months, Tuesday 14 March necessitates the transfer of Allardyce's attentions to Edgeley Park, where Wanderers take on Stockport County tonight. This is a real hectic British winter fixture list, and does not augur well for the Cup preparation. However, as we are perennially advised by all managers in lower leagues, "the league is what matters". And Sam has confirmed that he has banned talk of Wembley. 0-0 is the final score. Tense Claus Jensen came closest to breaking the deadlock with a curling free kick, which cannoned off the bar, but Stockport missed plenty of chances.

Wednesday 15 March, sees the arrival of another one-week triallist, Finnish player Mikka Koltilla from SK Brann. Allardyce jokes:

"He's only here to keep Jussi Jaaskelainen company, but we'll have a look at him and see if he's good enough to keep him company until the end of the season."

Sam pulls a couple of pre-match surprises out of the hat on Saturday 18 March, with Dean Holden on the bench and John O'Kane coming in at right back. Mark Fish is rested and Dean Holdsworth replaced by Bo Hansen. Allardyce explains that he is trying to utilise the squad rotation system in this most hectic part of their season for fear of burning players out. And it is also the case that Hansen has scored 3 goals against Grimsby in 2 meetings this season, one of which was on the Wanderers road to FA Cup glory.

In the Spring sunshine, relegation candidates Grimsby start without 7 regulars and Wanderers are by far and away the favourites to take the points. But within 3 minutes of the start Jaaskelainen is called upon to pull off a tremendous save. Wanderers cannot get it together at all and the Finnish keeper saves the day again shortly afterwards. The passing is not its usual self and Hansen and Gudjohnsen seem to have no edge up front. 5,289 witness Bolton scrape this barely deserved 1-0 win, which sees them defeated only once now in 12 matches and six points behind a play off place. And Sam proves that you can go to Grimsby, leave out a player called Fish and still come away with the points!

Another day brings another match, this time the visit of Sheffield United on Tuesday 21 March. But there are other special guests at the Reebok tonight, a delegation of Polish council leaders, representing around half the regional councils in Poland. Their trip to Bolton is part of a process in which they hope to prepare for their entry into the European Union in 2003, by checking out how English councils operate. This is part of a larger fact finding mission in which they are conducting research into the political structures of modern Western countries. The visitors arrive at the Reebok having spent the day witnessing various presentations at the town hall followed by a visit to Middlebrook and Horwich Leisure Centre.

They witness an even but hotly contested game, which Bolton look like winning, but then the taste of imminent victory turns slowly sour for Sam. First up, Warhurst receives a badly gashed leg and is carted off for stitches. And hardly has Holden entered the fray, when he is involved in a 50-50 challenge with Lee Sandford, which puts him in hospital with a suspected broken leg. The early news of the two casualties is that neither is likely to be involved in the Semi-Final. Wanderers go on to a somewhat Pyrrhic 2-0 victory.

On Sunday 26 March, the Wanderers squad is gathered outside the Reebok to be whisked off to a classified destination that will not be revealed. But they will be back on Thursday for a pre-Wembley press conference.

"We've done all we can in the league," says Sam. "Nine points out of nine is all I could ask for, and now we'll forget about the league for this week and concentrate on the Cup. And yes, now I'll allow talk of Wembley!

"And I'll tell you what. A lot of sides struggle in the run up to such a big game. But we've hit form! I know we're the underdogs and that suits us. Its back to that old saying isn't it, we've got nothing to lose. But believe me, we're not going there to lose!"

At their secret Leicestershire hideaway, preparations focus solely on the job in hand. Jaaskelainen has turned down the chance to be in the Finland squad for tomorrow's friendly against Wales, in front of 60,000 at Cardiff's Millennium Stadium. He explains that he would prefer to rest and focus entirely on Sunday's game and to ensure he becomes the first Finn to play in an FA Cup Semi-Final.

Sunday 2 April, and finally the big match arrives. Sam and the boys arrive to a tumultuous welcome from the Wanderers fans outside the ground and the players reciprocate with cheery waves and nervous smiles, as the coach drives through the massive gates into the stadium.

"Go on lads, fookin' stuff the Brummie bastards!"

Meanwhile referee Mr Elleray is doing his much-needed PR bit, meeting both sets of fans. Some indulge in playful banter with him:

"Yow ain't gunnah cost uz this one an'all are yow Dyevid?" laughs a claret and blue clad joker. The Harrow man smiles back and continues signing an autograph for a little boy also sporting Villa colours. And he comes out with a quip of his own:

"I'll only sign it if you promise not to shout at me today." The lad does not commit himself.

Around the vast expanse that is the exterior of Wembley Stadium, the crowds are beginning to swell. And from outside the ground, hordes of smiling faces can be seen making the trip along Wembley Way, banners flying high, with a seemingly high concentration of claret and blue checked flags on view. Many carry teddy bears and various good luck items adorned in the colours of their allegiance and some have faces painted accordingly. There are a fair sprinkling of the currently popular jesters hats and a Bolton fan probably in his 40's passes by waving his own little replica of the FA Cup, made of cardboard and silver paper, bearing the inscription: BWFC 2000. The scene itself could be the final, but it isn't. And not everyone believes the semi-final should be held here, not least of all Nat Lofthouse himself. "This should only be for the final itself", he tells the press

Many of both persuasions are chilling out whilst consuming overpriced burgers and fizzy drinks on the grass verges that line the exterior of the stadium and refreshingly certainly more so than the prices of the aforementioned reinvigoration products, there appears to be no hint of trouble.

With kick off almost upon us, Wanderers cult-figure Nat Lofthouse walks in front of the Bolton ranks and receives his usual rousing welcome. And clearly putting his comments about the use of Wembley for a Semi-Final to one side, reciprocates with the now statutory 'Wayne's World' style, 'we're not worthy' gesture. Those nearest return the motion with gusto.

Memories come flooding back to one author, who smiles as he remembers a less complimentary Wembley welcome for the great man, courtesy of a Bristol City banner in the 1986 Freight Rover Trophy Final, which read 'Nat Lofthouse, Big Shithouse.' Well, you had to be there.

Having endured the Wembley MC and his pre-match entertainment package, it is at last time for the teams to come out. Flanked by his assistants, Mr Elleray leads the procession, performing the noble art of gripping the match ball underneath his right hand and somehow preventing it from falling to the ground. Who does he think he is, Pat Jennings? The sides come out to a massive welcome and are hit hard by Bolton-related noise as it is the Lancastrians that are situated at the tunnel end, albeit with one or two visible gaps within the ranks. Bolton actually sold only 25,000 tickets for today, compared with Villa's 36,000:

"They're saving their moneh while t'Faahnal," explains one particularly large, jubilant and clearly optimistic gentleman sporting a yellow Bolton away top and moustache. But he can barely make himself heard over the cries:

The teams warm up in the sunshine, Wanderers in white shirts, dark blue shorts and white socks and Villa in wide, vertical claret and blue striped shirts, with claret shorts and socks. Complete with taped-up earring, as per Mr Elleray's orders, Carbone removes his 'necklace' and reveals it to be a hairband, which he transfers to his barnet accordingly. Julian Joachim then kicks things off among echoing cries of "Villa, Villa," from the retaliating claret and blue hordes, who are now the louder of the opposing forces.

Villa give a signal of their intent in the first minute as Carbone, in his golden boots (a change from the blue sported in the Cup victory against Leeds) receives a delicate chip over the top inside the Bolton area, but he is offside and the panic is over.

A Bolton fan then declares:

"One time you had to be European Footballer of the piggin' Year to have t'boot that colour!"

Then Bolton get into gear, as the ever-inspirational Whitlow gets things moving on the left. He plays a ball in to Holdsworth's feet. Holdsworth wrong foots Ehiogu on the edge of the box and curls in a shot, which lands comfortably in the arms of Tony James. Relatively harmless. But a shot across the Villa bows from Holdo, on this, his Wembley debut. And he is really on fire in these early stages, as a cross comes in from Johnston on the left. Flanked by the Gareths, Barry and Southgate, Holdo gets up first to despatch a glancing header from just right of the penalty spot. James leaps across his area, but the header goes agonisingly wide. Bolton could be one up and Holdo knows it. He puts his hands on his head, looks to the skies and shouts, "oh fuck!"

In the midfield battle, George Boateng gets a hamstring pull and is replaced by Steve Stone after only 10 minutes.

Next up, the Villa right flank is being attacked again as Johnston rampages down the Bolton left. This time he plays it in to Gudjohnson's feet on the left edge of the Villa box. The Icelander ingeniously flicks the ball into the box between Ehiogu and Southgate and runs onto it to put himself clean through. He picks his spot to the right, just inside James' far post and side-foots a well placed shot with his right peg. James is beaten and the ball is heading goalwards. But somehow left midfielder Allan Wright appears out of nowhere behind James and twists his neck to head the ball behind, saving a certain goal in the process.

The corner comes to nothing, but with around 20 minutes gone, Bolton are well on top.

But Villa are quickly back to the other end where Carbone is causing problems for the Wanderers back line. A frustrated Whitlow obstructs the Italian resulting in an exchange of words, starting with the Bolton man offering Carbone the ball in the palm of his hand, the significance of which, nobody seems to know. Whitlow however, continues the fracas by pointing at Carbone and mouthing off and receives a flick across the face from the Italian for his troubles. A brave act from the Villa man, as his target is the archetypal, uncompromising defender and does not look the kind of bloke whose face you would flick in a pub on a Saturday night. Although, Whitlow has been around long enough to know when a player has got a giant sized key in his back.

John Gregory was banned from the touchline on 25 November, after an exchange with newly promoted Premiership referee Andy D'Urso. But after a remarkable upturn in Villa's fortunes during the ban, decided to stay away even after it had been served. He is known to put this down to the fact that his ranting and raving can place unnecessary pressure on players and upon asking them whether they would prefer him to return to the dugout, admits to being greeted with a unanimous 'no' vote. His anger is still vented in the stand as he kicks the wall following a Joachim miss.

Villa's pace is starting to tell, but half time comes scoreless. Predominantly however, this is due to a couple of Finnish saves. Bolton re-start the stronger though, and a distant Gudjohnsen shot goes close.

Paul Merson is not enjoying a fruitful day and surprisingly his control lets him down on a couple of occasions. Meanwhile the Bolton fans are winning the exchanges on the terraces.

With around 20 minutes left, Dublin duly enters the fray, although the exit of the man he replaces is met with boos from the Villa faithful. And Carbone is none too pleased either. He goes off with a face like thunder and after crossing the white line, boots a trainer's bucket into the air. The press box love it and speculation of this being the final straw which breaks the contractual back of his Villa career reaches fever pitch.

As we approach the end of normal time, Holdsworth is skinned by Boateng and clips him from behind to halt his progress, just inside the Bolton half. He enters Mr Elleray's detention book accordingly. Southgate floats the free kick in to Dublin, who heads just wide and misses the chance of a fairy tale. This ends the dull game with an equally dull scoreline.

Both sides go into huddles as Sam and John do their motivational things. Carbone meanwhile, is nowhere to be seen.

Both managers return to the sidelines and we're under way again for 30 minutes of extra time (not golden goals) followed by penalties if the matter is still not settled, the Semi-Final and Final being the only ties not designated to go to replays.

Half chances come and go. The crowd raises the tempo. Villa are more interested in Birmingham City than Bolton however, with the ever popular 'My old man said "be a City fan". I said fuck off bollocks you're a cunt!'

The extra time grinds into the second period, and eventually the excitement comes from the dismissal of Delaney for two quick fouls.

Holdsworth strides up to take the free kick and smashes it against the post, in tune with frenetic excitement and movement on the benches. Then the moment by which this semi-final will be remembered. Gudjohnsen hares down the left, James spots the danger and comes off his line. Gudjohnsen awaits his arrival and skilfully takes it past the keeper's flailing leg just to the left of the Villa box. He travels the short distance to the by-line and pulls it back for the oncoming and unchallenged Holdsworth. Barry and Southgate stand helpless on the goal line and look ready to accept the inevitable. The Bolton fans behind the goal are ready to hit the roof. With the goal at his mercy, Holdsworth connects near the penalty spot and smashes it somehow over the bar!

PENALTIES

First up is Steve Stone. He faces a cavalcade of Lancastrian boos from behind his target, but scores.

For Bolton it is Dean Holdsworth, of all people. We the authors do like this guy. He has got a heart as big as a bucket. The Villa fans help him on his way with a wall of sound specially created by boos and catcalls. Given his earlier costly miss and others prior to today, can he really do the business under such intense pressure? Yes! He sends James the wrong way and punches the air in recognition of Bolton's equaliser and his demonstration of 24-carat character.

Lee Hendrie strolls up for Villa. He is 20 years old and has not kicked a ball yet today, having entered the fray as a late, late sub. The odds are stacked against him. "Fuckin' come on," he mouths as he approaches the penalty spot and places the ball. He shoots and Jaaskelainen gets a hand to it, but it sneaks in and Villa have the upper hand again.

Then Johnston for Bolton. He hits it to James' left. James dives the right way...And saves!

Sam is expressionless, his only motion the chewing of gum. Gregory punches the air along with the Villa huddle.

Another youngster, Gareth Barry comes up for Villa. He tucks it away and Bolton's light is fading.

Johansen is next for Bolton. He hits it to James's right, but it's another save. Match point Villa and Sam must be writing his "if only" lines. Holdo consoles Johansen, who indulges in Bolton's regular activity of the day, looking to the skies for salvation. And Gregory is poised to explode.

Villa need to score this one to go through. And who else to win the day than the fairy tale king himself. It's Dion Dublin, juggling the ball, super-cool on his way to the spot. He places the ball, makes his run and bang! No mistake! It's there. The Villa huddle breaks up leaps in the air and run as one to congratulate the hero. And of course, David James.

Villa are in the Final and Bolton have failed at the last hurdle again. But there is no despondency on the faces of Sam or the Wanderers players. Firstly they stay in their huddle in true contemporary post-traumatic motivational style. There is still a job to do in the league. Then they go to their fans to give thanks and receive rapturous applause. Sam returns the applause and there is hardly a sad face amongst the Bolton faithful basking in the sunshine. They know their side have given a good account of themselves and that better things may be around the corner.

Dublin of course is surrounded by urgent hacks:

"Nerve racking? Yes very. But David James was the hero today. The job had already been done by him when I scored. And yeah, it wasn't the best game, I know. But we're there!"

By now James has also been gathered in:

"That's right, it wasn't the prettiest of games and Deano could well have wrapped it up for them. And yes in retrospect perhaps I shouldn't have come so far off my line to try and stop him. But we've done it and whilst it would have been nice to have gone to a replay so we could experience it again, I'm glad we won!"

The celebrations continue on the pitch and in the stands as the PA belts out Quo's Rockin' All Over the World. They may be struck off the Radio One playlist, but there is no such luck at Wembley.

First out of the changing rooms and into the valley of death by media is that man Dean Holdsworth. The world's press converges, but all credit to him as he shows that he is big enough and bad enough to handle it:

"I looked up, saw two of theirs on the line and thought, 'I've got to get a good connection here.' But perhaps it was too good a connection (shrugs his shoulders). It was just one of those days."

"The penalty? Yeah, I was confident. I wanted to level things and I was delighted to do that. But I thought we gave a good account of ourselves today. We ran them pretty close. Y'know, they had a few good chances and so did we, but overall I thought we had a really good game. Sometimes you wonder if you're gonna get the rub of the green. We couldn't have done any more today. It just wasn't gonna be our day. I just wish they could have moved the goalpost over another couple of inches, then my free kick would have gone in!

"Yeah it was my biggest disappointment in football, especially as we'd done ourselves proud against a top-six Premiership side. But it won't take me a long time to get over it. I'm a strong character. I've been through a lot of other things and I'll get through this. I know I will. I'll bounce back for the sake of Bolton Wanderers!"

Eventually in walks Sam, complete with sick dog expression in overdrive, but positive attitude still intact:

"Disappointed? Of course I am, but at the same time I'm proud of the players. They played one hundred and twenty minutes against a top six Premiership side and didn't concede a goal. We've graced the big stage and we want to do it again!"

"Deano's chance? Yes I thought you might ask me that! It was the most intense moment of the day for me. One of those split-second situations where your heart stops and a lump comes into your throat. You think, 'this is going to be it.' Then you feel the disappointment, when you know you should have been feeling the elation of scoring a goal!

"But you can't be critical of anybody. Dean did everything right. He did what he had to do and took it first time and I suppose if you were going to back anybody to score then you would've backed Deano!

"And when he hit the post with his free kick he was very unfortunate and I have to say he was a brave man to take the first penalty after that. And he put it away very comfortably, which settled our nerves."

Authors' thought: Yeah, so much so that all the other penalties were missed.

"But what about our fans eh? They were brilliant right from the moment we arrived. And they were at the tunnel end of the ground, which meant the support for us was deafening when the teams came out. Looking around at the mass of blue and white in the stands really made the hairs stand up on the back of my neck. It was fantastic. They gave us a great reception after the match too. I think because we played so well, it gave them the heart and spirit to get off their seats and sing, which helped us an awful lot. It's just a pity they couldn't suck Deano's shot in!"

Meanwhile, Mr Elleray sums up: "If I'd made a mistake today of the same proportions as Dean Holdsworth's, I'd have been pilloried for life!" Good point Dave. Now back to your homework, please.

17

Hello Brian!

THE FINAL

ASTON VILLA

V

CHELSEA

20 MAY 2000

ATTENDANCE 78,217
(Last 100,000 attendance was 1985 – Capacity now 80,000)

@ WEMBLEY STADIUM

The bi-product of Cup Fever of course, is the presence of half the world's press and its brother, which have now descended in unison upon all things Villa Park and the luxurious training facility at Bodymoor Heath in Sutton Coldfield. And never will there be such a diverse cross section of media presence, as in the build up to an FA Cup Final, especially the last one to be held at Wembley. Apart from the local and national press and web site hacks, we have seen a presence from the likes of Shoot, Match, Total Football and numerous other glossy publications, not to mention Villa's number one fanzine 'Heroes and Villains'.

There is nothing like a cup final to get your name on the map, except of course that Villa's is already there, large-style. This is indeed a big set up, Villa Park is simply massive and having never been here before, it becomes clear to us that Villa are quite simply, a massive club. If it ever gets to the stage where a small number of 'super-clubs' break away from the rest of the domestic scene for whatever reason, you can be sure that this lot will not be left behind.

The attention of the cup is also affecting a holidaying Royal family, as Prince William gives an impromptu press conference whilst away with his father and brother.

"The Cup is definitely secure with Aston Villa!" declares the future king. Well, that interested everybody then.

Nobody knows why the club has the Royal seal of approval, although speculation points to a tradition with pupils at Eton, which consists of supporting an 'untrendy' football team. This is clearly a somewhat tenuous connection, as we all know that Villa pull support from all over the country. And Arsenal fan Prince Harry, is certainly in need of a better excuse. Back in Birmingham meanwhile, Doug Ellis is equally bemused:

"I don't know either," says the deadly one, "but when it was first made public, I sent a couple of souvenirs down to him, via his father's office and they wrote to me to confirm they'd got them. Next thing you know, he's all over the papers with a Villa hat on! But don't worry, there's no truth in the rumour that we're replacing the Trinity Stand façade with a 'By Appointment' logo!"

Villa's build up includes a match at Sheffield Wednesday, where the once mightily injured Dion Dublin is maintaining his return and hope for a Wembley appearance. Dublin staked his claim with an impressive performance and hit the post twice. Villa's Italian genius, Carbone is dropped for the game after an anti Wednesday tirade related to his treatment at the club. Meanwhile his semi-final substitution that brought about a famous tantrum has been explained away as the physio noticing "his run had changed" and suspecting an injury. Benito has bought this explanation.

Villa are due to meet Leeds next, immediately after the deaths in Istanbul of two Leeds fans who travelled to the UEFA Cup tie against Galatasaray. The commendable consensus among many Villa fans is that differences should be put aside and maximum respect shown. Indeed, some recall their own experiences including the flares that were fired into the Villa support in Milan, the baton-happy cops in La Coruna and the kid who got his skull fractured in Madrid, and they have come to the mass conclusion, 'there but for the grace of God.'

On Sunday 9 April, the many tributes laid by both sets of support outside the Witton End of Villa Park, underlines a moving and poignant occasion, in which both teams wear black armbands. The minute's silence, which the Leeds players spend in a huddle, is immaculately respected, provoking a tribute from boss David O'Leary, although he did add that he was sure the reaction would have been the same anywhere in the country.

With Thompson on the bench in spite of netting the midweek Sheffield winner, Villa nudge past Leeds 1-0. This comes courtesy of Joachim taking advantage of a defensive lapse just before half time, some fines saves by James and a Leeds miss, described by a Villa website contributor as being of "Holdsworthian proportions!"

Joachim had put in a lot of hard work at Bodymoor Heath, since the disappointing misses against Bolton and is understandably delighted with his reward. But Thompson is a somewhat less-happy chap after being left out again. "I'll not stand in Thommo's way if he wants to go," says Gregory post-match, "I've never been one to hinder someone who wants to improve themselves. But my message to him is simple:

"Make me pick you for the Final!"

JG is obviously trying to generate competition for places, but anybody who has ever been in Thompson's position at any level, will suspect that, barring injury to one of the blue-eyed boys, the writing is on the wall.

Back down at the proverbial twin towers of course, the second Semi-Final is set to determine who will provide the opposition in the May showpiece. Can Newcastle overcome Chelsea and avoid a hat trick of Wembley losses? In a nutshell, No! A brace from Poyet secures a 2-1 victory and to quote the ever, more amusing website man:

"We are to be spared six weeks of melodramatic nonsense about good old Bobby, the fanatical Toon Army, no real trophies for forty years and the Holy Shearer!" And so say all of us.

Instead we get "Poy Story 2" headlines.

The first response from Chelsea HQ comes from the struggling Chris Sutton "Yeah, Villa are a resolute side. Difficult to play against. We've had two tight games against them this season and I haven't managed to find the net in either. Then again, there's a lot of sides I haven't scored against this season!"

Back on the claret and blue side of Brum, the never-ending talk is of tickets, travel and tipple arrangements for the big day. Indeed the club has now announced a system for fairer ticket allocation once the season ticket holders have claimed their fill. Stubs from Villa home games for this season will each be worth a certain amount of points and punters accruing the most points will get first bash, it is as simple as that.

A selection of executive rail, coach and even limousine charters are of course also available through the club, with the coach in particular presenting excellent value at £17 a throw. For the more well-heeled, £139 will secure the train trip, which offers a champagne reception at Villa Park, followed by a luxurious journey to the twin towers, with proverbial Full English Breakfast (copious cholesterol thrown in free). And it does not end there, the return journey incorporates a 3 course evening meal, with silver service and vegetarians catered for to boot. A far cry from the 'Football Specials' of the Seventies, which were regularly smashed up by 'feather-cut' sporting yobbos, in flared jeans and ribbed 'star' jumpers, as T Rex blasted from the carriage speakers.

Inevitably, and to be fair, understandably, the Cup Final merchandising sales push is now in full swing, with all types of banners, wigs, shirts and retro regalia available from the 'Villa Village,' which basks in the momentous shadow of the stadium. A club of this stature of course has no problem setting up 'on-line' sales arrangements for punters with access to PCs, and the strapline, 'Wembley is Only a Click Away,' is born.

Meanwhile, Graham Poll is set to officiate his first FA Cup Final. And in verification of how highly rated he is, a couple of weeks after the Wembley showpiece, Mr Poll will be flying out to join UEFA's finest in Euro 2000, where he will be the only English referee.

Like any manager of a successful side, Gregory is having to contend with his stars getting called up for international duty at increasingly inopportune moments. Accordingly, Joachim's recent efforts have been rewarded by a call to duty for St Vincent and the Grenadines in a World Cup qualifier against St Kitts and Nevis. And on Friday 14 April, he is sitting in Heathrow Airport ready to fly to St Kitts for the action.

In the meantime however, FIFA have contacted the St Vincent FA to warn them that Joachim is ineligible due to competing for England in the World Youth Championships in 1993, thus committing himself to Blighty for ever. The FA phone Villa and Gregory makes a frantic, but fruitless call to Heathrow. It is too late and 'Jocky' has boarded the plane for his pointless trip. Four hours into the flight, the captain is at last contacted and relays the news to Jocky, who is not best pleased as he desperately wants to play international football. So the worthless flight goes on, with only a few hours on the beach and a family reunion ahead to soften the blow. Needless to say, this does little to assuage the anger of JG and the powers that be at Villa, who are far from happy at losing their man for tomorrow's game.

Villa are now off to the Capital for a warm up with Spurs, and JG will be staying over as he is set to make his second appearance in the London marathon. "I've been running six to ten miles every night round Sutton Coldfield for practice," explains Gregory. "And I've got some rousing stuff on minidisc to help me get round, including all my Bruce Springsteen albums, but I won't be running in a bandana!"

JG has a great love of music which he shares in particular with Villa secretary-director Steve Stride, and it has been known for them to sit up until the wee small hours together, strumming Beatles tunes on their guitars.

And Saturday 15 April proves to be a profitable visit to the capital in more ways than one. Many of the Holte End crew that we have got to know over the weeks describe the trip as "good practice for Wembley".

After about an hour of action, Villa minus Southgate and of course Joachim, are 2-0 down and on the ropes. But all is well in the end as they find their feet from nowhere courtesy of a 4 goal spree in 12 minutes, starting with a controversial penalty for Dublin. He follows this up almost immediately with a spectacular overhead kick. Next up Dublin turns provider for a classic Carbone effort and the comeback is topped off with an Allan Wright screamer, leaving Villa to run out 4-2 winners, and no further injuries into the bargain.

The press conference provides further entertainment, as referee Rob Harris comes into the spotlight. Bearing in mind the old adage of a good official being one that is not noticed, a referee will normally only attract such attention for the wrong reasons. And this is no exception. Harris is of course the chap that was suspended earlier in the season, for allowing an extra Tranmere man on the pitch, during their FA Cup Fourth Round victory over Sunderland and grabbing all the Sunday headlines in the process. And today he was at it again, allowing Villa back into the game with a controversial penalty, for which it appears he did not see the (handball) offence being (allegedly) committed by Tottenham's Iversen. He went by the word of a frantically signalling linesman, but neither party could identify the culprit and the press are having a field day. Dublin gratefully slotted away the spot kick to spark off the Villa revival and convert Mr Harris's name to mud, at least in North London. Even Gregory, who benefited massively from the decision cannot resist a (traditional) dig:

"Yeah, the penalty put us right back in it. But Iversen should've been sent off for the handball, except Mr Harris didn't know who the player was that did it. He got the minutes silence right at the beginning though!"

On Sunday 17 April, JG is all set for 26 miles of torture and punters interested in more detail would do well to read his autobiography 'The Boss". He describes everything from how he was done for speeding on the way there, to his innermost thoughts during the race, including how he focused his mind on Villa lifting the Cup, as inspiration to beat the pain. JG completes in 5 hours 5 minutes and nets 10 grand for charity.

Good tidings have arrived at Villa Park as Gareth Southgate looks set to resurface, if not against Leicester on Saturday, then Sunderland a week later. He's made one appearance since March when he picked up an Achilles problem against Liverpool, and that was in the Semi-Final against Bolton.

With the injury situation in general looking a little on the dodgy side, JG insists that he will still take full-strength teams to both forthcoming testimonial trips. First up is Whaddon Road, home of our old mate (ooarr) Stevie Cotterill's Cheltenham Town on 25 April (10 years service for player, Chris Banks). And following this, an ironic trip to Swansea City's Vetch Field on 9 May, where a certain John Hollins, of Chelsea 1970 FA Cup winning fame is to be found in the hot-seat. But the match against the Swans will be in recognition of Keith Walker, their Scottish stalwart, who left to join Merthyr Tydfil earlier in the season for his first managerial job.

Cutting back to Cotterill, he deserves a special mention here, having taken loads of time out to chat to the authors when in their role of Non-League journalists in the Robins' more humble days. His prize quote from that era being:

"League status? Ooh, Oi dunno 'bout thaaat!"

By Thursday 20 April, League action is again on the horizon. This time it's prodigal sons all round as Leicester City are the guests, with a certain Mr Little at the helm plus an albeit laid-up Mr Collymore among his employees, which surely necessitates the removal of all fire extinguishers from the vicinity.

Further spice is added to the forthcoming attraction, by the fact that Villa have never beaten these particular Midlands rivals in the Premiership, or for the last 12 years for that matter. And Leicester knocked Villa out of this season's Worthington Cup at the Semi-Final stage, so there is incentive a-plenty and a little 'edge' is guaranteed.

Collymore in the meantime, will not be drawn on the subject of Gregory, but does insist that after bagging a hat trick for the Foxes against Sunderland, he received congratulatory phone calls from Dublin, Hendrie and Villa backroom boy Steve Harrison!

"We've got two challenges on Saturday," declares Gregory. "One is to keep this fantastic run of ours going and the other to bloody well beat Leicester for once. And as for Stan, I hope his fracture doesn't keep him out for too long and I wish him well!"

The encounter of Saturday 22 April, has as much edge as promised, boiling over into a mass touchline brawl near the end, after Lee Hendrie pushes the self-destruct button, with a vicious tackle on Robbie Savage. Hendrie and Joachim were earlier brought on for Thompson and Dublin. Having twice taken the lead through Thompson and Merson, Villa are pegged back on both occasions and Leicester give a good account of themselves as they battle to a 2-2 draw and preserve the Villa duck.

In the press conference, Leicester boss Martin O'Neill is furious over Hendrie's foul, but JG simply states:

"These things happen. It's nothing to worry about. It's the first real setback in his life," explains Gregory. "It's been hard to accept, but he's coming to terms with it."

A relatively quiet week, culminates with the visit of Sunderland to Villa Park on Saturday 29 April and in front of 34,000, Villa dominate a good old fashioned '6 pointer,' but come away with a disappointing 1-1 draw, as Barry's second half opener is cancelled out by Quinn. Gregory's mood is boosted however, by a painless Southgate comeback, a standing ovation for Allan Thompson (obviously determined to 'make' JG pick him) and a stirring performance from Merson, spoiled only by a glaring miss.

After the game, JG and co pile into the Holte Suite for a lively and emotional Supporters Player of the Year 2000 Gala. And glaring miss or not, it is an emotional night for Merson as he scoops the award.

Gareth Barry wins the young player award and JG enhances this by adding that if there was any justice in the world, Barry would have ousted Harry Kewell and taken the PFA young player of the year award into the bargain.

Villa's penultimate league match on Saturday 6 May, ends with yet another late, expensive lapse. Having gone behind to an early Ehiogu own goal, they rampage back into a 2-1 lead thanks to the second half efforts of Hendrie and Dublin. But John Hartson, sent on out of desperation, delivers a kick in the teeth to Villa's chances of catching Chelsea in the Premiership table, as he nets a late equaliser and earns Wimbledon a stay of execution.

Meanwhile Chippenham Town's agonising FA Cup exit is put to one side as they take on Deal Town in the FA Vase Final and Tommy Saunders becomes the youngest manager ever to lead a team out at Wembley - a record previously held by Stevie Cotterill at Cheltenham in their Non-League days. And this feat is made all the sweeter by the fact that the Bluebirds enjoyed a couple of particularly glorious victories on the way. First up was the Quarter-Final against Bedlington Terriers, whose pedigree includes being last year's Vase runners-up and '98-'99 season FA Cup conquerors of Second Division Colchester United! And in the Semi-Final, Saunders' boys drove past North West Counties League high-fliers Vauxhall GM, whose Vase spec from this year includes a 5-1 drubbing of none other than red-hot favourites Taunton Town. It was no mean feat to dispatch either of these sides, but the 20,000 plus crowd, including quite literally half of Chippenham, witnessed a Deal Town victory, secured by a goal in the 87th minute. Rest assured though, that the boys still returned home to a veritable hero's welcome.

Taunton meanwhile, continued unabated after what was a massive Vase disappointment for them and have now won the Western League title once again. They cannot however be promoted, as ground improvements are not yet complete, so the runners-up will now be given that option. And we are pleased to report that our friends at Mangotsfield United have not only secured second place, but also been accepted into the Southern League for next season!

And this in many ways has been a successful period for many of the acquaintances made earlier in our journey, as Burnley today secure automatic promotion to the First Division, with a 2-1 win at Scunthorpe.

Despite the death of a Swansea supporter at Millmooor over the weekend, the scheduled testimonial goes ahead at Swansea City on Tuesday 9 May, but is overshadowed by excellent news for Villa, which bears out our theory regarding just how big a club they are. It has just been announced by Deloitte and Touche, the financial consultancy giants, that the club's pre-tax profits from season 98-99 come in at a cool £20.2 million, which is bettered only by Man United. "Sure, the sale of Milosevic and Yorke have helped," admits financial director Mark Ansell, "but it's such great news for the club and it proves that our ambitious policies are now bearing fruit, both on and off the pitch! And what's more, we will carry out our responsibility to the fans, by making sure we keep signing the big names, to secure our status as a big club, without putting up prices!"

Meanwhile at Vetch Field, Villa despatch the newly crowned Division 3 Champions 3-0. After the season's second poignant ceremony, the Swans put up a brave show, but are simply outclassed by a Villa side containing the big names that JG promised. Wright, Carbone and Joachim inflict the damage and Hendrie, Dublin and Taylor all come through unscathed to increase their chances of involvement on the big day. The game is played in good spirits, with Swansea's keeper ending up at centre forward and Hollins and his assistant John Curtis also getting a run towards the end. And at the final whistle, 6,000 Swansea fans swamp the Villa players in search of autographs and photos.

The next day the club announces the arrangements for those not yet ticketed-up for the FA Cup Final. On a first come first serve basis, punters must use an official application envelope and enclose their home-game ticket stubs, so that scores and eligibility can be calculated. The points system is as follows:

Stubs for these Premiership games are worth 3 points:
Bradford, Derby, Leicester, Middlesbrough, Sheffield Wednesday, Southampton, Sunderland (!), Watford, West Ham and Wimbledon.

And the following Premiership matches, 2 points:
Arsenal, Chelsea, Coventry, Everton, Leeds, Liverpool, Newcastle and Spurs.

While these cup games will earn you a paltry 1 point:
Leeds, Leicester, Southampton, Man Utd, Chester and Darlington.

Consequently, you do not have to be a brain surgeon to understand that the higher your total scores on the stubs, the sooner you get to apply.

Meanwhile the marketing machine is in full flow, as next season's home kit is revealed in timely fashion, although some replica tops, complete with 'FA Cup, Wembley Final' embroidery, are available at 'vastly reduced prices,' due to 'slight imperfections.'

While all this is going on, some players, although assured of free entry to the game, are still wondering whether they will get to take their new suits off on the day. Steve Stone is one. He has missed the last 5 Premiership matches and the trip to Swansea and time is running out. This week, he and fellow Geordie

Hamstring victim Steve Watson have been undergoing a tough rehabilitation programme, while all around them, JG's Final touches are being put to the squad's preparations.

With punters camped outside the club offices to make sure of getting their tickets for the Final, it's time for a 'bit of a do' for the more privileged, on the evening of Wednesday 10 May, in the form of the Players Poll Winners Party.

And in a carbon copy of the supporters' equivalent, Paul Merson scoops the player's player of the year award, ahead of David James, while Gareth Barry is again honoured as the young counterpart.

Gareth Southgate gets Clubman of the Year, which presumably has different connotations in professional circles to the poor guy that wins the 'parks' equivalent, that being the mug who turns up every week, runs the line, washes the kit and still doesn't get a game!

Alan Wright wins, Goal of the Season for his 25 yard volley at White Hart Lane, a late contender, beating Carbone's best of 3 against Leeds in the FA Cup Fifth Round.

Having woken up to tabloid stories of how Saturday's referee, Graham Poll is a Chelsea fan, around 40,000 pack Villa Park on Sunday 14 May to witness the visit of the almighty Man U. A lacklustre game ensues, with a Sherringham goal separating the sides. David James is absent due to a "slight knock." Hmm. Well, hopefully it isn't too bad, as Kevin Keegan has given him the nod for the squad at England's forthcoming first-team friendlies, against Brazil (Wembley), Ukraine (Wembley) and Malta (Valetta). He is to join regulars, Seaman, Wright and Martyn in the party, which KK will look to whittle down to the final Euro 2000 hardcore, on the night of Ukraine's visit.

As we move into the final week of our journey, JG gets a phone call from Graham Poll, assuring him that yesterday's stories were complete fabrication and of his complete neutrality. Having given counter-assurances that this was never in doubt, Gregory goes off to join his players within the ever-increasing realm of press conferences, radio/TV/newspaper interviews and webcasts.

As the week progresses, the pressure does nothing but intensify. JG however, handles it and protects the players.

The Grims Dyke Hotel, Harrow is the retreat for Villa pre-final day. JG is looking forward to this as it allows for proper preparation away from the press. Prior to their departure however, David James is asked relentlessly about his

Final appearance with Liverpool which culminated in a bad punch resulting with United notching their winner. He confidently assures everybody there will be "no gift wrapped opportunities" this time around.

The training on Friday 19 May, takes place at Broughinge Road, Hertfordshire home Borehamwood FC - current residents of the Isthmian (Ryman) League Premier Division and after the tactical discussion, JG leaves a simple message on the tactic board:

'HISTORY IS IN YOUR HANDS!'

Sky Sports Cup Final build up provides the sole entertainment for the Villa Boys on Friday night. It is not a patch on Brian Moore's Seventies equivalent; 'Who Will Win the Cup'. Older readers will revel in the memory of Brian and guests awarding points to both sides for various attributes and totting them up to give their prediction for the following day - all over dinner and awkward conversation at the Moore residence. Oh, great TV.

Tonight the coverage is admittedly much more thorough, although, surely that is what Cup Final Grandstand and World of Sport used to be for and while we are on the subject, whatever happened to "Cup Final, It's a Knockout"? Anyway, so comprehensive is tonight's TV that we are even treated to footage of Graham Poll having his hair cut.

Eventually, the morning of Saturday 20 May arrives, with, of all things babies, dominating the news, courtesy of headlines declaring the pregnancy of Zoe Ball and early morning news programmes, announcing the birth of Prime Minister Tony Blair's fourth child, Leo, just after midnight. The behaviour of Arsenal fans in Copenhagen before last Wednesday's UEFA Cup Final against Galatasaray, also receives plenty of copy. But the back pages and pullouts are of course, in FA Cup overdrive:

Opening with a shot of James and de Goey holding a cake in the shape of Wembley Stadium, and the headline 'Piece of Cake'. The Mirror plays on the perceived brash and arrogant attitude of Gregory and Vialli's more softly spoken nature, billing the Final as 'Smashie v Nicey.'

It also features a major piece entitled 'Goodbye Wembley,' focussing of course on the highs and lows of the great amphitheatre of sport over the years and its impending destruction.

Meanwhile, at the Grims Dyke Hotel, Steve Watson, Alan Thompson,

Najwan Ghrayib, Neil Cutler and Richard Walker learn that they will stay in their suits for the whole day after being named as the unlucky squad members not to make the bench.

Outside Wembley in the surrounding streets, all the pubs are packed to the rafters, with clientele spilling out onto the pavements. The Post House, is clearly a 'Chelsea' boozer. A banner hanging from the upstairs window, announces this, and blue shirts squeeze from the doorway. Trouble would seem to be a home banker as a number of pubs are 'mixed' and it becomes clear that Chelsea fans are in the ascendancy. However, police uniforms are numerous and the number of people mingling with the crowd holding 2 way radios spell a large presence of plain clothed officialdom.

Coming back in towards the stadium, we see the latest craze in action, everyday punters travelling in hired limousines. One goes by with a blue and white scarf hanging out of the window. Further on, the first signs of unrest. A heated verbal exchange is taking place between two groups of supporters regarding the merits of their respective sides and along the way a Chelsea fan sits on a wall with blood trickling from his head.

The ubiquitous cup final message!

The perennial wigs and hats (jester–style seems still to be the most popular) are of course out in abundance. One Villa fan though, has gone above and beyond the call of duty, with (shaved) head, face and neck, all fully covered in wide bands of claret and blue paint.

Immediately outside the Twin Towers, the numbers are gathering. The police are trying to control the flow of human traffic, but at one awful point it seems as though there is going to be a major crush. We duck out of it and fight our way to the side. A police officer demands to know why we wish to leave the flow. "Panic attack mate!" He is happy with this and lets us out. We stand on a grass verge and wait. Thankfully, the crush comes to nothing.

And amazingly, despite the Villa and Chelsea songs ringing through the air, the unashamed display of club colours and the addition of alcohol, there is no further evidence of trouble.

We eventually fight our way to the media and hospitality area to sort our press passes out. A clerical cock–up means that we get to see the game, but may not be allowed access to the press conference. Bloody typical. We come back down the steps, past Brendan Batson, then Brian Moore. Bet they don't have these problems. "Hello Brian" we say, as if he was our lifelong mate. Brian is still the consummate professional though, and cheerily says "Hiya lads" in return making us feel really important.

So then it's a final walk to our entrance. Once more past the money–grabbing portakabins. What? Ten quid for a programme? Then through representatives of the British Olympic Team, reduced to begging outside football grounds for funding. Surely the National Lottery is supposed to cater for such things?

If only they could win 11 gold medals or something, they might be worth supporting.

Inside the stadium, we take our seats and discover the gratis, 'Last FA Cup Final at the Original Wembley' pennants beneath them. And as the announcer goes banging on forever about "this historic day at the twin towers," Geoff Hurst leads 72 schoolkids around the track, all dressed in the colours of the previous FA Cup winners. AXA of course have taken their rightful advertising space and the centre circle is dominated by the Cup sponsors' logo. While the ex–England hero does his Pied–Piper act, both teams are out on the pitch in their New Suits as befits the tradition, Villa in grey Hugo Boss and Chelsea in dark blue Armani.

On the pitch, Leslie Garrett belts out her version of 'Abide With Me,' the fireworks at last erupt and it is time for the teams to make their grand entrance.

Led by Adrian Titcombe, who unbeknown to him has graced both the beginning and end of our odyssey, they emerge from the players' entrance, and are immediately hit by a wall of Villa sound, provided by the fans at the tunnel end. Looking around at the bubbling oceans of claret and blue, JG is visibly overwhelmed.

And in front of him, 10 year old Matthew Stride, son of Club secretary Steve and mascot for the day looks around in wonderment.

Then the drum roll leads into the National Anthem and seeing Zola, Weah, Poyet, Desailly, Vialli et al, squaring up against him, JG shouts over his famous quote to Dennis Wise:

"Oi, sing up Wisey, you're the only bugger who knows the words!"

The sides line up in traditional colours. Villa in this season's thick, claret and blue vertical stripes, with claret shorts and socks and Chelsea in blue shirts, blue shorts and white socks.

The stage is finally set for what many predict will be a dour contest, between the fifth and sixth placed Premiership clubs, with seven league points between them.

Mr Poll, is all set in the middle and away we go. The largely home-grown Villa (or 'Little England' as dubbed by some in the press box) from our 'second city' with their mixture of youth and experience, versus the cosmopolitan capital boys, with one Englishman and only two players under thirty.

It does not take Boateng and Wise long to get up close and personal, as the former stops the little man in full flight and sends him sprawling, with a shuddering tackle–cum attempt at leg amputation minus anaesthetic. To his credit, Wisey gets up and gets on with it, giving Boateng a friendly, ' I forgive you, it's a man's game after all' – type slap on the back (whilst no doubt already plotting revenge). Graham Poll decides a free kick to Chelsea is in order and the Villa bench (and a somewhat more elevated JG) rise as one in disgust.

Meanwhile Ian Taylor, making his first start since the Bolton game, is charging about as if to make up for lost time, and registers his intent with a brace of 'robust' challenges on Deschamps and Melchiot respectively.

And Chelsea take not a minute longer to show theirs, as white–booted Weah and Zola exchange passes to violate the Villa danger zone, but James is quick to demonstrate his own agenda, and is there first to make a determined clearance. Buffered only by a gift from Leboeuf to Carbone, which the Italian blasts too close to Desailly from outside the box, James is shortly at it again, comfortably clutching, a crisp, long–range Wise volley, set up by good combination play from Poyet and Zola. The shot was struck with such ferocity that James was forced back a pace, but he was never going to let go and looks solid as a rock, so far!

It is difficult to establish any superiority with almost inevitably, both sides struggling to find their rhythm.

Then, bang! Wise exacts his inevitable revenge on Boateng, but the referee plays the advantage, and a poor Chelsea clearance is pounced upon by Merson who blasts a volley just over. But Mr Poll has not forgotten the illegal challenge and Wise goes into the book.

JG takes a trip down to the bench, to brief ex-Liverpool man Kevin Macdonald, who will relay all messages onto the pitch.

Nothing brings the game to life though. And the first half ends minus entertainment and goals.

The quality and negativity of the game brings smart-arse journo comments "Let's just cut straight to the penalties!"

Meanwhile, the ubiquitous Cup Final band do their thing during the interval, to keep the pageantry going until the last. But towards the end of the break a young fan from the Villa end, jumps off his seat, scales the perimeter and charges onto the now empty pitch. The boys in the luminous coats are soon chasing him of course and he leads them a merry, if not pointless dance for about a minute, before an unforced error makes him lose his footing and security are able to pounce on him. Without wishing to seem ungrateful for the break in monotony that the lad has graciously supplied, we have to ask from his point of view, why did he do it? It is so obvious that he will miss the rest of the match and have to go through the hassle of whatever charges are pressed against him, not to mention the alleged risk of a good kicking! A Villa fan puts forward a theory:

"Perhaps he wants to be the last person to get chucked out of Wembley!"

As the second half continues where the first half started, Villa's driving force of Boateng and Taylor shows signs of losing it's organisation and Merson's runs are just not penetrating today. Slowly, but surely Wise and Deschamps begin to dominate the midfield and Chelsea wrestle the initiative away. Then James' worst nightmare happens. He fluffs a low Di Matteo cross and the ball runs loose to Wise, who blasts it in. Wise sets off on a celebratory run, that takes him virtually half way round the stadium, only to be brought down from Cloud Nine, the referee's assistant having raised his flag for offside against Weah. James, has a look of massive relief on his face, as though he is experiencing that great feeling when you wake up from a bad dream and realise that everything is OK after all!

The game slows, probably due to the infamous strength sapping turf. Short of match practise Southgate receives treatment.

Chelsea pressure starts to build and James drops a free-kick straight to Roberto Di Matteo who slams it first–time into the roof of the net. This prompts well over half the stadium to erupt, into what is, quite simply, the biggest demonstration of support we have ever witnessed, for any one club, at any game we have attended. And having scored the fastest FA Cup Final goal at 43 seconds in 1997, he may also now have notched the last one at Wembley. Twenty-five yards last time. Two point five yards this time.

With the kind of urgency that only being 1-0 down in an FA Cup Final with eighteen minutes to go can provide, Villa set about redeeming the situation. Their efforts are rewarded by an error from De Goey, who parries the ball lamely to the feet of Carbone, presenting him with a glorious opportunity to level the score. A helpless De Goey looks on and awaits his punishment. Carbone shoots …but it's a real powder–puff effort and although de Goey is nowhere, Leboeuf is well–placed to easily clear off the line.

On the Villa bench, Joachim and Stone can be seen on mobiles and are shortly in action. Taylor and Carbone are off. No histrionics!.

As time ticks away, a couple of scrambles in the Chelsea goalmouth produce only adrenaline and the score remains the same.

But Delaney, having managed to stay on for the full duration this time, pushes forward for Villa regardless and sends a cross over. Ehiogu arrives, but he cannot direct his header at goal and it sails harmlessly over. Still all is not lost. Melchiot handles the ball on Villa's left flank, deep in the Chelsea half. Now James arrives in the Chelsea box, Schmeichel–style, desperate to atone. But his presence does not generate the same result as the red–nosed one's Champion's League Final capers and Mr Poll eventually ends the agony, or rather begins it for James, who promptly collapses to his knees in tears.

He spends a long while on his back, hands covering his face until Merson hauls him to his feet. But he wheels away and throws one glove about twenty yards to his left and the other a similar distance to his right, rushes to the touchline and collapses again, determined to be alone in his misery. A TV cameraman spots the scoop and circles him accordingly, but is sent packing by Taylor. James just sits there. Face buried in his jersey.

Similarly, frustrated by his ineffectiveness, Dublin too is seated on the turf, as

Southgate plays the captain's role, with his arm around the back of the striker's head as he tries to console the inconsolable.

In contrast of course, about 50 yards away, the Chelsea players are jumping all over each other and Vialli runs on to the pitch, grabs Wise by the ears and plants a massive kiss on his chops. And Desailly jumps up and down in the centre circle punching the air

Villa go up to collect their loser's medals minus JG.

In a display of insurgency as their heroes climb the steps, the Villa fans chant: "Eng - erland, Eng – erland, Eng – erland!"

But in a move unprecedented in Cup Final history, although in keeping with today's press-purveyed babe and suckling theme, a couple of Chelsea players grab their offspring and bring them onto the pitch. Absolutely sickening. What happened to the man's game where women and kids were seen but not heard! Consequently, Matias Poyet, plus Jade and Hugo Leboeuf, all in Chelsea kits are now celebrating on the lush green turf with their dads, a la David and Brooklyn Beckham, when Man United won the Championship a few days ago. A steward's attempt at dissuading Leboeuf from such activity is brushed aside. Having seen this, Zola follows suit and Wise decides he wants a piece of the action too. So he grabs five month old son Henry, from wife Claire and carries his tiny lookalike, in Chelsea top with 'Daddy' across the back and diminutive Adidas trainers, up the famous 39 steps, to collect the old pot from the Duke of Kent.

As Wise lifts the Cup aloft, with little Henry in the other hand, the roof is almost blown off the stand by the ecstatic cheers and wild celebrations of the Chelsea faithful. The players stand in a line and raise their arms to acknowledge the adulation. The youngsters old enough to mimic do likewise, while little Henry can only gurgle with delight in the arms of his father.

"I might never be able to do this again," gasps Wise, exhausted from 90 minutes toil and the carrying around of two heavy objects. "So when I saw Frank, Gus and Franco's kids, I really wanted to take Henry up there to collect the Cup with me. I don't think for a minute he will remember it, but he can look at it on video in years to come and say he was there at the last Wembley Final. I hope I haven't started a trend. It was just an off the cuff thing. But I'm delighted that I did it.

"Mind you, I thought I was going to drop one of them, so I had to cling on tight - to Henry that is. If I had to drop one, it would have to have been the Cup. Can you imagine the headlines otherwise?"

Musically, retro is big and obviously this message has got to the Wembley crowd.

"Blue is the colour, Football is the game,
We're all together and winning is our aim,
So cheer us all through the sun and rain,
'Cos Chelsea, Chelsea is our name."

The rendition of this by the fans, many of which will not even have been born at the time of its release, is truly deafening and we find ourselves tapping our feet and singing along. Even for us, as neutrals (give or take one author's boyhood flirtation with Osgood, Webb, Harris et al) this, among all the triumph and tragedy we have witnessed on our journey, is – perhaps fittingly - the most intense inducement for the rise of the hairs, on the back of our proverbial necks. This is some show from the Chelsea lot. Some show indeed. And the music goes on. When all the songs have been played, they are played again and then again. The sight of countless blue banners waving at the Chelsea end, not forgetting the pockets of their support among the Villa faithful is truly awesome. More success for Vialli and a long career ahead of him with the Blues is assured!

The Chelsea players and respective offspring link hands and charge towards their supporters, ending the run with a mass dive. This makes the fans go wilder still and in the Villa end a fat Chelsea skinhead takes off his yellow away top, turns round and waves it over his head, dancing all the while, like Buster Bloodvessell. A few yards away, his slightly more presentable colleagues mercilessly pester a half-tidy female steward for a celebratory, slobbering, 'snog.' She eventually consents to the middle ground of a hug, more to keep the peace than have any kind of physical contact.

Back on the pitch, the players link hands again for another belly flop, transporting their devotees to new levels of bliss.

In truth, for the neutral, again this has been a yawn–inducing Final of the highest proportions and were the cheers directly proportional to pure entertainment, you would be able to hear a pin drop.

Steadily increasing attitudes of tribalism however, dictate that to get one over your rivals is paramount and this is at least partially reflected in the intensity of the celebrations. But at the first sign of their subsidence, our next task is to get into the press conference, so we scamper to the media room accordingly. The boys in blazers are at the door, but (and don't try this at home) our silver tongues are soon in action again and entry secured accordingly.

The Wembley press–room is a somewhat Spartan affair, with no buffet, although we have reason to believe that one may have taken place in a separate hospitality area, to which, we subsequently failed to gain admittance, in a very poor show of blagging indeed.

The décor is atrocious. No wonder they are knocking the place down. The infamous interview area is bare, with school chairs, draughty windows, and sparse pictures of legends on the walls. These consist of a number of famous Wembley events, namely Henry Cooper standing over the prostrate form of Muhammad Ali; Alan Shearer in another Wembley defeat; Beckham & Yorke celebrating with said FA Cup on the pitch; and a black and white print of Nat Lofthouse holding the cup aloft in 1958. Behind the loosely assembled top table is a photo-montage of Dutch, Italian and German internationals and somewhat bizarrely a colour photo of Michael Jackson.

As Luca walks in, a Police patrol helicopter is creating such a noise outside, that when the press conference commences, the shy, softly spoken manager is being drowned out. A member of staff is swiftly despatched to close the windows, which improves things considerably, although leaving them far from perfect. Luca is now however, just about audible as he talks into his large knotted tie. "Well, it wasn't the most spectacular game and I think we won our victory today through the way we defended. I think all our defenders were spot on and the whole team worked really hard when they weren't in possession of the ball.

"It took a free kick to win the match, but even before that we had a couple of chances. I'm pleased, because the reason we put so much into this game is because we want to win things. It hasn't been a great season in the Premiership, but I think we have done marvellously well in the Champions League and now in the FA Cup as well.

"It wasn't easy to perform at our best because when you feel the pressure, your legs and brain don't work as well as they can. But we realised at half–time that we had to step it up to win the game. And we did.

"And you know, Desailly did a magnificent job as did all the other three in the back four. He was fantastic. He won everything in the air and we knew that was vital against Villa's long ball, which Dion Dublin was always looking to flick on

"We worked hard to get our hands on some silverware this year, so this is the best possible reward for a great season. It helps me a lot in terms of credibility. I'm a young manager and I've got to show what I say and what I try to do is the right thing in order to get the people at Chelsea to follow me and support me.

"We want to improve the team and while money will be a little tighter without the income from the Champion's League. I have to say that I had a meeting with Colin Hutchinson and Ken Bates the other day and we all came to the conclusion, that while this team are not the youngest, they are not too bad, so there's no need to do too much.

"I'm too demanding. I forget that 61 matches at their best is impossible and I get pissed off! Instead of coming fifth we can be very close to the top. But without the distraction of the Champion's League maybe we can be a little more competitive, especially when we visit the less-exciting places, which is something we didn't do this year and I feel we let people down in that way. But we will aim for the Premiership title next season!

"Right now I'm just relieved. I need a break and this win will allow me to recharge the batteries, wind down for a while and come back with a desire to be even more successful. I'm glad we didn't have to enter the InterToto Cup. It can affect the rest of your season if you start too early. Look at Juventus. They've collapsed over the last couple of months and I don't want that to happen to us. Without the InterToto we've more chance of winning the Title

"We are improving too and my thoughts would not have been different if we'd lost 1-0. We're a great team and a great squad. The fans love me and I love them. We are getting married soon! And there won't be a divorce!

"But guys, let's not talk too much about the future. It's been a long season and now we have to celebrate the win, then have a break. Now I have to say, I'm bloody tired you know!"

And with that he's off. A very pleasant, shy, articulate Italian who you wouldn't know had done anything worth a mention today.

The disconsolate figure of JG eventually arrives and takes position in front of those that displease him most. He is not the biggest fan of the press. It is not difficult to spot the immediate differences between the managers. Gregory speaks confidently, clearly and although with similar articulation, with a much more recognisable manager speak.

And the inevitable first question regarding how he feels come forth.

"I don't think we lost it. Chelsea won it," he replies. "They got a lucky break and we didn't and they took their half-chance. That's the only thing that's helped them to win the Cup, because I don't think there was anything between the two teams.

"I don't think we created enough goal-scoring opportunities, which has been our problem all season, but having said that we put in an enormous amount of effort in the first period and I thought we did exceptionally well during that time. Certainly at half time we thought we could get something out of the game. But we didn't get a break and they did. The lads couldn't have given much more, we were just beaten by a lucky break!

"It's going to take a long time to get over this one, if you ever do and I don't think you ever do. But it makes you more determined to come back and do it next time. We can definitely use today as an incentive for next season. We'll have another day and we WILL be back!"

As predictable as the first question was, nobody could have foreseen the second, which must rank as one of the most surreal moments behind Eric Cantona's seagull and trawler rantings, as a female reporter asks:

"Do you think Luc Nilis would have made the difference today?"

A pregnant pause ensues as the gathered journos exchange incredulous looks. "You're not from Belgium are you?" responds JG. "Yes how did you guess?" "Oh Just a hunch. Next question please!"

The conference continues along a more orthodox and predictable line.

"David James? Yeah he's very low. But my lot don't point fingers at other people, unlike some clubs in the Premiership, they hold their hands up. And David has openly come in the dressing room and done that."

"I still think he's the best English keeper. Yeah I'm slightly biased because I live with the guy, day in, day out, and if what he did today is considered an error, then that's two he's made all season, including today. Keepers always get the blame because they can't afford to make mistakes. But players can miss open goals at the other end and tend not to get criticised for it."

Authors' thoughts: Hmm. Dean Holdsworth may have something to say about that.

"The ball could have fallen to anybody when David dropped it. If it had fallen to Ugo it would have ended up in the back of the stand, but it fell nicely to Di Matteo. That's the way it goes sometimes. David's made enormous strides since his Liverpool days, when he got blamed for everything that went on in front of him. No, he won't get any stick from me. He's had an outstanding season. He's shown his worth to us and I'd say that he is one of the best keepers in Europe without any question.

"Without doubt, if he was called upon to play for England he would do a good job.

216

"And don't forget it was his saves that got us to the Final. He's done unbelievable things to get us here in the first place. I'm not going to criticise him or anybody else for that matter. No, our problem lay in the last third of the pitch. We just didn't do enough there and that's pretty much been the story of our season.

And you know you do find out more about players in this type of situation. I just wish it hadn't been today that I had to find out!

"Being at Wembley? That doesn't mean a great deal to me, because we've got nothing to show for it. There was a lot of blood, sweat and tears and fantastic support and a tremendous sense of pride in the bunch of blokes I've got in the dressing room. Our lads couldn't have given much more. But we got beaten with a lucky break. And I don't think I've ever seen anything like the atmosphere in our dressing room after the game. We were all so disappointed because we really believed it was going to be our day!

And now, perhaps the Interwhatsitsname lies in wait for us. I'll discuss it with the chairman and then we'll see. West Ham entered and had an exceptionally good start to this season and a terrible dip in form later on. Whether you can attribute either to their competitive appearances in the middle of July, I don't know. We might find out. But our main aim is the Championship!"

That is the end of the official conference, but remarkably JG is cornered again for a further 20 minutes before he can get out of the room, in a question session that seems to go over ground already covered. He then leaves the room when the journalists follow him again and hold a 3rd impromptu conference in the corridor. We never did find out why.

Back outside the emptied stadium, the Chelsea players can now be seen leaving the twin towers and entering their coach by osmosis. They largely ignore requests from the happy band of about a hundred fans, looking for crumbs from the rich man's table, in the form of autographs and the like. Scraps were subsequently given however, in the form of a £10,000 cheque from the player's pool, to the children's ward at the Chelsea and Westminster Hospital, the birthplace of young Henry Wise and a certain master Leo Blair to boot.

Villa board their coach to be greeted by Champagne, which does little to lift the spirits.

Back in civvy street, 99% of the departing crowd seem in good spirits, but there are pockets of discontent. A heated exchange is taking place between two groups of couples, all seemingly in the thirtysomething age group and certainly old enough to know better. Incredibly, time is being wasted on a discussion over who has had the better season and one Villa woman is screaming her head off about it:

"Well you'll do fuck all in Europe!"

On the next street corner, a couple of middle-aged men, one Villa, one Chelsea cannot agree on whether the latter's team deserved the win today and this one looks close to blows as well.

And finally, a family group of Chelsea walk past a number of 'thirtysomething' Villa blokes, one of which stops a little Chelsea boy, aged about seven, to give him a Villa flag:

"Ere yow are son, here's a souvenir for ya!"

Harmless enough in print maybe, but you have to be there to realise that the guy is taking the piss.

"No thanks. Yur. Rubbish," screeches the youngster. "Villa crap, Chelsea forever!"

"Go on son, take it."

"Look, fuck off mate!" Instructs a Chelsea elder.

"I was only bein' friendlaye," says the Villa bloke.

"No you wasn't you was taking the piss!"

And so it goes on, with more of each group gradually becoming involved. We take a while to get past them but the argument rages on ad infinitum.

And amazingly, there are more of these 'conversations' at various points on the way back, all at various levels of 'friendliness', but each totally partisan, with no-one seeing reason, let alone the futility factor. However, none of this is hardcore violence and there are no exchanges of blows to be seen. Certainly if fists do fly, it will be 'spur of the moment' stuff.

Villa end their day at The Grosvenor House Hotel in London, with the obligatory Villa post-match banquet. It isn't a party and nobody is looking forward to the civic reception planned for the next day.

On Sunday 21 May, in Birmingham's Centenary Square, the 'homecoming' is greeted by another ocean of claret and blue as around 5,000 Villa fans turn up to welcome the lads back to the second city. Mercifully for James, the papers have centred mainly on the boredom factor associated with the Final and relatively little has been made of his gaffe. All is forgiven it seems and good cheer is once again in the air as Dave Woodhall of Villa fanzine, Heroes and Villains jokes:

"As we've been saying all week, Villa's name was on the Cup. Unfortunately, we didn't realise that it had been spelt wrongly!" Even David James is out to face the journos. Even so 'Calamity James' headlines seem inevitable.

The Chelsea tour is somewhat more celebratory. As it reaches Stamford Bridge, the beaming boss disembarks and takes the Cup along the perimeter fencing, allowing fans to touch it as he goes. The enormity of winning the FA Cup may be under severe scrutiny this year, but try telling that to any of this lot.

"Now for the Title," is Vialli's rabble–rousing message.

As a final postscript to the Chelsea victory, our opening concerns regarding the current validity of the Cup are illustrated in fine detail. The manager who has won the once most coveted cup in British football is sacked, effectively for failing to achieve a top three finish in the league. The famous silverware was not even considered as Mr Bates wielded another axe and terminated Gianluca's reign at the Bridge, while they still held the Cup. Still, at least they will defend it in the first Non-Wembley final since 1923. And even Manchester United may be entering.

Chelsea fans in buoyant mood

The Players

CHAPTER 2

Mangotsfield United

Tony Court, Gary Thomas, Danny Hallett, Lee Barlass, Dave Elsey, Gareth Loyden, Neil Rosslee, Nigel Gillard, Martin Boyle, Darren Edwards, Noel O'Sullivan. Subs: Nick (Zubey) Wilson, Paul Cichy, Gary Davies, Andy Black.

Hungerford Town

Alan Churchward, Daniel Gray, Jamie Matthews, Andy Wollen, Martyn Churchward, Jason Brizell, Gary Horgan, Paul Donnelly, Mickey Durkin, Chris Brown, David Gee. Subs: Mark Jordan, Steve Thomas, Danny Stevens

CHAPTER 3

Mangotsfield United

Tony Court, Gary Thomas, Danny Hallett, Lee Barlass, Dave Elsey, Gareth Loyden, Neil Rosslee, Nathan Rudge, Martin Boyle, Darren Edwards Noel O'Sullivan. Subs: Nick Wilson, Nigel Gillard, Paul Cichy, Andy Black.

Odd Down

Mark Batters, Matthew Pike, Duncan Fear, Dave hare, Steve Fuller, Francis Hodges, Rob Lardner, Glen Witts, Shaun Wiles, Paul Keen, Dean Book. Subs: Jason Maggs, Jimmy Jordan, Alan Newman

CHAPTER 4

Odd Down

Mark Batters, Matthew Pike, Duncan Fear, Dave Hare, Steve Fuller, Francis Hodges, Rob Lardner, Paul Keen, Glen Witts, Dean Book. Subs: Jasom Naggs, Jimmy Jordan, J,Riccio

Mangotsfield United

Tony Court, Gary Davies, Danny Hallett, Lee Barlass, Dave Elsey, Gareth Loyden, Neil Rosslee, Nathan Rudge, Martin Boyle, Darren Edwards, Nick Wilson. Subs: Nigel Gillard, Paul Cichy, Noel O'Sullivan, Andy Black.

CHAPTER 5
Chippenham Town

Ian Jones, Richard Thompson, Nick Tiley, Iain Murphy, Lee Burns, John Woods, Lee Collier, Lea James, Tony Bennett, Steve Tweddle, Steve Campbell. Subs: Simon Charity, Mike Godwin, Tony Fortt, Darren Hobbs.

Mangotsfield United

Tony Court, Gary Davies, Danny Hallett, Lee Barlass, Dave Elsey, Neil Rosslee, Nathan Rudge, Noel O'Sullivan, Darren Edwards, Nigel Gillard. Subs: Paul Cichy, Marcus Bloomfield, Bradley Andrews, Andy Black, Robert Wrolley

CHAPTER 6
Chippenham Town

Ian Jones, Richard Thompson, Nick Tiley, Iain Murphy, Lee Burns, John Woods, Lee Collier, Lea James, Tony Bennett, Steve Tweddle, Steve Campbell. Subs: Simon Charity, Shane Andrews, Darren Hobbs, Steve Brown, Ian Harris.

Worthing

Lee Bray, Miles Rutherford, Mark Knee, Mark Burt, Adie Miles, Guy Rutherford, Simon James, Paul Thomas, Marc Rice, Simon Funnell, Ben Carrington. Subs: Lee Weston, Rob Craven, Gareth Donnelly, Neil Francis, Matthew May

CHAPTER 7
Worthing

Lee Bray, Miles Rutherford, Mark Knee, Mark Burt, Paul Kennett, Guy Rutherford, Simon James, Paul Thomas, Marc Rice, Simon Funnell, Ben Carrington. Subs: Adie Miles, Lee Weson, Matthew May, Tony Holden, Lee Cox

Chippenham Town

Ian Jones, Richard Thompson, Nick Tiley, Iain Murphy, Lee Burns, John Woods, Lee Collier, Lea James, Tony Bennett, Steve Tweddle, Steve Campbell. Subs: Simon Charity, Shane Andrews, Darren Hobbs, Steve Brown, Mark Cutler.

CHAPTER 8
Worthing

Lee Bray, Miles Rutherford, Mark Knee, Mark Burt, Paul Kennett, Guy Rutherford,

Simon James, Lee Cox, Marc Rice, Simon Funnell, Ben Carrington. Subs: Adie Miles, Lee Weston, Matthew may, Tony Holden, Paul Thomas.

Dover Athletic
Paul Hyde, Joe Dunne, James Virgo, Scott Davies, Lee Shearer, Jake Leberl, Dave Clarke, Simon Wormull, Mark Hynes, Steve Brown, Neil LeBihan. Subs: Matt Carruthers, Steve Norman, Joff Vansittart, Stuart Munday.

CHAPTER 9
Dover Athletic
Paul Hyde, Joe Dunne, James Virgo, Stuart Munday, Lee Shearer, Jake Leberl, Dave Clarke, Simon Wormull, Joff Vansittart, Matt Carruthers, Neil LeBihan. Subs: Steve Brown, Steve Norman, Mark Hynes, Scott Daniels, Andy Iga.

Worthing
Lee Bray, Miles Rutherford, Mark Knee, Mark Burt, Paul Kennett, Guy Rutherford, Simon James, Lee Cox, Mark Rice, Simon Funnell, Ben Carrington. Subs: Adie Miles, Lee Weston, Paul Thomas, Tony Holden, Matthew May.

CHAPTER 10
Rotherham United
Mike Pollitt, Will Varty, Paul Dillon, Kevin Watson, Brian Wilsterman, Steve Thompson, Rob Scott, Darren Garner, Leo Fortune-West, Paul Warne, Trevor Berry. Subs: Paul Pettinger, Paul Hurst, Gary Martindale, Chris Sedgwick, Andy Turner.

Worthing
Lee Bray, Miles Rutherford, Mark Knee, Mark Burt, Paul Kennett, Guy Rutherford, Simon James, Lee Cox, Paul Thomas, Simon Funnell, Ben Carrington. Subs: Adie Miles, Tony Holden, Matthew may, Lee Weston, Rob Craven.

CHAPTER 11
Burnley
Paul Crichton, Dean West, Gordon Armstrong, Micky Mellon, Steve Davis, Mitchell Thomas, Glen Little, Paul Cook, Andy Cooke, Andy Payton, John Mullin. Subs: Ronnie Jepson, Graham Branch, Lenny Johnrose, Chris Brass, Alan Lee.

Rotherham

Mike Pollitt, John Varty, Brian Wilsterman, Steve Thompson, Kevin Watson, Paul Dillon, Rob Scott, Trevor Berry, Darren Garner, Leo Fortune-West, Paul Warne. Subs: Paul Pettinger, Chris Sedgwick, Vance Warner, Gary Monkhouse, Paul Hurst.

CHAPTER 12
Derby County

Mart Poom, Horacio Carbonari, Darryl Powell, Tony Dorigo, Dean Sturridge, Rory Delap, Avi Nimni, Steve Elliott, Vass Borbokis, Giorgi Kinkladze, Craig Burley. Subs: Russell Hoult, Seth Johnson, Deon Burton, Lars Bohinen, Mikkel Beck.

Burnley

Paul Crichton, Dean West, Gordon Armstrong, Micky Mellon, Steve Davis, Mitchell Thomas, Glenn Little, Paul Cook, Andy Cooke, Andy Payton, John Mullin. Subs: Ronnie Jepson, Len Johnrose, Paul Weller, Chriss Brass, Graham Branch

CHAPTER 13
Coventry City

Magnus Hedman, Paul Williams, Robbie Keane, Gary McAllister, Moustapha Hadji, Paul Telfer, Carlton Palmer, Stephen Froggatt, Gary Breen, Youssef Chippo, Cedric Roussel. Subs: Noel Whelan, Runar Normann, John Eustace, Steve Ogrizovic, Tomas Gustafsson.

Burnley

Paul Crichton, Dean West, Mitchell Thomas, Micky Mellon, Steve Davis, Gordon Armstrong, Glen Little, Paul Cook, Andy Cooke, Andy Payton, John Mullin. Subs: Lenny Johnrose, Ronnie Jepson, Graham Branch, Paul Smith, Paul Weller.

CHAPTER 14
Coventry City

Magnus Hedman, Paul Williams, Robbie Keane, Gary McAllister, Paul Telfer, Carlton Palmer, Stephen Froggatt, Gary Breen, Runar Normann, John Eustace, Cedric Roussel. Subs: Richard Shaw Laurent Delorge, Gavin Strachan, Steve Ogrizovoc, Tomas Gustafsson.

Charlton Athletic

Dean Kiely, Chris Powell, Graham Stuart, Richard Rufus, Shaun Newton, Mark Kinsella,

Andy Hunt, John Robinson, Steve brown, Martin Pringle, Greg Shields. Subs: Sasa Ilic, Paul Konchesky, Andy Todd, Charlie Mcdonald, John Salako.

CHAPTER 15
Bolton Wanderers
Jussi Jaaskelainen, Dean Holden, Robbie Elliott, Gudni Bergsson, Mark Fish, Mike Whitlow, Michael Johansen, Claus Jensen, Alan Johnston, Eidur Gudjohnsen, Bob Taylor. Subs: Steve Banks, Dean Holdsworth, Ricardo Gardner, Franck Passi, Paul Ritchie

Charlton Athletic
Dean Kiely, Anthony Barness, Chris Powell, Graham Stuart, Richard Rufus, Shaun Newton, Andy Hunt, John Robinson, Steve Brown, Martin Pringle, Andy Todd. Subs: Carl Tiler, Mark Kinsella, Sasa Ilic, Paul Konchesky, John Salako.

CHAPTER 16
Bolton Wanderers
Jussi Jaaskelainen, Gudni Bergsson, Paul Ritchie, Mike Whitlow, Michael Johansen, Claus Jensen, Robbie Elliott, Alan Johnston, Eidur Gudjohnsen, Dean Holdsworth. Subs: Steve Banks, Paul Warhurst, Bo Hansen, John O'Kane, Franck Passi.

Aston Villa
David James, Ugo Ehiogu, Gareth Southgate, Gareth Barry, Mark Delaney, Ian Taylor, George Boateng, Alan Wright, Julian Joachim, Paul Merson, Benito Carbone. Subs: Peter Enckleman, Dion Dublin, Lee Hendrie, Steve Stone, Jlloyd Samuel.

CHAPTER 17
Aston Villa
David James, Ugo Ehiogu, Gareth Southgate, Gareth Bary, Mark Delaney, Ian Taylor, George Boateng, Alan Wright, Dion Dublin, Paul Merson, Benito Carbone. Subs: Peter Enckleman, Jlloyd Samuel, Steve Stone, Julian Joachim, Lee Hendrie.

Chelsea
Ed de Goey, Celestine Babayaro, Frank Leboeuf, Marcel Desailly, Mario Melchiot, Roberto Di Matteo, Didier Deschamps, Dennis Wise, Gustavo Poyet, George Weah, Gianfranco Zola. Subs: Tore Andre Flo, Jody Morris, Carlo Cudicini, Jon Harley, John Terry.